Born in 1943 in drab East London, Michael went to sea with P&O at 16 to see the world and for seven years saw life, shipping and the world profoundly change. His sea-going experience was multi-faceted, world-encompassing and intellectually stimulating.

VOYAGES TO MATURITY

Seven Years Before the Mast with P & O

MICHAEL FROST

Austin Macauley Publishers™
LONDON • CAMBRIDGE • NEW YORK • SHARJAH

Copyright © Michael Frost (2019)

The right of **Michael Frost** to be identified as author of this work has been asserted by him in accordance with section 77 and 78 of the Copyright, Designs and Patents Act 1988.

All rights reserved. No part of this publication may be reproduced, stored in a retrieval system, or transmitted in any form or by any means, electronic, mechanical, photocopying, recording, or otherwise, without the prior permission of the publishers.

Any person who commits any unauthorised act in relation to this publication may be liable to criminal prosecution and civil claims for damages.

A CIP catalogue record for this title is available from the British Library.

ISBN 9781528900324 (Paperback)
ISBN 9781528900331 (Hardback)
ISBN 9781528993128 (ePub e-book)

www.austinmacauley.com

First Published (2019)
Austin Macauley Publishers Ltd
25 Canada Square
Canary Wharf
London
E14 5LQ

To All the Women in My Life

I would like to thank Melinda of Go West Design Group, without whose graphic and artistic expertise there would have been far less to the tale.

~ Table of Contents ~

Foreword..10

   1. Khyber...12

   2. Mantua and Malwa..58

   3. Arcadia and Himalaya...84

   4. Mid-Apprenticeship Release.......................................106

   5. Oriana, Comorin and 2nd Mates' Ticket...................126

   6. Chitral, Salsette and Cannanore.................................158

   7. Canberra and Cathay..190

   8. Leadenhall Street, Canada, West Star & CPR...........232

   9. Postscript...258

Glossary..261

~ Foreword ~

Most people have lives of some, or great, interest, though it is often not realised that that is the case until a large portion of it has passed by and 'thoughts recollected in tranquillity' foster the realisation that one's life is only a brief moment of time that all too easily slips into the abyss of forgotten history. Such was the case with my recollection of my parents' history, for they grew up during one of the most cataclysmic of times, both being born in 1913 and being in the 'prime of their lives' during the World War II, near the end of which I was born (and about which I have often wondered when they knew, or whether it occurred to them, that the Allies were definitely to prevail and that the time had come to pass on their genes).

During that war, the family home was in the general area of Woolwich and Foots Cray, prime areas for bombing during the prolonged Blitz; they were boroughs adjacent to the London Royal Docks, munitions factories, and the River Thames, by whose reflection bombers could see their way to the prime targets of Westminster, St. Paul's Cathedral and Buckingham Palace. My father's sight was poor, and for that reason he was enlisted as a fireman, and my mother became an ambulance driver. Twice their home was destroyed by bombs, once our collective lives being saved by a Morrison Shelter, a steel construction that served both as a shelter in case of the collapse of one's house and as a dining table.

These things I know because of the incident of my being bundled under the table and the side 'cages' being lowered just in time as my father heard the V1 coming and knew that it was for us. This was the stuff of frequently-recited family legend ... but very little else was. When she died in 2005, my mother was starting to write some recollections of a life that started ten years after the Wright Brothers first flew and ended two years after the Concorde was to fly for the last time. Nothing else was saved from two long lives; a few photographs survived, occasional memories periodically surface, and no letters remain, despite what I venture to say are thousands written.

With time and great good fortune having provided to us five vigorous grandchildren, I was brought to task one day when my daughter-in-law found my personal tale sorely lacking in specificity, what I had done when and where being almost entirely unrecorded. Fortunately, this was not quite the case, having gone away to sea when eighteen years old and at that time being given a five-year diary by a kindly family friend. I was far from diligent in keeping this up, there being gaps, sometimes months long. But in retracing these times with that template, a great deal of detail came back to me that I had thought forgotten but could now recollect with sometimes remarkable, though perhaps not always entirely accurate, clarity.

Maturity is not only what I hope that I attained, but some of what the nautical, political and intellectual worlds gained during this so-brief moment in history. In this respect, what follows is not my story but part of a huge fabric but one corner of which I was privileged to witness.

The *Khyber*

1 Khyber

This was not at all what I had expected. It was October 1961 and from my home just over the Thames I had joined *Khyber* as a navigating (deck) cadet at the P&O berth No. 1 in the King George V Dock in London's Royal Docks. I was eighteen years old and had recently completed a one-year course at the School of Navigation at Warsash, Hampshire, from where I had elected to join P&O. The selection of this company was not fortuitous; it operated glamorous ships that went to glamorous places. But *Khyber* was a stranger to glamour of any sort.

For a number of years my family had lived in Woolwich, south of the River Thames, but within a hundred yards of the river itself. My brother David and I could see from our bedroom right across the river to the docks, at that time the world's biggest commercial docks. There, right before our eyes, we could see the splendour of the world's biggest merchant fleet, with an array of vessels trading to Africa, North and South America, the Far East and everywhere between. One of the more splendid fleets was that of P&O, whose *Corfu, Carthage, Canton, Chitral* and *Cathay* stood out with their sparkling white hulls and yellow funnels, bound, we knew, for Ceylon and Malaya (as they then were), Hong Kong and Japan. Because of our ship-recognition books we also knew of the more mundane aspects of the company, comprising basic freighters carrying cargo to much of the rest of the world. However, due in part to the lure of these sparkling passenger

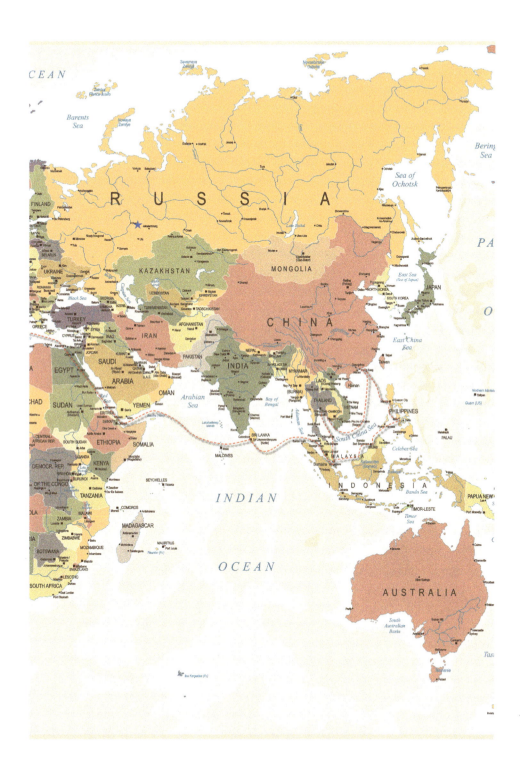

ships, and also because at Warsash, P&O had the reputation of being the most difficult company by which to be accepted, it was P&O which I felt held the best prospects for me (there were, of course, other quality companies, such as Royal Mail, Blue Star, Blue Funnel – alias Alfred Holt – Ellerman Lines, Cunard etc.).

My expectations when Father drove me over to the ship itself were, therefore, not prepared for what I then saw before me, a vessel of a type never before seen by David or me, a black-hulled, black-funnelled ship topped by a slim pencil-like funnel that looked, well, silly. I could count this among the ugliest of ships that I had ever seen. I had certainly seen P&O cargo ships with this colouring (*Salsette, Cannanore* and many others) but none had so ill-mannered an appearance.

However, I was there, about to start my career, so it was hardly the time to cavil about mere appearances. I climbed the gang-plank (itself no easy task – this was a very utilitarian ship) and was told by the quartermaster (aka 'helmsman') at its top to report to the chief officer (again, not an easy instruction, the deck crew being from Maharashtra, and my Hindustani at that time completely unformulated), nobody having told me that, apart from the deck crew, the engine-room was manned by Pakistanis (Urdu), and the steward's department was Goanese (English, Portuguese, Konkani and Hindi).

The accommodation structure was, again, very utilitarian. It was thus very easy to find the mate's cabin (the usual term for the chief officer). He, David Hannah, quickly found the 2nd steward to direct me to my cabin. He, Des, in turn explained that the reason for no evidence of life on the ship was the fact that it had only arrived from the Far East that morning, and with the advent of wives and lovers, there was not going to be much of a showing from the officers.

The cabin to which I was introduced was like something out of a Roald Dahl novel. It was evident that when the ship was constructed, there was no intention to accommodate cadets. It rather appeared to be a converted cargo office, but both its location (at the fore-end of the superstructure and on the extreme port side) and its facilities (small portholes and three iron bunks with two uncomfortable chairs) seemed hardly sufficient for three young men. Fortunately, there was a very small adjoining office. Formally, cadets were apprentices who required four years of sea service (one of which I had already served at Warsash) before being able to take a succession of 'tickets' (2nd mates', 1st mates', masters', and, if one chose to teach, extra masters', the possessors of the last rarely, if ever, being found employed on a seagoing ship). I had, of course, not gone to sea for the creature comforts (having been to boarding schools since being nine years old, privation and lack of personal space were features of normal life), but for three people living cheek by jowl for three to six months at a time, this looked like an uncomfortable squeeze indeed.

As nothing seemed to be particularly required of me at that time, I looked around what was probably to be my home for a considerable time. I looked for the wardroom and dining saloon but found that the Spartan nature of the ship allowed only for a 'dining room' that was a bunch of immovable tables that bore more of a resemblance to a cafeteria than anywhere where one would sit and chat. The utilitarian nature of the ship seemed to be absolute.

I ventured out onto the deck. One of the best features of the Royal Docks was that ships' loading and discharging was carried out, and overseen by, local crews or gangs specially chosen to take over these duties at the home port, ships' deck officers usually carrying out these tasks in foreign ports. (By happenstance, my maternal grandfather had headed one of those specialist gangs for a number of years, but he had died before I had had the urge to go to sea so imparted no relevant wisdom to me.) On this occasion, all this was naturally quite new to me. I saw a lower hold full of chrome ore, smelled the odiously sweet aroma of heated palm oil in the deep-tanks (both from Malaya), saw some of the tobacco (from Indonesia) being unloaded from the secure lock-ups, watched the curious task of unloading the 'ingots' of rubber (a bit like handling tea-chest sized jelly cubes covered with talcum powder, this to prevent the rubber degenerating into one congealed wobbly mess), this from Borneo and Sarawak, and saw numerous miscellaneous oddments like cinnamon sticks from the Philippines. I began to feel that I was about to learn what world trade was all about.

Little, therefore, needing my attention, I walked home (one could walk under the Thames by foot tunnel, ferries being much slower than walking through the drab – and very smelly – passage that was well located both to get to the docks and to our shop and home on the south side of the river). Mother was very surprised to see me – I think that she expected me to be on my way to India by that time – and we had fish and chips for dinner, the last time that the family ever dined together in Woolwich.

A few words are necessary here about the ships and the changes in the nautical environment of the sixties, a time of huge change in most aspects of life in the western world but particularly within the seagoing fraternity.

World War II could not have been won by Britain at sea but could easily have been lost. The British Merchant Marine in 1939 was, by some way, the world's largest. But it was extremely vulnerable; there were many months when U-boats sank an unsustainably large proportion of those ships endeavouring to bring supplies to the country. Fortunately, the US perceived sufficiently dangerous a time coming for it to enter into the Lend-Lease programme, whereby for the use of certain overseas bases it allowed some of its obsolescent and unneeded vessels to both carry cargo and hunt for U-boats operating in the Atlantic. But it was not for nothing that Churchill, born of an American mother and a distant relative of President Roosevelt, declared the war to be won when Hitler, in one of the more asinine of his many senseless decisions, declared war on the US almost immediately after Pearl Harbour; Churchill, evidently unlike Hitler, was fully aware of the enormous productive potential of the US. Indeed, by that time, it had already begun to produce a basic freighter, to a British design, that could be assembled in about two weeks from parts made all over North America; these were known as 'Liberty' ships. Well over 2,000 of these ungainly vessels were launched (as were a number of other designs, including tankers, but of these the Liberties were the most numerous). But they were slow (whatever else they were, U-boats were also slow but not much more so). Therefore, an improved rapid-build vessel was designed; it could manage seventeen knots as opposed to twelve, and of these, over 500 were constructed (they were termed 'Victory' ships) before 1945. The British Government bought many of these (and finished paying for them, in a bundled-up debt, only in 2006). At the war's end, companies were given some ships to replace wartime losses; P&O received two Liberties (*Dongola* and *Devahna*) and two Victories (*Khyber* and *Karmala*). And as the wartime life-expectancy of these types of ships was perhaps one or two Atlantic crossings, any luxuries were eschewed. Thus, no windows, no wardroom, no dining room (or mess, whatever one prefers) and often a gun platform resolutely placed upon the bow or poop to deter any submarines foolish enough to surface (few did); the ships had only what was strictly necessary. At the end of the war, shipping companies were in no financial position to replace the ships lost, thus giving these crude but effective ships a longer life than they really deserved. In our gilded age, my determination that *Khyber* was ugly would be roundly condemned by many seafarers, as the ships were a triumph of function over form, but even so, there were still some beautiful ships around, those of the Blue Funnel (Alfred Holt and Company) and Union Castle Lines being particularly noteworthy.

These deprivations did not particularly concern me; as I have said, British boarding school tends to harden the critical faculties and the arteries, for that matter. And I soon found that ship's food wasn't so bad, even occasionally including roast duck.

But duty called, and the following morning, I was back aboard. There were no other cadets yet (they were still on leave), but I met the 2nd mate, a rank charged with navigation and cargo disposition. He, Mr Foote, was a cool and collected man who seemed to actually relish a sea-going existence (a preference which I subsequently found declined with many as seniority increased). I recall that he introduced me to his wife; I then understood why, for so long, I had not seen him around on deck.

The loading of a ship can be a tiresome business at times. Of course, I knew nothing of how to load various cargoes in the order appropriate for the voyage's ports, and the stevedores really did not much want a callow cadet walking around trying to look as though he knew what he was about. As a result, I spent a good deal of time sitting in my sorry little cabin. One morning, while I knew that the forthcoming voyage was to be to the Far East, I was somewhat taken aback when Foote asked me where Iloilo was, he just having seen some crates for that port being loaded. Being the navigator, I felt that that was probably something that he should have known! To me, the same question arose with the ports of Jesselton and Rajang, equally obscure, and today probably more so than Iloilo. One has to remember that in the days before the Internet, this sort of information was not readily available except from charts and pilotage books (wherein immense amounts of information was available but which was mainly directed to navigational issues). I had already discovered the ship's library (provided by the Missions to Seamen) but this comprised only about fifty books that looked as though they had come from someone's garage sale (although I also noted a copy of 'Crime and Punishment', presumably for some light reading during the longer ocean passages), a situation that I had immediately rectified by bringing from home a few of my larger books that I had yet to read.

'Home' had, however, now forever changed. For some months, Father had been negotiating (though this was a poor word for the London County Council's immovable position on compensation) on the question of expropriating the shop/home premises; the Free Ferry (something of an historic icon, a free ferry having been located there for several centuries) was to be replaced by new vessels whose berth was to be moved upriver to a spot right in front of our building, which was therefore to be demolished. To David and me, who had crossed the Thames many hundreds of times on *John Benn* and *Will Crooks*, splendid coke-fired steam-reciprocating paddle-wheelers that displayed for foot passengers wonderful brass pistons that not only kept the ships warm but were also in themselves endlessly fascinating, this was a major childhood loss.

Fortunately, however, that did not mean that we had no home; some years before the enforced move, my parents, deciding that East London was no place to bring up a family, had purchased a cottage in Sussex, a wholly delightful 16th century house that provided peace, quiet and clean air. The latter was important; as Britain was in reality insolvent after the war, the government had decided to export its one important commodity – high quality coal – and condemn the British themselves to subsist on the lowest quality of usable coal consistent with warmth and the needs of industry. The result, especially in London, was immediately apparent; a foul-smelling smog besmirched the city whenever there was a temperature inversion, and when there was not, the prevailing westerly wind ensured that the smell and the particulate nature of the fog fell upon the poorer and more industrial eastern part of the city. This became personal. David as a youth was a sickly boy, and the wise Dr Lucket opined that without fresh air, he would possibly never truly get better. At the time, this seemed realistic enough, and in the fullness of time, it proved truly prescient; at the time, the British Government decided not to publish the figures for 'smog deaths', but there is little doubt that many thousands of Londoners in particular suffered restricted lives, if not a fatal lung cancer, because of this policy. Both my maternal grandmother and my mother herself suffered grievously from what seemed to be asthma, the latter recovering only after moving to Sussex. As for David, it was decided that he had to go to school where the air was pure, so *I* was sent to Westbrook House School (a 'preparatory' boarding school) in Folkestone, Kent, to see if the air was good enough for David, and two years (our age difference) later, he joined me. He never looked back; the good doctor, one trusts, received his reward in his heaven (he was Egyptian, and therefore probably has a different heaven where I don't expect to go. This was typical; Britain lost its doctors to the U.S., and the third world lost theirs to Western Europe, a loss of expertise that they could ill afford to lose).

In part, this sort of experience was what determined me to go to sea. Living in Woolwich perhaps gave one a distorted view of the world, but it was real. The Royal Docks were very important in the delivery of wartime supplies. Moreover, the town harboured Woolwich Arsenal. Though not as important as in the past (legend had it that the guns that defeated Napoleon at Waterloo were cast at that arsenal), it was still an important aerial target. And up the hill lay the barracks of the Royal Artillery. Being in the south-east corner of the country, Woolwich had been a large and close target for the Luftwaffe and virtually without any ability to hide, because although there was a strictly enforced blackout, the Thames reflected all available light. The Luftwaffe had a 'lighted' path that was easily followed; it could not be masked.

For most of the war, my parents had lived on the north side of the river,

Father being a fireman and Mother an ambulance-driver. Twice they had been bombed out of their homes, firstly by a simple bomb (which they heard coming) and secondly by a V1 (which could be heard flying in. When the engine was heard to stop, one took cover; at that time, Londoners spent a great deal of time in air-raid shelters and the underground!). All this mayhem produced a vision of hell in eastern London, whole rows of houses being demolished; public services were out of commission for weeks, and strict food rationing was enforced. We, living in the 1950's in a confectionary/tobacconist shop, could still witness the poverty and the shortage of means; eggs and milk were still largely powdered, and rabbit was more often the meat of choice than were chicken and lamb.

However, not only was the city covered in grime, but it remained unrepaired. It was still replete with bomb-sites, derelict houses and the detritus of a war that had left the country, and particularly the industrial areas, ragged and disconsolate. The mood, certainly of East London, was a definition of pyrrhic; victory over the Axis seemed tantamount to defeat.

While I was at school, I had enjoyed geography in particular (enjoyment not enhanced by the buffoon of the geography/careers teacher, Mr M, who taught the subject, I believe, because during the war he had joined the Royal Navy and had even been on an MTB as far as the coast of France), and I had determined that a seagoing life looked a lot more interesting than working in, say, a bank, which Father thought the epitome of a secure and worthy lifestyle. At that time, the U.K. offered very little chance of attending university to middle-class families such as ours (although a few years later there began a period of growth in the number of colleges and polytechnics being upgraded to regional universities). As careers master, however, Mr M had no idea of how to join the Merchant Navy (he gave me a few ragged brochures) so I wrote to many of the better-known companies and was gratified to receive a number of encouraging replies. All that I had to do was either attend a residential nautical training school and then be indentured for three years or otherwise complete a four-year apprenticeship 'before the mast'. I was quite happy, as were my parents, for me to apply to Warsash to begin the first route. At that time, it was not difficult to see how Britain was changing; during the early 1960s, the government eliminated the whole concept of Resale Price Maintenance, a step that represented the death-knell for small businesses such as was my parents'. Needless to say, however, taking over their business was the last thing that they would have wished for their sons; they were happy to send me to Warsash.

It was from that setting that I had embarked upon the life of travel, reasonable pay, and what I expected to be a bit more comfort than *Khyber* obviously offered.

The processes of unloading and then loading cargoes were labour-intensive and long-winded. *Khyber* was by that time a fairly old ship (twenty years of seagoing was an average ship's life, especially if trading in some of the world's more rugged environments) and when I joined the ship, much maintenance, particularly to the engine, was required before leaving London.

Captain Adie joined the vessel, quietly and unostentatiously. With the other officers, I was introduced to a taciturn and gentlemanly figure who had been captain of other P&O ships, and probably did not see the appointment to *Khyber* as a favourable step in his career path. Nor was the list of ports very stimulating; our first port of call was to be Newcastle-upon-Tyne, a city of which I had no knowledge but which lay in one of the more impoverished parts of northern England.

A few hours after Captain Adie joined us, we set sail. I had always expected a departure from a ship's home-port to be more symbolic, perhaps with some splendour, but this departure, in drizzle, was drab and gloomy. With the prevailing north-west wind, and the cold sea funneling the waters into the narrow English Channel, the North Sea is notoriously nasty, often fog-shrouded, and full of small coastal vessels and fishing boats who believe in their divine right to have navigational priority at all times. The unruly weather has in the past resulted in tidal surges that have caused many devastating floods and mayhem, leading to high dikes in the Netherlands and the construction of the Thames Barrier in Woolwich.

Leaving London, on November 8th, introduced me to one of the worst periods of North Sea weather. I found myself on the 8-12 watch, but one needs to be ready for anything in the eastern reaches of the Thames, so 'stations' on the foredeck were maintained for over two hours. I finally climbed into my bunk only after 2 am.

The following day dawned cloudy, misty and very cold. The whole morning was spent learning about the radar, at that time a comparatively new navigational tool but surprisingly to me, quite a delicate one; it was very easy to lose small vessels in the sea 'clutter', which one could only eliminate by reducing sensitivity, thus losing the very echoes of those small ships that one was trying to enhance. Therefore, certainly in that day and age, human eyes (and ears, the collision regulations requiring vessels whistles to be sounded at intervals which depended upon a number of factors, particularly whether the vessel was stopped or underway, rules almost universally ignored by small boat mariners) were often far more reliable than electronic aids. This 'lookout' task had to be carried out from the open bridge wing, a chilling experience that made me look forward to the tropics.

But the ship itself was warm enough, so I was back in reasonable spirits for the evening watch. Unfortunately, the weather proved even more chilling than it had in the morning. At about 9 pm, we arrived off the River Tyne, but because of thick fog we were obliged to anchor, as I saw it, right in the middle of nowhere (this was where radar was definitely of value, for one could maintain position by reference to jetties, buoys and other fixed objects). However, very soon the pilot came aboard and, fortuitously, the fog lifted, we raised the anchor ('the hook') and entered the river. It was a surprise to me how narrow it proved to be; for one of Britain's great ports, it appeared that it would be difficult to squeeze between its entrance piers.

Because of the conditions, the 2nd mate and I had to remain on the forecastle in case we needed to drop the hooks in a hurry, and I was glad to find myself with the job of keeping him, the ship's carpenter (whose job embraced being responsible for operating the anchor winch/capstan) and myself supplied with cocoa – I was in the warmth almost as much as I was out in the chill night. But this did not last, for no sooner had fresh cocoa been prepared than the fog again descended, and with some difficulty, a tug, appearing from nowhere, assisted us in turning around, and we again proceeded out to sea, where we anchored. However, almost immediately the fog again cleared, the pilot decided that we could now proceed; we raised the hook and entered the river. I was sent up to the bridge to see how things looked, but as I got there, fog returned.

This time we were too far up the river to safely turn around, so the pilot indicated that he would locate a berth, any berth, where we could safely tie-up for the night and await the sunrise and, we hoped, clear weather. I climbed between my sheets at about 3 am. Luckily, the morning was bright and clear, though very cold, and we berthed without difficulty.

In 1962, Newcastle might have been said to have been one of the U.K.'s fading glories. In earlier centuries, an important bastion of political rectitude, it declared for the Royalists in the Civil War and was promptly sacked by the Puritans (few movements had been so ineptly named). It was some centuries before the Industrial Revolution revived the region's prosperity, but the nearby coalfields and riparian access to a large local workforce eventually favoured the entire area (Northumberland and Durham), allowing it to become a major regional economic power. This prosperity had, in the fullness of time, faded; by 1961, it was facing hard times. While the coal industry was apparently flourishing (reality was otherwise, however, for the truth was that it was on its last legs, though few knew it), the shipbuilding and engineering enterprises that had been its engine-room had begun to disappear because of the endeavours of Japan and Korea to formulate a new industrial base, which, it was clear to those who chose to look, those societies could successfully effect with their substantially lower costs and highly motivated working classes. The old saw of "Who won the war?" was common in areas like Newcastle and nearby Sunderland, where heavily bombed and devastated neighbourhoods felt that they were competing with yards in Japan that enjoyed a completely reconstructed infrastructure; those countries' bombed cities were razed while ours were merely damaged, the former rebuilt (there was no choice), the other withering because of the shortage of public money.

A note should be made here respecting ship size and the progress of ships' design and purposes. Firstly, while *Khyber* had a gross tonnage of 7,674, this figure is not easily compared with other vessels. The ship had a 'net' tonnage of 4,592, but small tankers, in most respects much larger ships, were of 12,298 gross tons (*Mantua*) and 24,266 gross tons (*Malwa*). Later, I served on *Oriana* (41,915 gross tons, then a large passenger ship) and *Chitral* (a passenger/cargo ship of 13,821 gross tons). By way of comparison, *Titanic* had a gross tonnage of 46,328 and a displacement tonnage of 52,310. Nowadays the scale is, many would say, simply warped, *Allure of the Seas,* a cruise vessel, weighing in at 225,282 gross tons.

Secondly, all of the tonnage specifications have their particular purposes, and one cannot directly compare gross, net, deadweight, cargo and displacement tonnage; some are best suited for passenger ships, one or two for tankers, and one for bulk and LNG carriers. Tugs and warships enjoy their own measurements.

And thirdly, there was likewise substantial variety in ships' propulsion. While only the Woolwich Ferry and a few old ships (and even British admiralty tugs) were propelled by paddle wheels with steam-reciprocating engines, the variety thereafter included steam turbines (then the norm). Additionally, there was a growing number of diesel-powered motor ships, some turbo-electric and even some nuclear; though the USS *Enterprise* and *Savannah* were nuclear, less than 200 nuclear-powered commercial ships have been built, the major exception being the very fine *France* (in its declining days *Norway*) which was designed to be converted to nuclear power but which modification never actually occurred. There were some oddities as well, tugs that had propellers which could operate in any direction, jet-like nozzles, even new-style sailing ships!

The main transformative maritime changes that were beginning to occur in the 1960s were, however, more readily apparent. Most notably, the containerisation revolution had started and was becoming significant. This transformation of cargo-handling affected the huge number of ships of *Khyber's* generation, which relied upon the very inefficient handling by ship's gear or shore cranes of individual crates or pallets. Damage was expected (crates of whisky could simply disappear during unloading) and idle time was the norm (at which time a ship was earning no money but was spending it profligately) with piecemeal cargo-handling. It was to be five years before P&O organised its fleet to include custom-made container ships, but soon, shipyards were hard-pressed to meet demand. Consequently, the second revolution was in ship sizes. Rapidly cargo ships became virtual behemoths, fast, usually manned by a crew similar in manpower to *Khyber*, and which rarely remain in the new specialised ports for even a day. One obvious result was that, almost overnight, cargo damage was substantially minimised. Other specialist ships, for example car carriers (the most ungainly of all ship designs), by driving cars up and down ramps, eliminated damage occasioned to cars hoisted into the holds of ships like *Khyber*, where scrapes or dents were almost inevitable.

These factors contributed to fundamental changes to commercial and to working lives. The Royal Docks very rapidly fell into terminal decline. Something less than twenty miles from the North Sea, these docks were in a shallower and narrower part of the Thames than large container ships could safely navigate, and they simply stopped coming, though the docks actually remained open until 1981. Needless to say, this progress necessitated huge social changes to dockworkers, but inevitably, the rules of commerce prevailed; today, there are merely three rather sinister large bodies of water lying parallel to a short-runway airport. Necessarily, ports like Newcastle, with their narrow entrances, became transformed and in need of substantial government aid. But for those who got the good and difficult jobs, (container-crane operators and the like) the cargo revolution was wholly good.

Other changes that were occurring were more gradual but inevitable. While ships of all types were still being built in the UK, their numbers declined quite rapidly, although the P&O *Canberra* (Belfast) and the Orient Line *Oriana* (Barrow-in-Furness) were both launched in 1960, British yards being generally obsolescent and unable to easily compete with builders in developing countries (at that time most notably Japan, but many others wished to get into such profitable lines of business). There were also a number of specialised ventures that, often with government help, saw opportunities that in the past would have gone to British entrepreneurs; the Finns became adept at constructing the most exotic of passenger ships, and their success was closely followed by both Germany and Italy. Ship-breaking, in the past a British specialty, was taken over by Pakistan and Taiwan, and had it not been for oil rigs, oil-servicing ships, warships and ferries, the dramatic decline in British shipbuilding would have been the greater. Seafarers themselves were aware of all this turmoil, though only vaguely.

And most obviously affected by these profound changes were the north-east coast ship-building communities; Newcastle, South and North Shields and their hinterland. The Tyne was narrow, but daylight revealed that *Khyber* was of a size that was easily accommodated. Thus, on the morning after the berthing in places unknown, we proceeded up the river to our anticipated dock, which we reached at about noon. As the main cargo to be unloaded was chrome ore, (a dark, heavy sand-like substance that required special 'scooping' cranes) there was little enough for me to do. So, I walked ashore and took in the sights. Frankly, they were of no great moment. In fact, the scene was one of almost as much desolation as was Woolwich. The city had, of course, been heavily bombed during the war, and, obviously, there was little enough money to effect much reconstruction, so I returned to the ship to while away a bit more time.

But not for long. I was called up by the mate and told that the second mate's wife was shortly to join the ship for the coastal trip, which was to include Rotterdam and Antwerp. The significance of this event was that there was no longer sufficient capacity in the lifeboats for all of those on board. Therefore, I, the junior person aboard, had to go home.

A few hours later, I was on a train. My first 'voyage' was over; arrival in London on October 1, then a two-day trip up a fog-enclosed North Sea and finally to a departure back home on November 10. Needless to say, my family was quite surprised to see me, the anticipated tales of adventure on the high seas being little other than standing in freezing weather waiting to watch how to drop the anchor. (However, I did learn that one did not use an anchor to hitch onto anything, in fact very much the opposite, for it was the weight of the anchor and cable that kept the ship roughly where it should be. Snagging a submarine electrical, telegraphic cable or simply another old discarded anchor chain with a ship's anchor could result in a long and arduous recovery task.)

I remained at home until November 26, when I re-joined *Khyber*. Meanwhile, my companion cadets had arrived. The senior, close to the end of his apprenticeship, was Plumridge (in the British social structure the Old-School tradition eschewed the use of first names; their use, particularly in a highly structured society like a ship, would be most peculiar, not so much gay as effete, and quite abnormal except for persons of similar 'rank'. Des, however, was plainly 'proletarian').

I introduced myself. I quickly realised that this was someone with whom sharing a cabin was likely to be a generally unpleasant experience. He was a heavy-set fellow who had evidently come from a fairly rough life-school, appeared to be devoid of a sense of humour, and, because he was soon to take his 2nd mate's exam and then become an officer, seemed intent on demonstrating to me that he was a superior sort of person. Four months with him in cramped quarters looked pretty undesirable. However, boarding school leaves one with several useful traits; one becomes adept at ignoring those who deserve it, and, additionally, keeping to oneself becomes almost second nature.

I was, however, happy to see that the other cadet (Young), though a few months senior to me, was an altogether different sort of person. He was a physically slight, cheery sort with an interest in things other than the ships and the sea. One of Young's interests was (target) rifle shooting, and because while I had been at Cranbrook School, I had been in the school eight that had shot against hundreds of schools at Bisley, this sport was of interest to me. (Cranbrook, in fact, won the coveted Ashburton Shield in 1939 and thereby held the title longer than any other school in the country.)

However, there was no choice of companions; we were stuck together, like it or not. The jobs that we were required to do were twofold. Firstly, we had to learn watch-keeping, and this was accompanied by practical training in navigation. The watches almost always kept on deep-sea ships were 12 to 4, 4 to 8, and 8 to 12; four hours on, eight off. The second role was to learn seamanship. This was 'learn by watching' rather than by example, for neither the Serang (bosun – the head of the deck crew) nor the Tindal (assistant bosun) knew much English, although I was glad to see that the mate spoke fluent Hindustani, and a few of the deck crew spoke a little English. I had not anticipated the need to learn other languages; however, while the big passenger ships were generally British-manned, the engine-room crew were mostly Pakistani, stewards were Goanese, and perhaps four of the white ships were Chinese-manned. And I mean 'manned'; on passenger ships there were FAPs (female assistant pursers), nurses, female stewards, and a few children's hostesses, but anything feminine was completely absent elsewhere. It was inconceivable that there could be female officers (all of those just named were of officer-rank) on cargo ships, tankers or any other commercial ship; it just couldn't be done, a view to which I subscribed.

With quick stops in Rotterdam (a surprisingly modern city with facilities that made London look like something from the 1930s) and Hamburg (grim, dirty brown buildings with ever-present rain), on December 7th, we finally left the cold northern winter – or so I thought. Our first port was Genoa, in the perennially sunny Mediterranean!

Several days of unpleasant weather ensued, sixty-foot waves being reported in the English Channel, which though that might seem strange in so relatively small a body of water, was not uncommon when northerly winds and the tide so dictated. The main issue was, however, that *Khyber,* because of being lightly loaded (cargo comprising machinery, manufactured goods and special items like whisky), sat high in the water, and thus bounced over rather than cut its way through the waves. We, being on the main deck and on the port side, bore the brunt of the waves crashing against the superstructure as we pitched our way south across the notoriously rough Bay of Biscay. Thoughts that I might not be seasick were quickly dispelled; most meals were left barely touched. This situation was made the worse by a portent of things to come, when speed had to be reduced to ten knots (a knot is a nautical mile per hour, the 'mile' varying over the globe because of the earth's shape) because of boiler problems. Watches brought little relief from the unpleasantness. In fact, rather the opposite; twelve or so meters above the sea merely made rolling worse. But at least it was fresh air, and gradually, the nausea went.

But December 11th brought relief. It was a bright sunny day, and early in the afternoon, Gibraltar was passed. Be it recalled that this impressive rock was then something of a bone of contention. Though ceded in perpetuity in 1713 by the Treaty of Utrecht to Britain, Spain had never become reconciled to its loss, and given the poor relationship between Britain and Franco's Spain, the rock had undergone some painful sanctions from its large neighbour. But reading history from books sometimes gives one a poor sense of reality. Sailing past Gibraltar made one see how strategic a place it would have been in wartime. Though large, it could not be described as massive; it is 426 m high compared with, say, Cape Town's Table Mountain at 1,095 m. But its domination of the narrow (fourteen km) strait and its height in relation to its surroundings rendered it mightily impressive. And, obviously, had this formidable fortress been in the hands of the Axis, that wartime theatre may have very differently played out.

The calming of the weather, however, is not always a good thing. When the time came to repair to the bridge that evening, an unpleasant sea had given way to the sea not being visible at all; we were enveloped by a thick fog and total silence. Of all the conditions that mariners dislike, fog is the worst. Safety demands extra lookouts and technology requires constant reference to the radar. The latter, of course, was far from reliable, small vessels, especially those without radar reflectors, simply being invisible, and fog-horns often inaudible. And the term 'radar-assisted-collision' had come into maritime parlance, *Andrea Doria,* the pride of the Italian trans-Atlantic merchant marine, having been sunk in

1956 by a collision with *Stockholm*. Both vessels were ultimately found to be at fault, but had the captain of the Italian ship either made a substantial course change or maintained it without deviation, the ship would probably not have gone down (there was substantial loss of life). The 'hold your course' doctrine, which that captain favoured but failed to follow even though he had full radar information, may ironically have been the right idea; in 1912, had *Titanic* hit the iceberg head-on instead of altering course, the damage to its bow would have been very severe, but the watertight compartments would not have been compromised by the ship being sliced open along its length, thereby letting the sea into compartments that would otherwise have retained their integrity. (In the watch-keeping 1st officer's defence, it has to be said that practically every mariner in that situation at that time would have acted in the same way.) In fog, to know not quite enough is worse than knowing nothing other than what one senses; Captain Adie had a long night.

Two days later, we arrived in Genoa. A fine harbour gained one entry into an almost mediaeval city (being brought up in the British tradition, one tended to think of Alfred the Great and Danegeld as the beginnings of Western history, but this city had been a thriving settlement in the sixth century BC). Unfortunately, as I learned so often, my ethnocentrism was profound, the British education system having an unerring ability to downplay the achievements of lesser breeds – which is to say, everybody else. I noted in passing that one of Genoa's most notable doges was a certain Andrea Doria.

But this was not to be a quick stop, though the repairs to the engine rather than the volume of cargo prevented a rapid departure. We loaded hundreds of Vespas (two-stroke mini motor-bikes) and boxes of Martini & Rossi vermouth, and I took a stroll around the city. The war had caused much damage to the original buildings, but the larger ones had obviously been reconstructed with care and reverence. This was a typical Italian response to cataclysmic events; immediately after hostilities ceased, the people of Milan began reconstructing the La Scala Opera House, and on May 11th, 1946, it reopened to enormous acclaim even while the city was without transportation and was more rubble than buildings. All this passed me by, my main desire being for a proper coffee. This may seem strange, but on *Khyber* I had quickly discovered that the water carried on board, and on which we had to subsist, produced a singularly awful brew; at all the schools that I had attended, if we had had coffee at all, it was Camp Coffee, a chicory potion that was cheap and contained no discernable coffee. It was quite horrid and virtually undrinkable, but ship's coffee was almost its equal. However, I knew that if Italy could do anything properly, it was making coffee.

Consequently, I found a likely-looking coffee bar in a nearby piazza and ordered a brew. I was surprised when along came a minute cup, not much larger than a thimble and with it, a glass of water. Not really knowing how to handle this (I had never even heard of such a drink in my favourite coffee bar in Tunbridge Wells), I sipped the thick brown liquid. This, one is apparently not supposed to do, but how could I know? I spent twenty minutes on this (expensive) experience, found out why I needed the glass of water, and, as elegantly as I could, left the scene knowing that I had a few culinary things to learn.

The departure from Genoa was accompanied by a marked change in the weather. My imagination had long accepted the Mediterranean as a calm and languid sea, but other than a few hours of fog, the weather had done its best to make me wish to return home; now it had another go. Even though we were close to the Italian coast, the wind was strong and the sea enough to renew mal de mer. But interest lay elsewhere. On the 19th, we passed Stromboli, fortunately at night, for one could see the flames coming from the volcano. It rather resembled a fiery Hades, although the pilot book told me that about 1,800 people lived on the island; it did not look like the safest of places. And then, as we were entering the Strait of Messina, we hit a water-spout. I was on the bridge with the 4th mate, who himself had never experienced one of these phenomena, a savage demonstration of the power of nature; we literally slammed into a wall of solid water that obscured everything for some minutes, and then we were through. It occurred to me that in the days of the Phoenicians and Ulysses many a vessel would have quickly succumbed; it was something that I was never again to witness ... perhaps fortunately.

The following days were, I am glad to say, much more calm, though the temperature was more like Newcastle's than North African. However, there occurred one of those unfortunate incidents that, trivial though they seem in retrospect, I have not forgotten.

On one of those rare occasions when all three of us were unencumbered by watches, I was sitting in the cabin reading when Plumridge entered. The cabin contained three chairs, all of jumble-sale quality. I was sitting in that with a steel frame and plastic webbing, but when he saw me, he said, "I'm senior cadet, and I get the best chair!" We had never discussed such an idea, and although we were but two meters apart, he moved towards me in a vaguely threatening manner.

I had attended boarding school since being nine years old. Rather than put me in extra-curricular piano classes, Father decided that, not wanting to put us through his experiences of much-disliked piano practice, David and I would be enlisted in boxing classes. I quite took to this sport, eventually becoming the school boxing captain. We had enjoyed being taught by Mr Mallard, a PT teacher of the highest quality, who taught us that, properly coached, one need not be fearful of most things that at first glance might frighten or seem dangerous. So effective was his teaching that when I went on to public school, I could with ease fulfill all the gymnastic requirements that few of my class-mates would even attempt. At Warsash, there was no real sporting activity, but we were taught self-defence by a formidable Royal Marine sergeant (their barracks being nearby), whose first advice was that, especially when overseas, one's best defence is a good pair of heels (too true, as I later sailed with a second mate who was stabbed to death in Houston because he refused to hand over $25 to three thugs, and he actually possessed a black belt in judo, second dan, I believe; his feeling of security was entirely chimeric). Additionally, during the first term at Warsash, one of those in our 'cabin' of six was Al-Husseini, a heavily built young Iraqi of somewhat fearsome appearance. On one occasion, he expressed a visceral hatred of everything Jewish. I remonstrated, some of our London friends having been decidedly and proudly Jewish. He rose to what he regarded as bait, but remembering basic principles in confined spaces (hit target – bridge of nose, throat, bottom of rib cage – not often, but first, and as hard as possible), I stood ready. He stepped back; how often does one have to learn that bullies abhor defiance? (To give balance to the tale, there was another senior Iraqi cadet in the school. He was very much a civilised gentleman; actually, one learned a great deal about other nationalities at Warsash – which were things one certainly did not learn at boarding school – because there the government subsidised the training of foreign students. We even had a Swiss cadet, hardly a nation known for its merchant marine!).

Thus, when presented with a threatening Plumridge, I had a choice. I knew that he was quite well-muscled, but I felt that I could take him on fairly easily, as I knew that I had a heavier punch than most and I had a target probably not much accustomed to dissent. But, on the other hand, although I had a witness to all of this (Young was with us), it would certainly be unseemly and hardly likely to generate much favour amongst all those with whom I then worked and would undoubtedly work in the future. The downside seemed too considerable for any minor demonstration of macho superiority.

I gave him the seat … somewhat to my personal regret in later years.

Back on the bridge, however, I was not inspired by the eastern Mediterranean. Far from it being semi-tropical, there was a continuous cold north-easterly wind, and when we finally arrived at Port Said, we had to anchor and have a constant watch to ensure that we maintained our position. However, we weighed anchor at 4 am, but not before we had had our logbook taken ashore and examined by the authorities to ensure that since it had last visited Egypt, the ship had not touched in at any part of Israel. As it had not, we set out southwards in a large convoy towards the Red Sea.

I was intrigued by the Suez Canal and what it represented. Although built by the French and initially owned by Egypt, the Khedive of Egypt (at that time part of the disintegrating Ottoman Empire) had in 1875 offered to sell its shares in the Suez Canal Company to Britain, a purchase for which Prime Minister Disraeli was at the time roundly criticised. (It is of passing interest that the first ship through the new canal was a P&O liner). I, like every Englishman at that time, was acutely aware of the October 29, 1956 Suez crisis in which the British, French and Israelis had colluded in the invasion of Egypt. Because of America's negative reaction to the invasion, (in retrospect, because on November 4th the Red Army had invaded Hungary, the morality of the west's options suddenly became a decisive factor, though perhaps a further significant motivation was the perceived need to keep the mercurial Nasser in the Western camp, futile though that hope proved to be) Britain and France had been obliged to suffer a humiliating withdrawal (not so for the Israelis, however, who, because of their efficient armed forces, aggressively led by General Dayan, triumphed against the ragged Egyptian Army and thereby gained land and immense prestige). Egypt, realising the manipulative ways of the West, and after its now effectively undisputed nationalisation of the canal, decided to turn its economic favours towards the Soviet Union and (for armaments) to its satrapy Czechoslovakia. In so doing, the company fired most of the canal's western employees and turned to Russian, Polish and other such countries for equipment, technical assistance and, particularly, canal pilots. This resulted in some rather alarmed jocularity among Western ship-owners as to how these un-nautical intervenors could hope to fulfil so great an undertaking in running so complex an organisation; hiring such pilots had until then been an almost exclusively western European privilege. The surprise, I understood before reaching Suez, was that it was now at least as well run as before the takeover!

Less than 200 km long, the canal was nevertheless a fascinating feat of engineering and seamanship. Little more than a sloping-sided ditch in the sand, its apparent width is somewhat deceptive, especially when compared to the Panama Canal. Several hundred ships per day could be accommodated, but as they could not pass each other, they were arranged in convoys, one of which usually waited in the intervening Great Bitter Lake for the other to pass. Actual transit was perhaps not as complex as might have been expected, for a pilot explained to me that a reasonably sized vessel, once in the middle of the 'ditch', would tend to stay there because of the water exerting constant equal pressure on both sides of the hull. That seemed reasonable, if perhaps a bit simplistic.

But just as importantly, we entered a completely different world of weather. The wind ceased, the sun came out, and the temperature rose to the mid-twenties. Unlike most cargo companies, P&O maintained dress standards that emanated from the passenger fleet. A basic blue uniform and whites were required in the cold and the warm weather respectively, but within those parameters there was variety, long white uniforms, mess (evening) dress being required on the 'white ships' and white shorts and a 'Red Sea rig' on other vessels. Even within those requirements, P&O had very recently merged with the snooty Orient Line (the companies had operated cooperatively for some years) and that company (which operated six big passenger ships) had its own dress code. (Getting properly rigged out for the enlarged company was actually quite expensive, almost uniquely with P&O-Orient Lines, but not quite exclusively; some of the 'smarter' cargo companies – for example, Blue Funnel Line – also required standard officers' uniforms.)

We were soon in the Red Sea, which could not be described as one of the more enticing parts of the world. Never rough, and usually basking under the hot sun, the only infrequent and unwelcome relief was a sandstorm. One tale arising from this type of trip and weather is the derivation of the word 'Posh'. Legend has it that in past decades the most comfortable way to India on P&O was to travel easterly on the port side of the ship and return home on the starboard side, thus each way avoiding the direct heat of the sun. It makes for a nice neat little aphorism and is probably apocryphal … but the myth unsurprisingly seemed a tale much favoured by P&O.

At the foot of the Red Sea lay Aden. Then still under de facto British rule, the port was of fading economic and geopolitical importance. It existed as a transit port for India and the Persian Gulf and was for ships bound for easterly or westerly ports an important refuelling (bunkering) destination, oil there being substantially cheaper than anywhere else between North Africa and South-East Asia. But it exhibited a sorry face to the world. Although of substantial size, the harbour was little more than a barren roadstead anchorage with no industry or commerce unrelated to shipping and, perhaps, the odious commerce in khat, legal in Horn of Africa countries, illegal virtually everywhere else (it is immediately apparent where it is commonplace – one has only to see the discoloured teeth of the male population.) I was told that Aden's duty-free status was significant, but that as we were going to Hong Kong, that feature should be by-passed. It was also where, upon walking ashore, I witnessed men openly walking hand-in-hand, something that I had not seen elsewhere, but which, it was explained (correctly?) arose from the practice of purdah, the country (a status not actually achieved by 1961) being largely Muslim. Women being thus secluded seemed bizarre, but I had, I knew, much to learn.

Fuelling over (one never filled up with Aden's desalinated potable water unless one was in extremis, so we took none on) we set out over the Indian Ocean. The next port was Penang, my first taste of the east.

The Horn of Africa obtrudes some way into that ocean, but first one passes to starboard the island of Socotra, a large bump on the horizon that is remote, hostile in environment and home to unique flora and fauna. I have never met anyone who has actually been there, but it is one of those mysterious places that one would like to see at least once in a lifetime (like Kerguelen and Pitcairn, among others). Entering the Indian Ocean, however, meant starting the longest, seven-day, part of the trip. Further, it was my first encounter with a monsoon. Being December, we were outside the notoriously rough monsoon, so a relatively calm transit could be expected.

But that mattered little. The mate, in one of his less benign moods, decided that the time had come to clean up the paint locker. This small hellhole, situated as far forward in the bow as one could get, contained all of the ship's used and semi-used paint and varnish. To say that it smelled terrible would be a severe understatement; today, to work in such a gaseous place would simply be impermissible. In fact, certainly in this respect, the working world has improved. The indenture system, not so very different from today's 'intern' logic, was and is inherently exploitative. In the case of the merchant navy, cadets constituted a class of educated personnel who worked in the same manner as certificated seamen but who were paid a derisory sum for work that would normally have been negotiated collectively (in fact, for officers, the Merchant Navy and Airline Officers Association did act as a partially effective representative group, but I never heard a word from it about representing cadets). While apprenticed, (and the P&O Group must have utilised close to a thousand cadets) we earned ten pounds a month, supplemented by a cheque for about sixty pounds paid at year-end (by way of forced savings), young cadets obviously being too irresponsible to be permitted access to money as it was earned. Our jobs included lookout duty (no sinecure, as I had learned), being helmsmen, and scraping and maintaining decks, superstructure and accommodation. And that, as will be seen, was not the end of it.

All complaints about the iniquities of life were, however, temporarily set aside by Christmas, my first away from home. Many would have liked to have phoned home, but this was practically impossible, especially when located in the middle of the ocean. All communications came through the Radio Officer (the R/O, an important role in a small ship) and all messages were by way of Morse code, which, with semaphore, deck officers were required to know. Spent thus, the season was enjoyed in somewhat lonely circumstances. However, the captain hosted a party, we cadets were given the day off, and dinner was more than acceptable with grapefruit, soup, fish, turkey, Xmas pudding, mince pie and nuts … and, more importantly, champagne (I had turned eighteen, nineteen days before!).

But being in the middle of a large ocean on a decrepit ship and having to do what at that time I took as a martinet of a mate, the only option was to knuckle under. I had also begun to wonder if we were going to get to our destination; twice on December 30th we had to heave to, wallowing away in a modest swell, while engine repairs were effected. The paint locker having been cleansed, (what we were supposed to learn from this horrible exercise still eludes me) we were back on the learning curve. While at Warsash, we had learned some of the principles of celestial navigation, but actually coming up to the bridge at noon to take sights was rather more complex a task than it had seemed in the classroom. However, noon was simple in comparison with the calculations at dusk. Firstly, actually finding the particular stars required was, in practice, quite difficult. And, secondly, there was little time to find those heavenly bodies, sunset being quite short because of the sharp angle at which the sun descended over the horizon in lower latitudes; once the sun had set, the horizon against which the angle of the stars had to be measured disappeared into the darkness in mere moments. As there was no second chance once there was no horizon, this could result in calculations indicating only that one was somewhere in the Indian Ocean. (Without seeing the sky, which could happen for long periods in, for example, the South-West monsoon, one was guided by 'dead reckoning', which means where one's course and speed, plus educated guesses as to the effects of tides and wind, would supposedly take the vessel. It could be an inaccurate sort of navigation; in 1707, Admiral Sir Cloudesley Shovell had lost a good part of a British Fleet on the Rocks of the Isles of Scilly because of faulty dead reckoning, this when the (Muslim-invented) astrolabe was in use, only some two decades before the sextant was invented. The lack of a reliable navigational aids was, however, alleviated by some extraordinary feats of seamanship; Captain Bligh and some crew were cast into a small cutter near Tahiti in 1789 and navigated over 3,500 nautical miles to Batavia, Java, a feat carried out with navigational equipment that was minimal even for that day.)

On January 1st, the oldest member of the crew, the chief steward, and the youngest, myself, brought in the New Year by ringing twelve bells (a tradition, eight bells being the norm for an eight-hour watch) after which, the R/O, a Scot, invited us all to a drink. This, be it noted, was my first encounter with Scotch whisky; I observe that my comment was to the point – "Vile stuff!" I noted.

But all was not well with the ship itself, it being obliged to go at minimum speed while engine repairs were again carried out. As the speed was much reduced, arrival in Penang was set for January 14th, a delay that resulted in minor water rationing. I also learned of the need for a clock-change virtually every day (an hour or half an hour forward during most nights). Time changes were of little moment, but not always logical (China, despite being in five geographical time zones, is across its whole width attuned to being eight hours ahead of GMT. Thus, noon in Chinese waters may see the sun well past its apogee). Meanwhile, I had begun to enjoy some of the ship's activities. On the 6th, we rigged a deck tennis court (a curious hybrid game of quoits and tennis, but very vigorous) atop one of the hatches, and in the evening, I played bridge with the R/O and the 1st and 2nd electricians. At this pastime, I was far from expert, but my brother rather fancied his bridge skills and I had picked up a few ideas from him. I enjoyed both the company and the game. I was actually beginning to enjoy things; each day was spent with watches, practicing signals, painting our cabin and taking morning, noon and evening sights, and time off-watch was fairly social.

On the 9th, I was overjoyed to see my first view of the fabulous east; away on the starboard side were the small islands sitting at the north end of Sumatra. To this day, I believe that I could smell the mangoes, papaya and passion fruit in the breezes wafting from the shoreline (I had, of course, at that time never seen any of these fruits; they simply never appeared in UK).

Arrival in Penang occurred before midnight. The port is more properly called Georgetown, Penang being the name of one of the Malay States that constituted Malaya, which Britain had begun to formally administer in 1824. It is less of a classic port than a simple roadstead, there being insufficient dock space for vessels of any size. But it was surprisingly busy; we arrived to find the *Arcadia* (one of the biggest P&O passenger ships), *Chitral* (a small P&O passenger/cargo vessel plying the London to Japan route), *Cannanore* and *Somali* (pure P&O cargo vessels trading with the Far East), and, of course, ourselves, a veritable fleet homecoming. Right away, however, I noticed the peculiar phosphorescence of the water and, when anchoring, was able to see that that light arose from a sea of jellyfish. Apart from flying fish, this was really the first unusual marine animal that I had seen; more were, of course, to come.

Overnight the two large ships left, and we unloaded our cargo. Taking the opportunity to wander ashore, I was much taken by the town. I took a rickshaw (entertaining, if a trifle close to traffic – I saw no evidence of driving tests being needed, nor experience a legal pre-requisite to controlling a vehicle) to the Seamen's Club (actually a rather pleasing place in which to pass some time away from the hubbub of the ship) and bought a 'Times' (it was surprising how much one missed the news, despite it being four days out of date and with an airmail edition that was printed on the thinnest paper that I had ever encountered) and the 'Straits Times', which was undoubtedly the world's most uninformative paper that I had to that time encountered (although my view soon changed). Returning to the ship, I found that the small amount of cargo for northern Malaya had taken little time to unload, but that again we were marooned without power … and in a port with scant repair facilities, I was very glad not to be an engineer. I knew very little about engineering, but I knew enough to know that replacing boiler tubes was a very unpleasant task. It was at this time that thought of going to Kaohsiung in Formosa (Taiwan) was abandoned, so much behind schedule had the temperamental boilers made us, but the omission did not much concern me; I knew that I would likely be back to see the place, perhaps many times (in fact, I never made it to Formosa; its geopolitical role – Quemoy and Matsu had for a long time been in the news – was of much interest to me, and I rather wanted to see the geography).

The passage from Penang to Singapore was in many respects rather pleasant. We were running on one boiler, the zephyrs were light and the traffic modest, (only some decades later did traffic lane separation become necessary) and as tanker behemoths had yet to be invented, we encountered no north-bound shipping problems.

We arrived in Singapore on January 18th, and I was interested to see that as soon as we arrived the unloading gangs arrived on board and commenced work. Overseen by a Chinese foreman, I rapidly realised that this was a very efficient and different sort of port. Lunch took minimal time, each gang split up into groups of four and had bowls of rice and a fish dish between them, and little time was wasted in getting back to work. Just as interestingly, while in Penang the divide between the Chinese (who did most of the visible ship's work), the Indians (who ran all the business) and the Malays (who were in nominal charge and through whom the ultimate authority seemed to have to flow) was quite apparent. But in Singapore, the Chinese seemed in control of everything, except that, essentially unseen, the British, through the army and the navy, had the final say. The major issue in South-East Asia was then the Vietnam War and the vestiges of French efforts there were still apparent; we frequently saw *Cambodge*, *Laos* and *Vietnam*, three smart passenger ships very similar to P&O's *Cathay* and *Chitral*, themselves throwbacks to the need for the Belgians to travel to what had been the Belgian Congo. The port was also home to quite evident numbers of British troops and sailors.

The work needed by the officers in Singapore was minimal (though not, of course, in the case of engineers), and I was thus able to see something of the city. One necessarily went to Change Alley, which, true to its name, was little more than a narrow, enclosed street, but which I quickly realised was little different from Aden, though a good deal more expensive. The city itself, or what little I saw of it, was not, however, very impressive. To put it mildly, Singapore had not had a good war. It had fallen precipitously to the Japanese, largely because of the ineptitude of the British Army and Navy (in 1941, two British capital ships had been sunk within fifty minutes by the Japanese air force, which lost three aircraft in doing so) in part because the supposed supporting British aircraft carrier H.M.S. *Indomitable* had run aground in the West Indies, and partly as a result of which humiliation the western colonial powers were thereafter perceived to have feet of clay) and the city/state had been but lackadaisically resurrected; there was insufficient money to keep even the United Kingdom in the front rank, thus so much less important were the outposts of empire. On the 21st, we departed this rather disappointing port.

Three days later, we arrived at the fabled city of Bangkok. It was, however, difficult to know what 'arrival' meant; the land was so flat that there was no evidence of having arrived anywhere. But I took the opportunity, upon anchoring, of going ashore to the Mariners' Club and was delighted to read a few reasonably current magazines and also, for the first time in many moons, be able to hear some proper music; there was a record of Leonard Pennario and L.A. Philharmonic (in Grieg, I seem to recall). The city itself made no impression upon me, a fact that did not worry me as I knew that I would be back to see the unique sights and ride in one of the long canal boats. (I need hardly add that I was never to return.) But I was also advised by Plumridge that the most onerous part of the trip was about to start … though it was usually a remunerative interlude.

The following morning, I saw what he was talking about. A lighter loaded with squealing caged pigs arrived alongside, all of which were to be loaded, four high, on the fore-deck (which is to say, right in front of our cabin). The loading with ship's derricks, was noisome, smelly and, to me, cruel, as the creatures could move only to stand or lie down. In all, 450 of them were loaded, and about 420 of them immediately needed to poop.

But this was not all; once finished with our porcine guests, 150 water buffalo appeared. I know practically nothing of water buffalo (having lived partly in the country for a few years, I knew something of cows, one thing being that they were not always as docile as reputed, but these animals looked bulkier and had very big horns). Needless to say, they also needed to immediately answer the calls of nature.

The mate then came to our cabin and explained that this cargo was some sort of P&O tradition unique to this route, and that the animals were destined for the abattoirs in Hong Kong, which was the next port and four days' sailing away (if, of course, the engine was up to it). The 'tradition' seemed to imply that the trade was not strictly authorised by head office (though the company's other vessels on this route carried the same cargo) and that we were doing our local shipping agents a bit of a favour. But for this task we were likely to receive some extra funds to use in the fleshpots of Hong Kong. However, that benefit we had to earn; the deck crew, being Hindu and Moslem, was unable to minister to the needs of the pigs and, therefore, we cadets were charged with feeding, watering and keeping the animals reasonably clean. The saving grace was that the crew was to assist in the care of the buffalo and did not mind their feeding and watering. In fact, it seemed to me that they rather liked it, and unquestionably, it was a change for the better from the usual painting, scraping and maintaining wires and cargo gear. Loading was completed in the afternoon and off we sailed. Bangkok, however, was one of those ports whose exit provided considerable practical navigational difficulties; there are ports wherein a pilot is absolutely essential and this was one such. Likewise, of course, there are others where they simply come aboard to get their bottle of scotch. (Fundamentally, the captain was always in charge, but I was seeing well enough that it was necessary to very carefully observe what the pilots did well before one became a captain.)

The next day was a heavy one. The pigs had to be sprayed (it was, of course, exceedingly hot), given fresh water and, in effect, cleaned. We had also been provided with food for them, but distributing the swill was not an enjoyable task; they had to subsist on a bowl of water and another of bran per day, and actually getting among the cages and giving them the necessaries was a distinctly odious task. But by the third day, the nature of the job had changed; by then five of the pigs had died, and throwing the bodies overboard was far from pleasant, for they all seem to have died from some parasite eating them from inside, and carrying them to the ship's rail was a messy and gory task. Fortunately, the buffalo proved more hardy, although we grew to believe that they had been dosed a tranquilliser before being loaded; as time went by, their need to butt us with their large horns as we passed by increased. Of necessity, we sweltered in our cabin; however, the zephyrs were now manure-laden and unavoidable.

Hong Kong was one of the major P&O ports and lived up to every expectation. The number and variety of ships, large and small, was overwhelming. Although I had attended a lecture at the Royal Geographical Society in London about the efficiency of the basic design of a junk, to see so many of all sizes was an eye-opener (more current knowledge may be found in Gavin Menzies' '1421') and frankly awe-inspiring.

Junk and Restaurant in Hong Kong

The cargo had to be discharged, particularly that which now had to be transhipped for Taiwan, and then an army of men came aboard for a mass chipping and painting of every rust-spot on the ship. It being almost intolerable to remain aboard, I decided to take in the sights and sounds of what was reputedly the most interesting port on the entire run.

Hong Kong: Junk in rain squall

The press of humanity was perhaps the first impression. The second was the traffic. The primary mode of transportation was the tram, a mode of carriage that in London had disappeared in the early 1950s, largely because of their inflexibility, noise and discomfort. I remembered having ridden on many in my youth, but by 1962, they were a dim and distant memory. I clearly remembered their demise, for they had been replaced by double-decker trolleys, large, imposing and rather elegant machines, the better for being almost completely silent. They, in their turn, had been replaced by Routemasters and their forebears, more flexible indeed, but noisy and polluting. Walking around the colony felt like being in another era.

One of my purposes in going ashore was to relieve the silence (a comparative term) of the daily on-board activities.

Sampan/junk life in Hong Kong

Deck work on Khyber while in Hong Kong

At sea, there was no radio, and little enough portable music. Some individuals had short-wave radios, on which every now and again one could pick up the BBC or Voice of America, but normal communication was through the occasional outdated paper and, of course, the R/O, who existed in a world of the Morse code. So I searched around for a suitable tape recorder store. This was not a difficult task, for every sort of store seemed to have a group of nine-year old salesmen who diligently followed around every European pedestrian whom they could find. I was quickly directed to a suitable emporium by a very alert little fellow, and forthwith saw that the prices here were not only far better than anywhere else but that they were also negotiable. Furthermore, if one wanted a tape with something on it, virtually anything that had ever been recorded could be obtained within the hour. If the requested item was too obscure, 'the impossible took a little longer'; the stores plainly had a miraculous jungle telegraph. I need not say that neither I nor they seemed greatly concerned about copyright issues. In fact, I was sure that the excellent English of most of the traders did not include any knowledge of the concept. I was, however, very happy with my purchase of a Grundig machine and a posse of illicit recordings. Money was running out, so I decided that the much-needed camera would have to await my return, and that this occasion did not warrant the purchase of one-day made-to-measure suits and shirts. Actually, on that point I never changed my mind, as my twenty-two-pound Austin Reed suit looked good until it disintegrated; the $10 suits that I saw others purchase from on-board traders even when new looked quite extraordinary but not in a good sense. By this time, I had gained some knowledge of what I liked, as our dress uniforms were of a fine wool, hand-crafted by Gieves of London and frankly expensive; they tended to make lesser suits look insincere.

By the time I returned, (unfortunately, without having sampled the food) life was different as all of the livestock had been unloaded. The rest of the cargo having soon been discharged, we remained at a buoy for deck chipping and hammering to continue well into the night (nobody seemed to need sleep!). Fortunately, the foredeck wire-brushing and painting appeared to have largely been completed during the daylight hours. More importantly, the mate appeared and delivered ten pounds to each of us for our animal husbandry. The deck officers simply enjoyed Scotland's main product.

The trip to Manila, while short, was surprisingly choppy, a glance at the map making it look as though the short reach for the prevailing westerlies would make for a short stern sea. But arrive we did on February 6th, and it immediately became apparent that while it seemed to be a totally disorganised place, (Manila Bay is almost the size of a small sea) it was decidedly American, much as Hong Kong was firmly British. The main form of transportation, in a city that seemed devoted to traffic anarchy, was a peculiar vehicle called a jeepney, a unique form of modified and highly decorated jeep that the Americans left on the islands in their unmodified state after the expulsion of the Japanese. With many skilled

Filipinos having been trained by the Americans, largely for equipping the US to fight the Japanese and, latterly, the Vietnamese, there was an abundance of skilled steelworkers within the islands; their mechanical skills were apparent on virtually every vehicle. However, none appeared to have been trained in the art of driving, and as we were berthed close to downtown, I had good opportunity to see something of the city; my primary impressions were simple, these being that Manila, particularly its traffic, was chaotic, that there were as many cinemas in the city as there were people (largely, I surmised, because they meant air-conditioning in the blistering and dust-laden heat) and, lastly, that there were more beautiful women there than anywhere I had ever been.

While we had miscellaneous cargo for Manila, I noted that the gangs appeared to take no time off, even for meals. To my inexpert eyes, the people seemed quite impoverished (and this in the middle of the American Empire when vast sums were being spent to destroy much of nearby Indo-China). To me, an odd, if bustling, city.

The journey to Iloilo was a day's sailing, but Iloilo is one of those ports not much in evidence even when one arrives, the city apparently being little more than a collection of huts. The enforced idleness was by no means unwelcome. We were anchored in a very secure spot, the hot days were alleviated by some pleasant breezes, and apart from those odd packages seen in London, our cargo comprised little other than vast quantities of urea. This cargo has one or two purposes, but it is mostly used as fertiliser, a product that was hardly likely to be broached and which therefore could be left to the ministrations of the unloading gangs. And as we were to be in port for at least three days, we could waste our time in feckless pursuits; the 2nd mate went sailing in a small, and somewhat crude, boat that he had loaded in London, all who wanted to could play deck tennis – always invigorating and hotly competitive – and, on discovering that the 4th engineer had his record collection with him, and that it included every bit of Sibelius' music that had until then been recorded, I set about his collection with alacrity. Of course, knowing that at a time not so far off I would have to know by heart the Collision Regulations, lying around time was not completely ill-used. Additionally, I volunteered to keep watches while the other two cadets took out a lifeboat for fishing; the exchange of that time allowed me ten hours sleep, an almost erotically pleasant interlude, six unbroken hours to this time having been all that I had been able to take.

Our final Philippines port was Cebu City, barely 350 km from Iloilo. Never having heard of it before, I was surprised to find it to be that nation's second city and virtually where the Spanish had originally created their colony. It was, however, notably scruffy, and as we had little need to go there other than to unload some excess urea, I took the opportunity to walk around. At that time, the city had no worthwhile skyline and a modest population, and the transportation seemed mostly to be horse-drawn carriages. I also noted a few bandy-legged men walking around with holsters by their sides, filled or empty I did not care to find out. We departed at about midnight, bound for Jesselton.

Few, I suspect, have been to Jesselton (now Kota Kinabalu). Though the capital of Sabah, it was a rather charming, and notably clean, outpost of the Empire. Our going there hardly seemed necessary for the small amount of cargo which was to be discharged, but presumably, the company had to ensure that shipping agents knew on which ships reliance for delivery could be placed, so the flag had to be shown, even though we were only there for eight hours. Historically interesting, it had been virtually destroyed by the Japanese and British armies, but the centre of what vitality there was (this was a sleepy corner of Empire) resided in the Jesselton Hotel, into which I took a brief look, and was for a moment transported back into Somerset Maugham's South-East Asian world. (One could note that Mohammed Ali visited in 1975 after fighting Joe Bugner in Kuala Lumpur, so the city was not as 'remote' as one might suppose.)

We saw another, perhaps more enlivening, view of Borneo (still in the state of Sabah) in Labuan, which we reached after steaming at only eight knots through the night. Once again, we were in a place without much name recognition, but in fact it was a fairly significant location. Taken over by virtue of (a doubtless iniquitous) treaty by the British in 1890 as a new Singapore, it first hit the world news when in April 1904, during the Russo-Japanese War, it became a temporary stop for Admiral Togo's battle fleet as it tried to make contact with the doomed Russian fleet, which had steamed all the way from the Baltic (see 'Hubris' by Alistair Horne). Additionally, in World War II, it became the Japanese administrative capital of their short-lived East Indies Empire. I was glad to see a bit more of this island when I was obliged to take two seamen ashore to hospital – a detour so pleasant that I decided that on my next visit I would take a guided tour.

Another overnight transit of some 575 km took us to Rajang, at the mouth of Borneo's longest river. I have already expressed some doubts about destinations really being 'ports', but this was a sine qua non of nothingness. We appeared to anchor in the jungle, for there was no sign of any habitation (the 4th mate, who had never been to the Far East, being an ex-BP tanker cadet, told me that there was a bar ashore. Alas, he was jesting – a particularly feeble one, a good jest requiring at least a scintilla of credibility). We were truly in a tropical jungle, however; it poured with rain all day.

Three days later, we were still at anchor. We were also sweltering, because overnight we had been assailed by a fleet of what must have been the world's biggest flying insects. They happily flew into windows and portholes, presumably attracted by the light, so all had to be kept tightly closed. I was pleased to note that the locals, who mysteriously appeared from somewhere each day in barges and small motor boats, had no bother with B-52-sized insects. The cargo too was uninspiring, comprising mainly big rubber ingots but supplemented by specialised timber, some exotic spices and some odd products quite new to me. We were eventually glad to leave this strange world for the civilisation of Singapore, though this time only to bunker.

The trip to Singapore was brief. We were in 'Singapore' upon our arrival, but at the Shell Oil terminal at Pulau ('island' in Malay) Bukom, the most uninteresting of destinations. Tankers being its natural denizens, there were no cargo-handling facilities and the berths were all far more fire-conscious and protected than any normal port, so there was a long pier to navigate when going ashore. But any oil terminal had little to see anyway, so I wondered how tanker crews ever saw any worthwhile 'port' at all. But we were in and out within a few hours, so the only excitement was the receipt of mail. The point is worth making, however, for the pattern of communications with the rest of the world was sporadic and mail from home was a crucial lifeline. Our problem was that at the beginning of the trip, the company gives to the crew members a list of ports and the shipping agencies, but our schedule had been so disturbed that we were receiving Kaohsiung mail in Labuan or even in Penang, though by this time the omission of Formosa had brought us nearly in accord with the original schedule.

The cargo-learning process was continued in Penang, at which port we loaded 3,000 tons of Ilmenite sand. This cargo, of which I had never heard, dropped into a hold from a considerable height, unlike soot landed with a dull thud and without any cloud of dust. It seemed to be fairly common material (all ships had a good reference library for the common and extremely uncommon cargoes that even specialised ships carry) and had some variegated uses – it is used in the production of bright white items, pigment for paint and extensively in the production of titanium. An ideal trouble-free cargo, (unless dampened, when it rapidly developed mildew) its loading usually meant the simplification of stability issues as it was very heavy for its volume. As if to emphasise cargo weight, we also took aboard a number of tin ingots. Although these were religiously placed in the ship's cargo lock-up, it would have been an absurdity to try to steal one of these sparkling silver slabs; I tried lifting one, and although I could do so, though at some risk of herniation, to move anywhere with it would have created material for Monty Python. All this took two days to load, after which we steamed over to Belawan, the second city of Sumatra and only six hours across the Straits of Malacca.

This port had been very important when Indonesia had been under Dutch control but was at this stage a run-down, though vibrant, city, full of people, odd products (I had never seen durian, dragon fruit and similar products) and numerous vendors of the largest prawns that I had ever seen (junior cadet got the job of buying a load for the officers' pot, a task that I could happily have carried out every day). And on board, after loading at a port where we had loaded the heaviest of cargo, we came to load one of the lightest; tobacco. These leaves were hauled aboard in large rattan bundles that were cumbersome but easily lifted by two persons. Because it was tobacco, it came on board with numerous guards, thuggish fellows who looked as though they might have divided loyalties. This cargo went into the lock-up with the tin, the keys to which were retained by the mate. (I never understood the lure of this stuff. While living in Woolwich, a good portion of Father's business was the sale of cigarettes. He did not need to emphasise to us the poisonous nature of the leaf; both grandfathers smoked like chimneys and virtually coughed themselves to death. Moreover, few seemed worried outside ourselves about the odiferous cloud which at all times accompanied each smoker.)

While the ship completed the loading of several thousand bales of rubber, (again, a cargo that hardly needed our attention, the bales being large, cumbersome and liberally covered in talcum powder, without which product unloading from a hot cargo hold would be barely imaginable) the officers decided that we would challenge another British ship (*Antenor*, a smart Blue Funnel Line ship carrying on a similar trade to ours) to a game of football. We unfortunately just lost 6-2, a trifle unlucky, our team agreed. But we decided on a re-match two days later. This time they won 7-2, but this was because one half of the pitch was swampland. Unfortunately, we had put quite a lot of beer on the result, so our ship's stores were somewhat depleted (strangely, the referee and touch-judges all joined in – Moslem scruples were undiscussed). In all, we spent six long days in Belawan; too long, but despite the great heat, an enjoyable sojourn.

From the daily routine of supervising the unloading and subsequent loading of the ship, (the trip around south-east Asia and Hong Kong lasted from January 10th to March 6th) we were at last homeward-bound, essentially without working ports until we were to arrive in northern Europe. This allowed time for studying, learning the art of paint-chipping, and various navigational requirements, including the eternal taking of sights and watch-keeping, during which the officer of the watch would sometimes insist on our practicing signals (frankly, not that fascinating a task with an aldis lamp – usually hand-held – to signal passing ships, always only to ask such scintillating questions as, "Where are you from?" and "How was the weather?" However, two matters of no little interest were, on one of the world's busier shipping lanes, how very few were the ships that we encountered, and secondly, that I recall no ship not being able to reply in English, something that could only reinforce our collective ethnocentrism). On our second day at sea, Ramadan began, a Moslem fasting obligation of which I had hitherto been unaware. This seemed to necessitate, after sunset, large and tasty meals for the engineering crew (being so close to the equator, fasting times were very similar in length to the night hours) but was not apparently limited just to Moslems – our mess steward was Christian, for example, and looked forward to celebratory evenings under the stars. These occasions seemed generally to be accompanied by meat curry, of which, I am reminded, we had a choice every lunch and dinner, a habit derived from P&O's origins in its trade with, and administration of, India.

Watch-keeping on a route such as that across the Indian Ocean could be tedious and unenlightening. The bridge had to be kept pitch-black (no reading or anything), the absence of crossing ships, and the mainly straight route between Sumatra and Aden until arrival at the tip of Ceylon, from where the course deviated to the north, resulted in our maintaining only two courses for seven days on end. (The Ceylon of the 1960s demonstrated some identity crises; it had earlier enjoyed being known as Taprobane, then Serendip, and more recently as Sri Lanka; I will stick with Ceylon, as it then was.)

But such time was not entirely wasted. On the twelve to four, we were fortunate to have as our lookout a member of the crew who was outside the norm. We knew him only as Kadar, but he spoke good English, and, of course, excellent Hindustani. Therefore, I could enjoy some good first-hand lessons in that language, on which subject we cadets were periodically tested (not a complicated language, but, as I discovered, with a country boasting some 200 languages, not actually as useful as expected). Just as significantly, he was quite anxious to take a 2nd mates' ticket so that he could graduate to the nascent Indian merchant marine. In 1961, it was obvious that India was a coming maritime power, there having been at Warsash two Indian cadets (I became quite friendly with one, a gentleman named Dadi Modi, an intelligent fellow whose abilities augured well for his nautical career) who, as with the two Iraqi cadets referred to earlier, demonstrated the way to a future that not all westerners accepted, even so long after the independence of South Asia's nations. The night-time discussions were, therefore, by no means uninteresting as, while Kadar was little 'educated', it was apparent that he wanted to take every opportunity to learn what he could but that he had already taken upon himself the need to learn something of politics, economics and philosophy (not that someone from his milieu would be ignorant of the latter; Indians had composed the Vedic texts several hundred years before Pythagoras, Socrates and Plato had begun to rationalise ethics, psychology and logic).

While the northeast and south-westerly monsoon seasons are usually very marked, March is, as it were, a sort of shoulder season. We were, therefore, on this section of the trip favoured with a markedly pleasing period of weather and enjoyed a 'calm sea and prosperous voyage', marred only by the revelation that our destinations in northern Europe were to be Bremen, Hamburg, Rotterdam, Le Havre, Antwerp (for dry-docking) and then London for five days. This seemed to me distinctly unfair; nearly five months at sea and then only five days at home. (The order of ports was confusing, as I could not see how loading cargo in the appropriate order could be accomplished if one did not know in what order the ship was to deliver its goods. The answer, of course, was a combination of lower weight (stability) and careful organisation of goods on the ship's three levels;

loading in Rajang and Belawan had to be carefully planned by the cargo officer, though the ilmenite had to be left aboard until late in the parade of ports.)

The brief visit to Aden was uneventful and we made our way up to Suez. This time, I was able to see much more of the Canal, the passage being made in daylight. In the morning, when we were truly homeward bound, we were also fortunate enough to witness *Canberra* heading south. But we finally left the heat of the Middle East on March 21.

Canberra transiting Suez Canal

The temperature and climate changed markedly almost immediately, but the notoriously bilious nature of the Bay of Biscay on this occasion was but a passing bother; we were on our way home (in those days, and perhaps even now, the Gibraltar to the English Channel transit is termed 'The Channels', a time when almost any unpleasantness, especially seasickness, seemed a mere inconvenience). This part of the world encompassed many of the world's busiest ports, full of coastal traders, fish-boats, channel ferries, warships and all manner of nautical oddments, there were major sandbanks, the whole arena narrowed down to some twenty-one miles at its northern end, there was always rainy fog, and no authority had at that time implemented any traffic-separation scheme. In short, it was chaotic – but time passed quickly!

The city of Bremen was a misleading term, for it was in reality two cities, the port being better known as Bremerhaven. The river Weser, being an entrepôt for western West Germany and for Bremen itself, is for that reason an important trading artery. The brief transit up the river to the terminal was by itself a matter of interest, there even being damaged but seemingly viable submarine pens immediately alongside the riverbank. However, it was a mixed delight to stroll around the city itself. Being aware that the end of the war came in part because of the bombing campaign that destroyed most of the military infrastructure of Germany, I was surprised to see that the area of the city adjacent to our berth was sparkling new in design and structure, with well-stocked shops and street vendors selling cream cakes the like of which I had not seen in England. It all looked new and prosperous. Recalling Woolwich, I could only ask myself the usual question; "Who won the war?"

Back on board, all was activity. The first thing to discharge was the tobacco. I was in the hold when the locker doors were opened, and those precautions had certainly prevented the cargo being broached. But what the doors could not do was keep out the ship's rats, of which I had over the past few months seen a number scurrying over the decks. Apparently, the rat guards always placed on the mooring ropes at every port had little effect … or perhaps they had, even worse, been effective, but simply allowed access to superior rats. Anyway, that issue was up to the insurance adjusters.

Over the next five days, much of the cargo was very efficiently discharged and we sailed the short distance up the coast to Hamburg. This was a larger port than Bremen, but its ambiance might as well have been from another planet. It was definitively grimy and drab, the rain was continuous, and all that we discharged was a huge amount of rubber. Less than a day later, we arrived in Rotterdam (one quickly realises, when there, how small is Europe), where I was delighted to find that officers' partners were arriving from UK – I was to be sent home! I was very happy with the lifeboat problem.

From being somewhat unhappy with the four or five days that were originally in view for this short leave, it now seemed that the period of recuperation would be some three weeks, not the few days originally proposed. This was a good thing … but only 'sort of'. The problem, which I soon found to be almost universal within sea-going staff, was that while one was at home resting-up, everybody else was either working or enjoying their normal lives. I had heard of mariners who came home and found themselves strangers in their own homes, but the reality was that one was a bit of an interruption to the daily lives of one's families; a wandering nomad with all sorts of interesting tales, (except that mine were by this time not that interesting, as I had written lots of letters home to tell my story as it developed, and after a few hours, there was little left unembellished) one plainly became rather quickly a bit tiresome. Additionally, we now lived in deepest Sussex, I was without a vehicle, and, even worse, without feminine company. David was at school and therefore absent, and both parents were out earning the daily bread.

Reflection, therefore, became something of the order of the day. I realised that the environment in which I had grown up was somewhat removed from the realities of the real world. The British system of public (which is to say, private) education presented one with a reality that was unequalled in its tautness. I had been to two schools that represented the best that our parents could do for us, and those institutions had tried to instil an understanding of life that was frankly myopic; the British had for long rightly been the ubermenschen, the Empire was inviolate, the Russians had merely helped us win the war, and the Americans were for the most part brash ingrates (in 1944-45, "The Americans are oversexed, overpaid and over here," was not by any means a silent lament). In boarding school, I and most of my companions had greatly enjoyed use of the library, for it contained such exemplars of the gilded age as the Biggles, Bulldog Drummond, John Buchan, G. A. Henty, Kipling and R. M. Ballantyne, the 'Nile' books of Alan Moorehead, the leisurely lives of Somerset Maugham's characters, and school curricula that emphasised the civilising influence of Speke, Gordon and Livingstone, all heroes whose lives were expended for the betterment of the uncivilised masses and from which we all, to a greater or lesser extent, had learned that we, the British, with the senior Commonwealth members, still had a job to fulfil in the world's affairs.

The problem was that so much of this belief-system was, self-evidently, based on sand. The independence of India and Pakistan had generally been unenthusiastically greeted by the British public, whose view was that those countries should be grateful for what the British had bequeathed them. Before reading a bit more history, for example, I had not heard of the Amritsar Massacre. In Africa, the Mau Mau Rebellion had caught the headlines during its currency, no views other than that it was a savage and entirely unwarranted uprising by disaffected ingrates having appeared in the news as the savagery went on, and elsewhere in Africa, the Gold Coast inexplicably had decided to forego the glories of the Empire and become the unknown state of Ghana. By this time, the Malayan Emergency had been defeated, but far from the world being more settled, the forces of apparent enlightenment were evidently on their way out; already, Indonesia had forcefully ejected the Dutch, the Vietnamese had displayed the hubris of the unknowing by siding with the French during the war but whose perfidy was thereafter demonstrated when they emasculated the French army, one of the world's finest. Further, most of French West Africa seemed restless, and the Congo was a bottomless economic and political mess. Even now I recall listening to the BBC announcing the fall of Dien Bien Phu. The import of this event was not lost on anyone in the Empire, or the newish euphemism 'the Commonwealth', as peace was collapsing in Cyprus, Aden was dissolving, 'trouble' was foreseeable in Southern Rhodesia and human rights were soon to remove South Africa from the concert of right-thinking nations. Fortunately, though, not all was dissolving; British Honduras (known as 'the armpit of the British Empire') was still a stalwart – though hardly anyone knew where it was.

But the time for reflection was soon past. I had been fortunate in having my leave extended to May 2nd but being at home was not all that it was cracked up to be when everybody else was living a 'normal' life. While I had seen and learned a lot on my first voyage, I was hoping that a bit more would come from the second. And indeed, it did.

Khyber departed London, destined for the same sequence of ports as on my first voyage. Once again, the Bay of Biscay transit was horrible, but a new book ('The Franco-Prussian War' by Michael Howard) leavened the time spent lying down, and also incidentally made me realise why the French were such a grumpy lot. But upon passing Gibraltar, the weather improved noticeably. Thereafter, we needed only about thirty hours in Genoa, and the trip to Port Said was accomplished by May 16th. And now that it was May, the weather was much hotter, but as the South-West Monsoon rains in the northern summer, the trip across the Arabian Gulf was unexpectedly pleasant – and with no engine break-downs, it almost felt like a cruise to the fragrant Orient.

But first, we had to drop into Colombo. This was not a part of the scheduled cargo run, but merely a pause in the voyage necessitated by a crew change. Colombo itself is an important port, if only because of its location, lying as it does between the distant big ports of Bombay (Mumbai) to the West and Madras (Chennai) to the east. As it was a port not normally on P&O routes, (though passenger vessels called there with some frequency) I would have liked to see something of the place, but the limited time in port did not allow walks ashore. The crew change (the entire personnel of all three departments changed almost completely) was accomplished with speed, partly because there was little to take aboard, the water being little better than the brackish stuff available in Aden, and fresh food being in short supply even in Ceylon itself (pretty hard to imagine such a lush tropical paradise being unable to supply every fresh food that one could wish, but this was well before improved crop yields transformed agriculture). The stay was therefore short, and as most of the new crew were old P&O hands, despite being newly aboard, it was quickly apparent that their knowledge of how things were done on P&O ships greatly exceeded mine. A short but not unpleasant stay.

Thus, early in the afternoon of May 27th, we weighed anchor and proceeded into the Gulf, en route for Penang. But at 3:26 pm, the engines unaccountably stopped and electric power was cut. As I was on watch at 4:00 pm, I went up to the bridge to see what was happening (with no power and no noticeable wind, conditions on board in such heat quickly became less than comfortable). We were only a few miles off the coast, but the water was deep, and we had emergency power, so inconvenience was more appropriate a term than difficulty. And so it proved; at 5:15 pm power was restored and off we went but only for about ten minutes.

Again, all power was lost, and the chief engineer, a man of consummate gloom, came up to the bridge to report that a small problem had occurred; apparently, the 4th engineer, charged with turning on the engine's lubricating oil, had forgotten to turn the requisite valve, and that, therefore, the problem was no longer minor. The engine could be repaired, but considerable time and work was needed.

This turned out to be not quite the case. As I was on the 4 to 8 with the 2nd mate, I was on the bridge for one of the most boring watches of my life. But, again, not for long; at 10:45 pm, power was restored and again we resumed our course. But only for an hour or so, as just before midnight we again came to a juddering halt. Again, the chief engineer came up to the bridge, and now was even more glum (come to think of it, practically every engineering officer that I ever knew was of dour mien – I think this was caused by the almost eternal high heat and the permanent loud noise, neither wholly relieved even when in port).

Now the R/O was the man of the hour (he was one of the very few officers who could normally rely on sleeping most nights, his enthusiasm for late night hours being self-evidently easily contained). He was, however, able to call up Colombo pilotage, who were able to inform us that a tug would be sent out to us right away and that we could expect it to arrive late the following afternoon (this, by itself told us quite a lot about the word 'urgent' in this part of the world; we were only 27 miles from Colombo!). So, we waited.

At 9:00 pm the following evening, the tug arrived. By then I had, of course, seen quite a few tugs in various ports, Rotterdam probably having the smartest and most handy, Cebu and Rajang undoubtedly having the smallest and least useful. However, *Hercules*, registered in Colombo, was huge. From the ship's bridge, it seemed to be about half the size of *Khyber* and looked as though many decades ago, half-way through construction, was converted from paddle-wheels to propeller (I have not omitted an 's'). Other surprises awaited, especially that it did not possess a radio; thus, all our signalling had to be in Morse code by night (by aldis lamp) and semaphore during daylight hours (and I had wondered why we had had to learn these arcane skills!). The actual towing preparation was no small task, as the anchor cable had to be run out and a shackle of cable, with the anchor, suspended from the hawse pipe, and a wire from *Hercules* attached to the remaining anchor cable. This created a heavy towing cable, but in deep water provided a sort of de facto spring, thus absorbing energy surges created by wave and ship inter-actions (and a new word – catenary – entered my vocabulary).

The tow continued all night with virtually every officer and deck crew awake throughout (and a cadet posted on the bow to see that all was well – actually on a balmy Indian Ocean night, not such a bad job). This was, however, too good to last long, for at sunrise we suddenly arrived on the Continental Shelf and the whole system had to be re-rigged to a simple wire; our cable was beginning to snag the bottom. Two pilots boarded to take us into the harbour, but after twelve minutes under their guidance, the wire parted. This did not much matter, for *Goliath*, another not-quite-so-huge tug, arrived, and we were alongside a repair berth in the harbour. At that point *Hercules*, with a tired crew and probably itself worn out, was relieved by *Samson*, a newish and much smaller tug with which I became much more familiar as time (and there was a lot of it!) passed.

Colombo is described in places as a natural harbour. In part, it is properly so described, but its northerly two thirds can only be utilised because of the extensive breakwaters that man has constructed. The openings in the breakwaters lead directly into the Indian Ocean, and because of the rough weather that can afflict the west of the island, there would not be much of a port if the natural southern inlet comprised the whole port; the west coast of the whole continent is not much given to good natural harbours; Cochin, 350 nautical miles to the north, is the nearest anchorage of any consequence, but in 1962 it was not a city nor a port of substantial international commercial consequence.

One advantage of Colombo as far as we were concerned, however, was that there was really no differentiation between the port and the city. And having such a reputedly exotic city a mere ten minutes' walk away meant that it was easy enough to get away from life on board. And increasingly, we needed to do so.

Hitherto, the manifest problems of which the deck department was aware related only to the ship's boilers. These, however, comprised only one of the many components of the ship's propulsion and ancillary machinery. The stops to date and to which I have referred had been numerous but not lengthy and consisted mainly of the replacement of water-carrying tubes in the steam-producing boilers, a steam-turbine propulsion being quite different in concept from the more modern diesel propulsion. The lubricating oil omission with which the present problem related occurred within the turbines themselves, these being numerous fine steel 'propellers' rotating within a high-pressure encasement and a parallel low-pressure turbine, their rotating being substantially reduced through a gearing-down system before being used to drive the propeller. In this case now before us, the repair was much more significant than mere boiler tubes. Part of the problem were the facilities available in Colombo; during World War II Ceylon had been very strategically located, particularly after the Japanese took Singapore and part of Burma. The need for facilities to repair warships, however, was initially greater on the eastern side of the island, particularly in Trincomalee, a naturally protected harbour that was a temporary home to a large number of Allied warships, that is, until the Japanese sank *Prince of Wales* and *Repulse*. Therefore, both for repair facilities and because of its superb harbour, Trincomalee would have been better equipped than Colombo to have handled the repair that was now required. However, parts and specialist engineers could be flown in, so delay was the only issue.

And it was indeed quite a delay; it was 42 days later that *Khyber* was able to depart Colombo for Penang. And what of Colombo?

Well, it was not the exotic city that legend might indicate. I could go into the town quite frequently, and indeed occasionally take longer trips, but both the country and the city were not in great shape. Firstly, Colombo itself was decrepit and the population impoverished. While I had seen a good number of poor people (in the Philippines for example), this city seemed to have an entirely disproportionate number of beggars, some in deplorable physical shape, and many with babies (though I was more than once informed that these babies were in fact rented out to the 'mothers', and looking at the apparent age of some of these would-be parents, this was not difficult to believe). Further, there was a famine afflicting the island, so the ship was unable to purchase much by way of fresh food from the local vendors; in fact, the only useful addition to the ship's supply was the occasional harbour fishing trip organised by the 4th mate that produced a few excellent crayfish. Additionally, within the city there appeared to be nothing worth buying, all bookstores having only used books on sale, and all other stores' supplies being quite deficient in everything other than saris.

The two exceptions to the lack of things to purchase were jewellery and currency. Everywhere one walked, one would be hounded by men, and children, to purchase rubies and diamonds at laughable prices (Ceylon being one of the world's most important sources of rubies). Obviously, one had to regard these bargain items with some scepticism, but eventually I did purchase two from a disconsolate child for a few pounds. Needless to say, upon having them looked at in UK, I was told that these had been cooked up in a pot for a few hours, and while quite decorative, were of no more value than pebbles on a beach.

The currency issue was more important. One obtained rupees from the chief steward at a rate of about ten to the pound. While walking in the city, however, I found that the initial offering of strange little men walking on the street was twenty-two rupees to the pound, and that it was not difficult to obtain twenty-eight after a bit of haggling. I, therefore, wrote home and asked for a couple of pounds to be mailed to me for my expenses, and upon their arrival was able to obtain a very good rate.

Of course, there was very little on which to spend this largesse.

There was, however, one exception; a tour. And on one of our days off (for the most part we were kept busy by the mate in chipping the decks, painting, and suchlike menial tasks) we cadets engaged a driver to take us on a trip to Kandy, apparently a truly exotic city and the ancient capital of this historic island. This was an all-day expedition and a truly enlightening one. While the road to Kandy from Colombo can only be described as very primitive, the traffic met, which included a number of elephants and oxcarts (not to mention the oxen), were of formidable size, necessarily dictating which gave way to the other. But this gave us the opportunity to see a good deal more of the people and the island, which we quickly realised was, in fact, a country of unsurpassed beauty. The road was mostly uphill to Kandy and we ascended into lush tropical forest and primitive but picturesque villages and were able to stop at a tea plantation. Tea being one of the country's main exports, there was a good number of these plantations to see, but watching the pickers (all women) one also became aware of the fact that tea-picking is a thankless and back-breaking task; one observation, however, was that the air was much cooler at these heights than in the foetid streets of Colombo, so physical work could be much less unpleasant than on the coast. In fact, one was likely to change one's whole opinion of Ceylon by this day's outing; the climate was much more equable, the people looked more prosperous, we saw no beggars, the population numbers seemed much more attuned to available resources, and the plantations added an air of industry to the ambiance. The crowning glory was, however, Kandy itself.

The country's second city and ancient capital, its main claim to fame is that it is home to the Temple of the Tooth. Ceylon being largely Buddhist (though with the north being largely Hindu, and the west coast the domain of the descendants of the Portuguese, Dutch and British colonists, it is in reality a multi-cultural community), being the repository of Buddha's tooth gives the nation a cachet that it would probably not otherwise enjoy. The relic is taken out of the temple once each year on the back of a special elephant in a splendid parade, at which time the city's population, needless to say, explodes. And far from Colombo's ill-repair, Kandy was in perfect condition, paint apparently being available, whereas this seemed not to be the case in the capital, and the buildings and the lake around which the main buildings cluster presenting a picture of tranquillity that reflected the reality of following what is probably the most gentle of the world's great religions.

While forty-two days in one port, and one of the less salubrious at that (even the Seamen's Club was run-down) is not the sort of thing that one generally expects on scheduled voyages, I have found that few experiences in life are of no moment, and in many respects the most unlikely situations can lead to the most unlikely of consequences, unforeseeable and random. So it was with this unfortunate breakdown.

One should not, however, simply dismiss Colombo as a cultural desert, nor as one deprived of access to more esoteric pursuits. I noted, for example, that on one evening the Colombo Symphony Orchestra was playing a program of Mozart and Haydn. This was to be held at the Lionel Wendt Hall, a cultural centre located close to the ship. I decided to give it a try and was quite surprised at the venue. A relatively modern, though small, concert hall, I quickly saw the great advantage of Mozart having composed twenty-seven piano concertos and Haydn having composed one hundred and four symphonies; there was an endless supply of music for a small stage and what was almost a chamber orchestra. Such an ensemble was unlikely to ever run out of music of the highest quality. I not only thoroughly enjoyed the evening for its own sake, but it opened one's eyes to the elegance of the sari when properly worn, and to the fact that in the right places, there was no shortage of beer and wine, as the cream of Colombo society came out in force (probably all expected Mrs Bandaranaika, the prime minister, who apparently lived nearby, to appear. However, I did not see her).

I also took the opportunity to walk around that part of the city and realised that the grubbiness of the port area was by no means symptomatic of the whole of Colombo. This was in reality a garden-like setting which treated its wealthier citizens quite well.

After a few engine trials, now apparently as good as new (which in many respects it now was) *Khyber* departed for Malaya, shortly to become Malaysia.

Of the two large bodies of water either side of South Asia, the Bay of Bengal is probably the more reliably benign. But to set against that is the fact that it is in effect a funnel for shipping coming from the rest of the world into the Strait of Malacca, one of the world's busiest waterways. For the burgeoning South-East Asian nations, the annual growth of trade and the volume of shipping was staggering.

But that did not much matter to me. Two days out of Colombo, Young and I were informed that we were to leave the ship in Port Swettenham (now Port Klang) and join *Mantua*, a tanker presently bound for Singapore. P&O itself (apart from subsidiaries) owned four tankers at that time, but I had never come across anyone who knew anything about working on this type of vessel. We were, however, going into this venture 'cold'; two of the cadets presently on the vessel had been caught selling some of the ship's fire-gear (unwise on any ship, but on a tanker!) to some local 'entrepreneurs'. We were simply to join as soon as we could; the recalcitrant cadets, it need not be said, were to be flown back to UK as soon as the ship docked, their sea-going career thereafter unlikely to be extensive.

Arrival in Penang was somewhat anti-climactic; *Mantua* was still at sea. On July 17th, we arrived in Port Swettenham (not much of a place, actually, though it subsequently became Malaysia's biggest port) and were whisked ashore by the local P&O agent. I was not unhappy to leave *Khyber*; in its personnel, it was a pretty easy-going ship but far from a comfortable one. And I had had enough hot and sleepless nights in a small and stuffy cabin. So, I looked back without nostalgia; I never saw her again, the ship reputedly being scrapped a few months later.

****

It is opportune to refer to three significant matters that were to profoundly affect the world of shipping but which at the time received little of the notice that they deserved.

The first occurred in 1956 when the *Ideal X* set sail. This, the world's first container ship, effected a revolution in cargo transportation that was of a significance not then apparent. Time and prosperity had boosted the world's trade to such effect that the world of freighters was, to those who could see it, an anachronism, unnecessary days being spent in port, the acquisition of qualified crews daily growing more difficult and the wastage to cargoes becoming matters of major concern. *Khyber* was a manifestation of that obsolescence; a new day had dawned.

Then in 1957, the Boeing 707 commenced to operate. Almost instantly the world's passenger fleets saw their livelihood evaporate, in particular Cunard Line and P&O. The process took time, but it was inevitable. Though slow (envisaging new types of ships, designing, and then constructing them could not be rushed), once commenced, the revolution accelerated. *Queen Mary* and *Canberra* rapidly became white elephants.

Thirdly, equally significant was the US Jones Act (of 1920). This legislation, designed to maintain the dominance of the US merchant marine by requiring trade between US ports to be carried in American ships that had to be manned by

Americans, had exactly the opposite effect; the American fleet was gutted. The effect of this protectionism, urged by ship-owners and unions, was (as should have been anticipated) most recently to reduce US private-sector ships from 193 in 2000 to 91 in 2016. (Britain has had similar legislation; it was repealed in 1849!). In effect, US merchant shipping, including cruise vessels, became a worldwide irrelevance; P&O would have been happy to promote this act!

2 Mantua and Malwa

The car ride up to Kuala Lumpur was very instructive; most ports offer a distorted vision of the country being visited, as they are unusually cosmopolitan. In most countries' ports, certainly in Malaya, the lingua franca might as well be English, and shops have available most things foreigners – crew and passengers – might want. Inland, Malaya presented a most attractive countryside, lush, well-ordered and interesting in its variety of plantations, unusual trees and shrubs, and, of course, acres of rubber trees.

At that time Kuala Lumpur, while a city of some significance, was very different from the concrete and glass jungle that an advancing economy has produced. The country had the benefits of political stability, was patently prosperous and had the advantage of being in sharp contrast to nearby Vietnam, Laos and Cambodia, where the escalating conflict demonstrated the clay feet of the world's greatest power. Indonesia was becoming an economic and political quagmire, Burma, shortly to be a reclusive military dictatorship, apparently descending into poverty, and Thailand was home to amiability but sharp social divisions. Malaya was helped by having resources of tin, rubber (earlier, and very successfully, transplanted from Brazil) and a well-educated population. The problem that could have prevented progress, that of the racial balance between the Malays, the Chinese and the Indians had apparently been resolved by a delicate agreement as to the role of each faction, the only recent issue of substance having been the communist insurgency which the British and Malayan armies had successfully

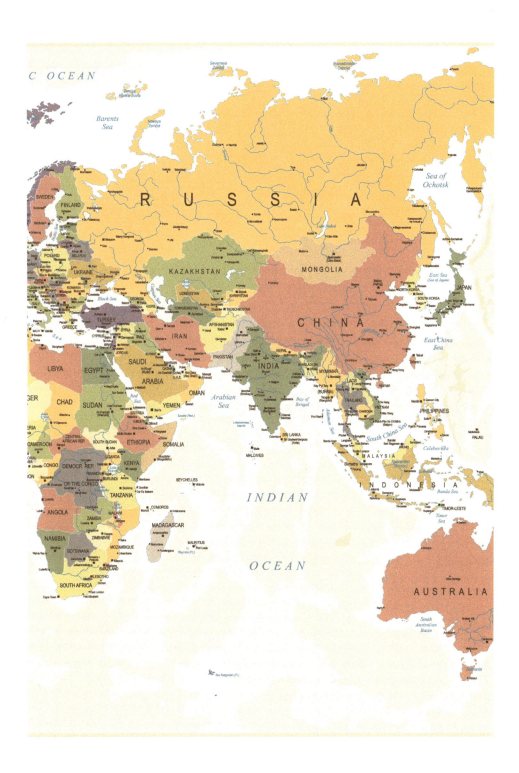

rendered impotent. Even from this conflict and its resolution, though, the Americans had in Indo-China drawn the wrong conclusions.

We arrived in Kuala Lumpur on a fragrant evening, and were able to see much of central K.L., a clean and modern city without evidence of poverty; it presented a pleasing contrast to the shambles that was most of Colombo. We were able to see much of the central district, as our train was an overnight to Singapore. While I had always been something of a railway fan – it was the way to get to school, but, more importantly, it was the way home as well – and the sheer magnificence of British main-line engines was the stuff of legend, especially when while at school in Folkestone we could nightly see the *Golden Arrow* steam past in the dusk on its way to deliver lucky passengers to the continent. The Malayan trains were not quite so glamorous, being more workmanlike diesels, but they were clean and fast (though I always loved the ambient scent of smoke created by the British behemoths).

And, indeed, they were very comfortable. Never having slept on an overnight train, this was my first experience of such a journey; I was overjoyed by the excellence of the fare that was served and then by the quality of the bunk (and, of course, by the blissful seven hours' sleep). If the new experience was any harbinger of things to come in this new chapter, then I was receiving a handsome introduction.

Singapore, then not as sparkling and grandiose as it became, was nevertheless far smarter and tidier than the Malayan ports that I had visited. But there was no time to dally; the agent drove us quickly to Pulau Bukom, where *Mantua* had by then arrived, and we climbed aboard, my first time on a tanker. Greeted by the mate, Mr Tate, we were shown to our cabin by one of the cadets remaining on board.

And this was a very welcome surprise. Not only was the cabin spacious, enormously so by comparison with the cramped *Khyber*, it was gloriously air-conditioned, as always much needed in Singapore, which is only some seventy miles from the Equator. The ship was of a then new, but obsolescent, design, had all the officers' accommodation in a mid-ship's 'island', and an aft superstructure containing the dining room, the electrical and engine components, storage, the galley and all of the crew.

The principal issue to be faced was, however, a bit more fractious and, indeed, delicate. On this vessel the whole crew, other than the steward's department (which was, again, Goanese) was Pakistani and, therefore, Muslim. Someone in London in 'Ship's Supplies' had apparently studied unusual economies and discovered that P&O was supplying toilet paper to ships with Muslim crews; it appeared that Muslims were prohibited from using toilet paper, or at least had some centuries before being so proscribed. (The issue is still contentious, but it is apparently one of those religious rules that in the fullness of time and in the face of practicality have been mostly eroded into oblivion). The 'economy' was ill-received; before we had joined, the whole crew had walked off the ship in protest, never to return (whether the order from London was ever rescinded, I never discovered). Already unloaded, we were a ship, for a time, without a purpose.

But for only two days.

On July 19th, the agency had rustled up a completely new, and Chinese, crew. This was actually not difficult to do, P&O having a solid presence in Singapore and being known by the seafaring community to be a good company for which to work. The only caveat to the crew situation was that very few P&O officers had worked with Chinese seamen and thus language differences were now to be something of a barrier between officers and crew (as a point of note, one observes that in Sherlock Holmes' novels the Lascar seaman makes frequent appearances, so well-known were they in East London from the early days of the South Asian contribution to the Empire). So, I got to explore the ship.

In any cast of characters on a ship, the story starts at the head; the captain. I met him after a very short time aboard, as he was a person who liked to be 'hands on' with his officers. A man of commanding stature – he was about seven feet tall – and commensurate girth, Captain Basil Thomson was the commander in every sense of the word. A tanker being more of a principality than almost every other type of ship, because it spent an extremely high proportion of its time at sea and not in port, one's circle of acquaintances for prolonged periods of time was very limited, and such was Basil's personality that he tended to dominate everything aboard. He was a Royal Naval Reserve officer (termed RNR, a sort of hybrid officer who would expect to be among the first to be called upon to become a naval officer in the event of war) and therefore was entitled to fly the blue ensign on his ship. This flag is the third in a trinity (white for the Royal Navy, red for the Merchant Navy, and blue for special category, including Australia and New Zealand (as modified), the RNR, and a few smaller members of the Commonwealth). But the privilege is conditional; depending upon current practice as dictated by the Admiralty and the Board of Trade, there needed to be a set number of other reservists on board, a number that has mutated over the years. Such strictures, however, were of little consequence to Basil. He was the only such officer on board but decided to fly the ensign not only while at sea, but all night as well, and then highlighted by a spotlight! Legitimate ... I think not, but nobody was about to tell him that.

Other peculiarities unique to him included the keeping to himself of all of the ship's Rose's Lime Marmalade, a peculiarly English type of spread that was everywhere very popular. At breakfast, however, it appeared only at the captain's table. Unusually, certainly for tankers, the epitome of utilitarian ships, he also insisted that officers wear caps when out on deck. This instruction was fairly sensible in places like the Persian Gulf but rather pretentious for normal life. He was also very conservative (a trait that can flourish in the cloistered world of ships), which led him to espouse, quite vigorously at times, that Britain was going to pot, in particular that the working class, whom he thought could barely speak the Queen's English, was becoming a bit uppity; the BBC, the divine repository of how to speak, was beginning far too eagerly to allow the lower orders (the Beatles not excluded) to rise above their station. As far as he was concerned, change should be gradual, and, if necessary, be imposed from the top of society downwards, Commonwealth citizens should appreciate how fortunate they were, and neatness was tantamount to Godliness (which he also liked, each Sunday conducting a wardroom 'service'). True to form, it was rumoured – there may have been a picture in his cabin – that his car was a vintage Bentley ... but that may have been wishful thinking, on our part, of an archetype that he seemed to represent.

But all that set aside, he was held to be an excellent (the need for the caveat will soon appear) seaman and he was committed to instructing cadets about the skills of their trade, even sending us down for a month to work in the engine-room (an idea that I did not know any other captain to follow, although I am sure that some did). And, despite his foibles, he was always polite to his officers, sometimes sternly so; such cannot be said of all captains, many of whom overtly enjoyed the imperium of a ship at sea.

The mate was of an entirely different order. Arthur Tate was a very small man, perhaps five feet six inches. This did not seem small generally, but set against the gargantuan Basil, when on the bridge, he appeared to be quite comfortably able to walk beneath Basil's stomach. He was also very taciturn, again perhaps in response to the effusive and booming Basil. The remaining officers called him 'half-a-mate', which fitted rather well. He did not keep a watch and, therefore, had a superficially easy job, because on a new tanker there was very little paintwork, ship's gear or rigging repair to effect. He was also reputed to be well acquainted with the gin bottle but never known to be drunk. His particular skill, however, was an essential one; P&O had two large and two small tankers, the first two, *Malwa* and *Garonne,* being for the carriage of 'black oil' (lightly refined, sludgy stuff that was for P&O refined largely in European ports) and the latter two, *Mantua* and *Maloja* being white, or light, oil carriers. They were more specialised, cargoes varying between the heavier grades (for example, diesel fuel) and the very light, the most volatile perhaps being aviation spirit, which was barely a liquid and therefore a dangerous cargo to carry. The problem with such a small tanker fleet was that very few officers knew much of loading or discharging oil products, and this was important; there were only four input lines into twenty-seven cargo tanks, and any type of product could be contaminated by coming into contact in the slightest way with a less-refined product. Therefore, it was always necessary to load the cargo from the most refined first to the least refined last – the latter, I believe it true to say, could hardly ever be contaminated except when very egregious errors occurred. On the other hand, the highly refined could easily lose all of its value by the slightest mixing, and for this, the mate was responsible. He, having had much tanker experience, was thus the link between the Cat-Cracker (where the product was refined) and the operation of the whole tanker enterprise. But he kept to himself; we saw him at mealtimes and when in port, but other than that, he was rarely visible. He was, in effect, at once the most efficient and the most misanthropic of shipboard companions.

Of the other officers, only the 4th mate was of significance in daily life (it seemed that whenever I was on watch-keeping, he was the one with whom I worked). His name was within P&O one to savour; Mr Hill was the son of one of P&O's senior captains, who, I believe, rose to be commodore (essentially, the senior, though not necessarily the longest-serving, of the company's captains; it meant little other than commanding the fleet flagship). Hill himself, however, didn't seem to fit the role very well. A heavy-set and large fellow, he had the face of a pugilist rather than an officer, rather reminiscent, I thought, of Henry Cooper, a British boxer of some repute. Moreover, I saw that he had the habit of punching cadets on the top of the arm in a rather gleeful way, and they were not light blows. I actually had many thoughts of how to deal with this quite inappropriate behaviour, either by sticking a thumbtack to my shoulder at the spot which he always hit, or by delivering a hard blow to his jaw, unseemly though that would be. But the right occasion never arose; for some reason, he never delivered such a blow to my shoulder.

A cargo ship in port was all hustle and bustle, lots of people, noise and things, like swinging pallets of cargo, to carefully avoid. A tanker, on the other hand, was on the face of it a sea of tranquillity. Below decks, however, each tank had to be cleaned and washed by sprays and, if necessary, by assiduous scrubbing. It was hard and filthy work and, on occasion, in part overseen by cadets who had no idea what they were trying to achieve. And it had to be done with speed. The first port was Plaju, a place of which I had not heard, but which was almost due south from Singapore and only some 200 miles away. There we were to load a cargo for Singapore, return there and then await instructions. And I quickly learned that on tankers, one actually did quite a lot of awaiting instructions, for the ship was on a long-term charter to Shell Oil, and that company, with its myriad of ships and ports, transported the oil from where it was found to where it was needed, taking into account the many types of non-interchangeable products that vessels could carry. It appeared to be a nightmare to manage from London, but only occasionally was there a major change of instructions (as will become apparent), though we had some days of steaming at reduced speed while thousands of miles away others decided on our destination. On this occasion, however, cleaning was completed relatively quickly, and we departed for the short trip to this unknown place.

That day, we crossed the equator. In the normal course of events, crossing the equator for the first time was a big event, assisted by Father Neptune and copious amounts of champagne. But on this occasion ... well, it was no occasion at all! We continued with the cleaning which, suffice it to say, was an unsophisticated job while at sea; we simply pumped water into tanks (judiciously, of course; filling up the wrong tanks and leaving others empty might put substantial strain upon the hull) and pumped until the water flowing upwards from the tank, out through the ullage vents and over the side, ran clear and uncontaminated – which states were not necessarily coincident.

This passage being short, we cadets were kept on the bridge, in part to steer. This need arose because, firstly, the usual helmsman was 'George', who was always the automatic 'helm' and, secondly, because the new helmsmen were completely unfamiliar both with the ship and with the officers' language. This was fine during the day because all was visible, but as night came and we bore closer to land, my familiarity with steering was really put to the test. (I had learned what I knew on *Khyber*, where nothing was automatic, the helm was a big old traditional wooden ship's 'wheel', and the length of the ship allowed it to respond very quickly to the wheel's turning; *Mantua*'s helm was smaller than that of a car, there was no feeling in the hands as the rudder responded, the wheel eliciting only electrically transmitted effects, and the whole ship responded only slowly to turns, it being much longer and more squat in the water than a conventional hull shape). I was also disconcerted to learn that Plaju was five hours sailing up a twisting river that, to my jaundiced eyes, made the Tyne look like the Amazon. And the pilot who boarded inspired little confidence; a tiny man dressed in a shabby suit, he completed an odd trio with the mate, who was by now on the bridge, and the enormous figure – and personality – of Basil. Furthermore, the river was apparently quite shallow, a matter for more future concern, as, fully loaded, our draught changed from a few to many feet. I was relieved to see, however, that Basil took this all in his stride. He allowed the pilot to assist (he was so short that he had to stand on a stool to see over the 'dodger' – the front of the bridge) but had no hesitation in taking over control whenever he deemed it necessary, as it frequently was. (I don't believe that the vessel had ever before been to this port, so this was quite a virtuoso feat). Much to my relief, we arrived without incident and almost immediately began loading (a tanker is only making money when it's transporting product from one place to another; dallying in port was almost unknown).

Morning came, and we began the return trip. Daylight revealed the river to be not quite the hazard that it seemed at night; nevertheless, I hoped that future ports would be a little more tanker-friendly.

Singapore again, but as usual in virtually all oil terminals, well away from the city; for relaxing off the ship, there was only a rather dull Seamen's Club. Highly efficiently, we discharged our cargo in a few hours and loaded our stores and victuals; we had been advised that we were bound for the Persian Gulf. At that time, most tanker routes led to the Gulf, but nothing that I had heard about that part of the world made me want to go there. (When at Warsash and choosing the company which I wished to join, several companies and destinations were rarely chosen by any of my classmates; Cunard, because of its eternal routine runs over the Atlantic; West Africa, because of its heat and chaotic city ports; Royal Mail Line, because of its destinations being exclusively in South America; and all tanker companies, because one saw very little of the world, despite going to numerous 'ports'). Moreover, I did not relish once again going across the Indian Ocean; the last such trip lasted fifty-two not particularly pleasant days.

And I was also back in the engine room. Having seen *Khyber's* turbines, I was somewhat familiar with the general principles of the steam turbine engine, but *Mantua* was built on a somewhat larger scale, and of course, was much more modern (at that time relatively few vessels were motor (diesel) vessels, and very few indeed were turbo-electric, as was *Canberra*). One issue, immediately apparent, was that such complex machinery, tucked away in as small a space as was practical, generated enormous heat, heat exacerbated by the warm waters of the Indian Ocean. There were large vents all over the engine-room, and air from on deck was continuously pumped down. But that air was, needless to say, very warm itself, so the relief, such as it was, was no different from standing under a very warm hair-dryer. The work itself was very routine, mainly comprising taking the temperatures of thousands of almost unreadable gauges, and, once a watch, cleaning the nozzles which forced the fuel into the boilers. This was a horrible job, as it required climbing up the front of the airless boilers and extracting these tubular jets. No engine-room watch could, I thought, ever be pleasant.

Another substantial difference from what I often enjoyed on the bridge was that one could not converse. I kept watch with the 3rd engineer, a genial enough northerner (like most engineers), from whom I could gain knowledge of what we were doing but with whom, because of the ambient noise, could not engage in any conversation. I was also obliged to keep the 12-4 watch, which was not my favourite – one never got five hours' continuous sleep. And I was scheduled to remain in the engine-room for about a month … barring a major change.

But major change occurred. On July 31st, at thirteen minutes past one in the afternoon the whole engine-room shuddered, and the telegraph rang, "Stop." Such an order is not expected half way through an eight-day voyage but is not difficult to effect. At least, it was for the 3rd engineer; I had not a clue what to do, but that did not matter, for I was instructed to go up on deck and see what all this was about. So, I again clambered up the front of the boilers, past the funnel, and out into the cool air, which was somewhere around a balmy ninety degrees. I was greeted with the sight of dry land; about a hundred yards from the starboard side was a palm-fringed island along whose beach I could see a line of excited gesticulating people. I knew that going back down and telling the 3rd engineer that we had surprisingly come alongside an island would not cut much mustard with him (besides which, the light vespers were pleasant indeed), so I decided to take a trip to the bridge (which, of course, was half-way up the ship).

There I encountered a quite chaotic situation. I asked the cadet what was going on, and he, knowing that he had to look as though he had something important to do, directed me to the chart, telling me quickly that we seemed to have run aground. This I had, of course, ascertained myself, but I looked at the chart and saw that our last charted position was near the south-western end of Kiltan Island, which I noted had last been charted in 1896, but about which there was a hand-written note (which notes are legitimately made on charts to reflect the latest marine developments) stating that 'coral growth' had been observed on the south-west corner of the island. I looked then at the Pilot Book (these provided much information about everywhere in the world) and saw that this was one of the Laccadive Islands and a leper colony administered from the state of Kerala; that was all that I and the 3rd engineer really needed to know.

This was, of course, more than enough for the engine-room staff, who by now had been joined by what seemed to be every other engineer aboard. This was now a chaotic place; normally, preparations for engine manoeuvres began many minutes before needed, as many adjustments to the whole system had to be made. However, those involved were more than up to the job, and, inasmuch as it could be a smooth operation in such circumstances, the Chief Engineer was fully in control. And he needed to be; the commands from the bridge were 'half ahead' followed moments later by 'half astern', this to produce a sort of rocking motion to effect release from the bottom (coral being sharp, but not very solid – assuming that it was, in fact, coral! – it could just be ground down. It is to be remembered that we were a light ship, having only a small tonnage of ballast water aboard, therefore with little to pump overboard to lighten the ship and raise us in the water). I had noted on the bridge that every interested party in the ship (P&O, Shell, local agents of P&O and the like) had been notified of our situation, but one irony did not escape my notice: Cochin was the nearest port that could offer some assistance, but the nearest port that had tugs of sufficient power and ocean-going capabilities was no less a place than Colombo!

Fortunately, the need to undergo the same experience twice did not arise; after an hour or so of slight, and then greater, to-ing and fro-ing, we made our own way off the bottom. I was by then on the bridge (the carpenter had ascertained by soundings that we were not taking on water, so the need for any emergency measures was avoided), but as we steamed slowly northwards away from Kiltan, we were disconcerted to note that a BP tanker appeared on the north-east corner of the island (hitherto obscured from our view). The Pilot Book informed us that that vessel had been aground there for three years!

There being no apparent damage to the ship, we headed towards the Strait of

Hormuz, the entrance to the Persian Gulf (at that time, Iran being the primary power in the Gulf, this was its name. However, because of the growing political importance of the surrounding Arab states, the name was shortly thereafter changed to, simply, the Gulf).

The voyage, now to be to Abadan and Bahrein, was accompanied by a rather more gloom-laden atmosphere than hitherto. It was also noted by some wiseacre that the masts, though small and barely to be noticed on a tanker, were no longer precisely in line; it was evident that some damage had resulted from the grounding. We did not yet know whether repairs would, or could, be carried out in the Gulf.

We saw little of the ebullient Basil. The 2nd mate, however, advised me that the grounding was not entirely unexpected, a similar incident having nearly occurred too close to an island off New Zealand earlier in the voyage, when Basil, anxious to take some photos for his wife, had taken the ship too close for the comfort of the officer of the watch. I had moreover already learned that deep-sea navigators very much dislike getting close to the shore, unlike coastal officers, who, on the contrary, became uneasy when out of sight of land. On that occasion things were close, but evidently the charts were at least current. No sequelae occurred, but unfortunately Basil had insufficiently learned from the experience.

The trip to the Gulf was made the less pleasant by the fact that we were traversing the Indian Ocean during the South-West monsoon, the effects of a beam-sea made even less pleasant by my remaining on engine-room duty. But the transition into the Gulf was dramatic, for that body of water almost never experiences a truly rough sea, though the already hot environment in the engine-room was made even more intolerable by our being surrounded by a sea degrees warmer than anything I had encountered to date.

As usual in oil ports, Abadan contained no facilities ashore that were in any way sought by itinerant seamen, even though the berth was actually alongside the shore itself. There was a Seamen's Club, but it offered nothing that anyone aboard sought, so we were simply left to our own devices under the hottest sun that I hoped never again to experience. However, given that there was a variety of products to pump aboard, and we were to load in two different ports, the pumping and diversion to of the cargo to discrete tanks was a complex exercise, both from the perspective of non-contamination of products and the constant need to be concerned about the balancing of empty tanks with the ones that were filling; we were all to a greater or lesser degree aware of mysterious (and not so mysterious) losses of tankers that had occurred because of intolerable strains put on these enormous hulls by full tanks wanting to sink and adjacent empty tanks wanting to rise. But, of course, there was drama elsewhere.

Waiting for us on the dock as we arrived was a delegation of P&O and Shell executives. They quickly boarded and disappeared to Basil's cabin, never to be seen again until they departed en masse, less one of their number. Basil was not seen again; one suspects that he said farewell to the senior officers and departed on the next available plane to London. Left aboard was a new, and very different personality; Captain Cowan.

****

There was a sequel to this sorry tale.

In 1976 I came across *Supership*, a book by Noel Mostert, a journalist who gravitated from South Africa to Canada and became something of a specialist in maritime matters. The book, published in 1974, appeared at a crucial time in the bulk-oil transportation business. The Suez Canal had again been closed because of Arab-Israeli conflict, an event which gave greater urgency, if any were needed, towards the modernisation of tankers and their ability to transport ever-larger quantities of oil products from the Gulf to the ever-expanding of needs of the industrial world.

The author had joined *Ardshiel* in Rotterdam. This vessel was a 214,085-ton super tanker owned by P&O, and, need I say, commanded by Captain Basil Thomson. It transpired that Basil had, as Mostert said, "…been found at fault in an accident and had left P&O…" and, I learned, subsequently joined Zim Israel Shipping as a master. Later, when in New York, he had been contacted by P&O to determine whether he would be prepared to re-join his old company. This was doubtless because the seagoing career was becoming increasingly unpopular among senior officers, and it was probably thought that the incident on *Mantua*, for which he had been fired, would not be repeated. In his book, Mostert indicated that Basil had thoroughly enjoyed working with 'the Israelites', as he termed them, because they had the high standards in personnel and ship maintenance that he had liked, though not unreservedly, with P&O. Mostert's voyage, from Europe to the Gulf, was of great interest to seamen, though the voyage itself was essentially without incident. Something of a Cassandra, the author feared that the world's insatiable oil demand would result in many more and greater marine catastrophes. He was right respecting the growth in size (there are today Ultra Large Crude Carriers that exceed 300,000 tons), but the limitations imposed by the depth of the oceans, and particularly the continental shelves, resulted in the practical size of these ships having probably reached a natural limit.

Mostert obviously believed that Basil had returned to his natural home (P&O) because that was the life to which he had over the years become accustomed; he was a stranger when at home in Brighton but knew a life on a ship to be thoroughly in accord with a life well-lived. The culmination of the writer's view was that;

"Her Master, according to P&O tradition, was a first-class seaman and he ran his ship according to older precepts, regardless whether they made him popular or not, which is what counts, because it is first-class seamanship and conscience that will help us save our seas, not polish and affability. If there were a Basil Thomson in command of every flag of convenience tanker afloat there would perhaps not be so much to worry about, except, of course, the very structure of the ships themselves…"

One has to wonder if this conclusion would be the same if the author of those words had known of the remote island of Kiltan.

****

As we were in the heart of the Gulf in August, one could only describe the weather as absurdly hot. There was usually a wind, but as it invariably came from the desert, by which the Gulf is surrounded, its effect was never to improve conditions on deck. Abadan was not a port which I ever wished to revisit, but it was quite a lot better that Bahrein, which had nothing to excite the senses. At the end of a pier, this port typified the sort of existence which tanker crews knew all too well. But we were soon loaded, and on our way to Durban, frankly, about as civilised a port as one could hope for; not that I found anyone on board who had ever witnessed its luxuries.

The trip through the Gulf required vigilance. Ports were not numerous, but tended to be spread about, thereby meaning that these cumbersome tankers had to constantly be on watch for large ships being on reciprocal courses or in dangerous crossing situations. Another unexpected issue was the heating effect of the constant sun. While we noted that most days would give rise to about 105 degrees on deck, the effect of this temperature on the cargo could be quite dramatic, and as a result seawater had to be sprayed over the whole deck for days on end. Otherwise, had the cargo expanded, we could have experienced some unpleasant, and perhaps explosive, consequences. (Other dangers, however, proved not as real as one might have expected. In the event of a blowout of one of the accesses to the cargo tanks – the ullage ports - the danger of fire was not great, the mixture arising from the ship being so rich, and almost bereft of oxygen, that it was not especially flammable. I had heard of a Shell executive, as a demonstration, actually throwing a lighted match into a full cargo tank and it simply being snuffed out in the liquid petroleum. The story might well be apocryphal, but I knew of nobody who ever wanted to repeat the experiment!)

The ship was now, however, a very different one from that which I had joined only a few days ago. A ship has its own character, of course, but the memory of a time on a particular ship leaves impressions of those with whom one sails, the places where one goes, and, only lastly, of the vessel itself. Basil was such a dominant figure, literally and figuratively, that he tended to shape to the whole social milieu. I had actually got on well with him myself, but he had a reputation for being obsessively particular (chart pencils had to be not only perfectly sharpened, but lined up with military precision, his binoculars and bridge chair had to be exactly in place at all times, bridge lights had to be lighted exactly as brightly as he wished, and one should not ignore the marmalade!). He could also get very angry, I was told, but set against that, he was regarded as a fair man, and as the Master of a ship usually 'at sea', steaming from one port to another, and thus a person almost uniquely answerable only to God, an unreasonable Captain could easily become the worst of martinets.

We soon learned that Captain Cowan was made of very different stuff, and frankly a very charming man. A good seaman and, I guessed, more generally experienced than Basil, he had an ease of manner that one could recognise as a man who probably knew little about tankers (and likely did not much appreciate being given command of such a vessel) but knew that it was a well-run ship and such a vessel needed only occasional assistance from himself, essentially only when arriving and leaving port and when ship's inspections were necessary. Basil seemed to enjoy visits to the wardroom, especially on Sundays, when he could talk with – or, more accurately, at – his officers. Cowan, however, did not obtrude into the personal space of others, and I do not actually recollect his coming down to the wardroom to converse. This is not to say that he did not do so, but that he made no effort to be 'the senior officer'. The upshot of these factors is whether *Mantua* can be said to have been a 'happy' ship. *Khyber*, in its own way, was, but Basil tended to make the whole ship's atmosphere uneasy, the officers' mess being permanently 'on edge'; our new Captain seemed to appreciate that each man was an island and wished to remain that way. The atmosphere was 'contented'.

Bahrein, as can be seen quickly on the map, is a very long way from Durban, a port very largely unknown to P&O officers. More to the point, however, I was now beginning to realise the differences between cargo-ship sailors and their tanker counterparts. The tanker, when fully loaded, is a fairly indolent beast; mostly, it ploughs ahead slowly, usually for voyages longer than those of cargo vessels, and with destinations mostly of very little interest. Few join tankers to see the world. Thus, life comprised keeping watches, the taking of sights twice a day, and accommodating to life on a ship that in comparison with my previously limited experience was very routine, and truth be told, could be quite dull. There was afternoon tea following the post-lunch nap (a tradition acquired, certainly in P&O, from the time-worn habit of life in India, where, as Noel Coward observed, "Only mad dogs and Englishmen go out in the midday sun"; an afternoon snooze was also one of Churchill's habits, gained, of course, during his service in India) and usually a pre-dinner and sometimes pre-lunch 'pour-out', where a few officers got together for a beer or two, or something stronger, though I still maintained at that time that scotch was almost undrinkable. Just as popular was the Pink

Gin, equally unpalatable to me, but which I understood to have been based upon the need to have something to consume that would make more palatable the daily dose of quinine. (Of Bourbon, Vodka and Rye I believe that P&O had never heard, in much the same way that the American Cocktail, an invention designed during Prohibition to make drinkable the moonshine made in domestic stills, had barely entered the English lexicon). But the days provided ample time for me to become well-acquainted with Bellini's 'Norma', whose nearly three hours soon became my favourite opera.

Cargo ship officers, however, had opportunities to see a great deal of the world. Most general cargo was slow both to load and discharge, the docking facilities were close to a town or city to which both stevedores and onward transportation had ready access, and, of course, many of them contained their own licit or illicit pleasures. It is also to be observed that the majority of the world's great cities, with some obvious exceptions, are coastal, and even many of those that are far from water have a major nearby port, such as Rome, Cairo, Tokyo, and Beijing, to name but an obvious few. Therefore, the crew facilities on tankers were usually much more comfortable than those characteristic of most cargo ships (though *Khyber* of necessity was well below even those standards, as I had yet to discover). After a few years at sea on a cargo ship, one could reasonably expect to have a good number of worldwide acquaintances; a tanker officer would probably know few other than port officials.

Despite the pour-outs and active wardroom it should not be thought that the life led by sailors was one sporadic drinking session; the consequences of overindulging were too severe. On a run from, say, the Gulf to South Africa, there were few ships to see, the Suez Canal being the normal route from the West to East; the immensity of the Ocean was a more common impression than how much seagoing traffic there was. This voyage occupied seventeen days, and the fact that little was seen of the shoreline rendered the occasional film, the wardroom activities, the high quality of the food and the need to study a life much more pleasant, at least for a while, than that enjoyed on a cargo vessel. Added to the ambience was the air-conditioning and the sheer comfort of the large cabins. With the passing of time, however, these lures have predictably declined in importance, for today it is difficult to persuade both men and women of the pleasures of a seagoing life, particularly on a ship that spends day after day at sea, and then briefly visits some very dull ports. A case in point was Southampton, a port of obvious attractions, but with an oil port that was situated miles up the Solent, rendering a trip to the city a major outing. As unloading a cargo was a quick and sometimes dirty business, the time was just not available to enjoy its fleshpots. But at least there was somewhere to go; I could not see any joy to be had anywhere near Abadan, Bahrein or Plaju.

The voyage down the east coast of Africa was, however, by no means unpleasant. It was hot, of course, but nowhere near as intemperate as the Gulf. It was a good time to catch up on the correspondence course and to get to read big books, although the period of seventeen days without a word from home, or indeed from anyone whom I knew, made me feel a bit glum. But there was one strange incident that seared itself on my memory.

On one after-lunch Sunday I was sitting in the wardroom with a number of the junior officers, including a couple of cadets, the 3rd and 4th engineers, and Hill, the 4th mate. As on all ships, most relationships between officers were distant, but generally amicable enough; a modus vivendi usually developed, though very few friendships ever formed, in an environment in which, in general, little happened. I was sitting opposite the 4th engineer, an amiable, bearded and slight young man, and saw that a bit of an argument about some trivial point was developing between him and Hill, who was standing directly behind his chair. Suddenly there was a sharp exclamation and I was astounded to see Hill violently punching with both fists both sides of the 4th engineer's head. Several people jumped up, but almost as soon as he had started, Hill stopped and stalked out of the room. The 4th engineer looked startled, but despite what looked to me like a quite vicious assault, seemed uninjured, though to me Hill had by no means pulled his punches. I felt that I should have done something, as I did not see this action as uncharacteristic of what I knew of Hill, but the group silently dispersed without further discussion, and, oddly enough, I never heard another word about this incident. This was to me a seminal moment; throughout life one is presented with many occasions taking just a second or so, but during which one is, as it were, frozen into inaction. Perhaps only heroes or fools can react with the decision about which they afterwards fantasise, but even today I still do not know what to make of it … but I was always more than a little cautious thereafter with someone who evidently had a very short fuse. In fact, after *Mantua*, I never heard what happened to Hill; I certainly never wished to sail again with him. Nor did I have to.

The arrival in Durban was not a moment of exaltation. As frequently occurred, the port was not ready to receive us. We therefore were obliged to anchor offshore awaiting a suitable berth, but with a calm sea and a rather kindly sun, this was not by any means an onerous obligation. In fact, rather the opposite, for in my youth I had never been inured to the pleasures of fishing, and this, it quickly became apparent, was one of the main pleasures of the Chief Steward. Miraculously a number of fishing rods appeared after he appeared on deck (a rare occurrence) with his gear and some fish from the freezer as bait, and a good number of officers decided that joining him might be a pleasant afternoon's pastime. The ship being fully loaded, we were only a few feet from the water, so I watched from the bridge (someone still had to ensure that we remained at our allotted anchorage) as a pleasant afternoon's fishing got under way.

It didn't happen. The few baited hooks quickly yielded a few interesting samples for the galley. But very shortly, the picture changed completely. Within fifteen minutes the ship was surrounded by sharks, ominously predatory, of which I had previously never before been aware (one sees dolphins, flying fish, sea snakes, even whales, but sharks infrequently appear to surface dwellers) and which readily yielded to the temptations of baited hooks, and when hauled on deck thrashed around in a violently dangerous way. But a few of our braver worthies quickly saw this as excellent bait and, chopping the thrashing fish with carving knives with dangerous expertise, found that there was much more flesh available than could easily be used. More heavy fishing rods rapidly appeared (from where?) and very soon the deck was running with blood, but the effect in the water was far more dramatic. By utilising the shark flesh as bait, the surface was transformed, for, within a few minutes, there appeared a host of hammerheads. These, surely among the more bizarre of animals, were large, ten to fifteen feet in length, but most obviously, driven by a terrible savagery; they attacked all and sundry around them, smaller sharks, other fish who happened to get in the way, and offal left by the dead and dying around them. All around the starboard side of the ship the sea was alive with the quick and the dead, huge sharks seeking food, smaller sharks dead or dying and many trying to escape the maelstrom. Although hammerheads move around in schools, and this predatory behaviour, including cannibalism, have obviously produced a very efficient machine, the afternoon's experience was to me akin to a vision from hell. Survival of the fittest was all very well, but to see it in action was sobering.

Next morning a berth was available, and we went alongside a pier that, as expected, was a substantial distance from the city itself. However, discharging the cargo was not complicated, it all being fairly standard product (though I was told not to be too complacent, the last cargo delivered by the ship within the Indian Ocean having been aviation spirit unloaded at Gan, a somewhat secretive British Air Force base south of Ceylon. That product that was more gas than liquid and thus far more dangerous than virtually any other normal product). But unloading in Durban occupied less than a day, after which we were sent to another berth, there to have our hull examined.

The hull inspection was by itself interesting. Immediately after berthing, there came aboard a gang to clean those tanks that were to be examined because of possible hull damage. I had previously had no experience other than by anecdote of the effect of apartheid, but it was immediately apparent to even the unenlightened how pervasive was this systemic cancer. The gang comprised about fifty blacks supervised by one white man, who patently regarded his charges with contempt. Curiously, the gang itself, though very unkempt in clothing and appearance, seemed quite happy, singing and laughing around the buckets of water with which they had been supplied for liquid sustenance, even though I saw little evidence of their careful preparation for descending into the tanks that we always experienced because of the known dangers that such descents could impose upon anyone who went into such gaseous environments without adequate backup (attested to by Mostert in 'Supership'). Reinforcing my reflections, I later came upon a book by Michael Caine about the filming of 'Zulu' (to me one of the finest of films, with him as a star or otherwise), in which he states that he very nearly left South Africa during the filming because of the gratuitous violence shown to blacks by supercilious whites.

But all was part of the day's work. It transpired that a split of fairly minor proportions had been discovered in the forward tanks (apart from the masts no longer being aligned as they should have been) and, on a surveyor's advice, 200 tons of concrete was pumped between the hull's forward longitudinal girders. The damage occasioned by the grounding ended here; thus repaired, *Mantua* sailed on until its scrapping in 1976, in reality long past its 'best by' date.

This being August 26th, my jaunt into the city was something of a disappointment, the day being some sort of public holiday. As this was one of those ports where the oil terminal is located as far from the city as it can be, the actual time ashore was fairly brief, and all that I managed to do was go to the local zoo. This was not unenlightening, however; I was particularly drawn to a large tank in which a number of fishes were kept. What again struck me, with the prevalence there of large and small sharks, was the behaviour of those animals, for if one needed a lesson in 'survival of the fittest' this was the place to see more of the savagery of nature. Quite often the biggest of the sharks, not all hammerheads, would simply bite their aquarium companions, often in half, and eating what they had bitten, simply glide elsewhere into the tank, presumably satiated.

But it was good to walk ashore, and good to have a coffee that was something other than the drek served on board. That, of course, was soon enough to be the norm, for we had the dull prospect that for another seventeen days we were steaming back to Abadan, a port for which my enthusiasm could scarcely decline; it was always exceedingly hot and dusty; its only redeeming feature was that mail was pretty reliable. But it got worse, for from the Gulf we were to sail for nineteen days to Port Elizabeth, one of the world's duller ports. Then we had to return to Abadan, thereafter, to take twenty-one southerly days to reach Cape Town. This, of course, was a wonderful city, made the better by the berth being in the city itself (certainly one of the world's most picturesque ports) and the taking on of fresh provisions (milk in particular, a welcome change from horrible powdered milk). Then, once again, we were bound for Abadan.

In general, being actually at sea produces a philosophical view of life. But occasionally real life throws an odd curve. The vessel being due for periodic maintenance, the last return to Abadan was notable for heralding the much-anticipated return to UK, a return that had looked as though it would never occur.

Cape Town Harbor

However, the port to which we were to return for painting and maintenance was North Shields, a grimy and depressed city close to Newcastle that clung to its significance as a shipbuilding centre, but which patently could not long hold on to its old purposes. Not that that much concerned me, for I was to be home for Christmas!

The Christmas of 1962 was a very unusual one in that it snowed. Snow is not, of course, unknown in UK, but this particular year it was unusually intense. Getting to Sussex by train was bad enough, but the snow didn't stop coming down, and country villages were without snow-removal equipment. I was due back on *Mantua* on December 27th, but as even the trains, particularly the local ones, could not handle more than a mere dusting, I had trouble even getting to the station, where I had to leave my luggage until the weather improved. A few days later it warmed a bit and I was able to get on the train and travel north. But this was not a happy time; upon the sale of the business in Woolwich, Father had invested in a small building company located in Sussex. The weather meant that all of the incoming work was stalled, but, of course, employees still had to be paid. Needless to say, the business failed, the only saving grace being that Father was soon able to secure employment in a retail wine merchant, a job that he could do easily enough, discipline and techniques in the confectionary and liquor trades not being much different. We sailed for the Gulf on January 1st, but this year there was an air of despondency on board; last year whisky for the first time … this year no celebration as we ploughed through the angry Bay of Biscay in ballast, cold and with a destination disliked by all on board.

We were scheduled to bunker in Aden, it apparently being cheaper even than was Iran, but along with a number of places around the colonial world, it was beginning to dispute the suzerainty of overlords. Unrest was beginning to infect many such vassal states, among which could be counted East Africa and the remnants of European empires such as Aden, Djibouti, Cyprus, Ghana, Malaya, the Rhodesias, Mozambique, and of course, Vietnam. Many hitherto safe ports of call were becoming too 'hot' for ships to visit.

However, for reasons that were not made known to those on board, we were directed not to go to the Gulf, but to proceed across the Indian Ocean towards Singapore, there to be given instructions respecting our next ports. And these were, to me, bizarre; we were to proceed to Borneo, but this, though the island is the world's third largest, was not known for the production of oil. However, in retrospect, it might have been portentous, for in Brunei, a tiny enclave on the island, there had been discovered some worthwhile oil deposits, which later proved substantial and were at the time being developed by Shell, who were, of course, our charterers. We were then to proceed from there to Liverpool, a port which I had never visited, but might present a good opportunity to transfer to a more interesting ship or route.

It was not to be. Two days later our orders were countermanded, the first time that this had happened in my limited experience, and we were instructed to go to Singapore itself, from where we to traverse the equator again and go to Plaju, then back to Singapore, and then perhaps on to Abadan; such are the travails of the tanker trade!

In Singapore we loaded a complex cargo, the most refined being kerosene, a product now needed in Penang, whence we proceeded. Penang having no berth of sufficient size, we were diverted to Butterworth, Perak, a port of which I had never heard, and, it transpired, of which I never need to have heard. 'Join P&O and see the world' was all very well, but what I was seeing constituted the armpits of civilisation; seamen's clubs had beer and outdated newspapers, but access to those luxuries was not why I had decided on this life. Furthermore, we still were unsure as to our destination, though it was obviously going to be the Gulf, though I now knew that this was a destination that brought only work and sweat.

On February 16th Ceylon hove into sight, from where we turned north-west towards Kiltan. But February 19th was a momentous day indeed; Captain Cowan allowed me to keep my first watch on my own (though I suspect that he also kept it from his cabin immediately beneath me). The vessel also passed Kiltan, but this time so far from it that it failed to even smudge the horizon. However, no discussion arose from that fact.

It now being confirmed that we were to load at Abadan, we were then advised that our destinations were to be Cochin, Madras (as it then was) and Calcutta (as it then was). While those ports were perhaps interesting in themselves, I was not particularly enthused at the news, but at least the oil terminals were unlikely to be remote from the cities. But even that plan was not to be, for shortly after leaving the Gulf, we were diverted to Karachi, though the diversion was not much off our original route. We were required to unload only 2,000 tons of product, which task should have occupied about three hours. However, it actually took nearly two days to do so, a typical time that presaged my subsequent visit to this chaotic city. I did not go and see the sights; we were at all times 'just about finished' discharging. But I did not see any lost opportunity for sight-seeing; I rarely saw so uninviting a port.

The trip down the west coast of India was a pleasant interlude, though it became the opportunity for work on taking sights, which is the job of finding out where the vessel was, or where it should be. By now I was supposed to be quite good at this task, but actually found that taking sights day after day was not easy in terms of consistency of results. But on March 4th, routine was again disturbed when we were advised that our destination had changed, this time from Cochin to Colombo. More importantly, at least in my view, London had decided that two of us had had enough tanker-training time and that we would be transferred to another P&O vessel wherever it was convenient to do so. We also discovered that Colombo was expecting *Salmara*, a cargo ship on its way to the Far East on a route similar to that which *Khyber* should have enjoyed. My enthusiasm was limited, as I would rather have been transferred to another homeward-bound vessel. Fortunately, this was not to be. On March 7th, a berth appeared in the harbour and we came alongside an oil terminal (this was one of the few ports where the terminal was right in the main harbour, an arrangement not altogether safe; shortly after arriving a port official walked aboard with a lighted cigarette in hand – we nearly threw him overboard!). *Salmara* appeared, but no orders to transfer came to us, although *Chitral* also arrived. This, a handsome small passenger ship (its capacity approximated 250 passengers), I thought that would have suited me very well. But neither was that to be, and we were then outward bound for Madras, a destination not greeted with joy, but at which *Cannanore*, another black-funnelled cargo ship, was due simultaneously with *Mantua*; this, again, I had no particular wish to join (a non-air-conditioned cargo ship in the Bay of Bengal was not on my wish-list).

Two days later we were in Madras, a stifling sort of place that, to me, had no redeeming features. *Cannanore* arrived, but again there were no instructions to transfer, and then we were off to Calcutta, the past capital of British India.

Cannanore in Colombo

This is, in many respects, a strange port. It lies amidst a vast accumulation of mankind, near the mouth of the Hooghly River, a tributary of the Ganges whose journey to the sea created an ever-expanding agglomeration of islands and tributary rivers that together constitute the world's largest delta. The arrival itself is to another of those ports that is barely visible from the sea, the land being exceedingly flat and low. It was also subject to many floods, a fortunate fact for agriculture, but far less so for its millions of inhabitants. Our destination was a berth at the wonderfully-named Budge Budge, a smallish city some 25 km from Calcutta itself. There we tied up but were told that we were to expect a tidal surge, and therefore to ensure that we were well secured to prevent a major marine incident. Nobody on board knew anything of tidal surges, so we secured ourselves to the wharf with every rope and wire on the ship and which were available from ashore. These surges were apparently quite unpredictable, so we prepared for a six- to seven-foot wall of water (in fact, when it came, it was a sorry little thing indeed, being about four inches high and so quickly past that few noticed it. But that was a surprise that was quite welcome, not a disappointment).

As I indicated earlier, mail became one of the primary pleasures of life on board, and here I received an interesting missive from Mother (she was always my main correspondent, for she liked writing letters about what was, I suppose, a fairly dull existence in a somnolent Sussex village; from Father, I recall only two letters in total while I was at sea, this simply not being his forte). In it she stated that one of her friends (one Vera Hayworth, a rather austere but elegant lady with whom she and another friend had invested in a rental property in Brighton in Sussex) was stationed in Calcutta with her husband, an executive with Imperial Tobacco, and that I should see if I could contact her. Mother had given me her phone number, so I decided to take the opportunity to see them and something of this part of the world. Phoning, however, was not something that one undertook lightly in West Bengal, for the connection, even once accomplished, could not have been more jumbled and muddled if the other person were on the Moon. I did, however, speak to a maid, and eventually found that Vera was that afternoon at the Calcutta Golf Club. I therefore left the ship and found a convenient taxi, which, I seem to recall, was a large black 1948 Austin. Although in terrible condition, its engine seemed to work, and if none of the windows would go up or down, this mattered little in light of the uncomfortable humidity.

The ride itself was an exercise in ingenuity. Though there were few cars on the road, if the track over which we drove could be so termed, there was an abundance of cows, harnessed to carts or otherwise free of any constraints, elephants and bicycles, and, of course, what seemed to be many thousands of pedestrians, all of whom obviously knew nothing of any rules for traffic or for personal safety. I believe that we arrived at the Club without actually maiming anything or anybody, but of this I cannot be certain.

The Club itself was splendid, with buildings redolent of the Empire at its height. Although it called itself the Golf Club, it was in effect a club for all sports, most notably cricket, which while India fielded a notable team at the time, had achieved nowhere near the cult – and indeed betting – status achieved only a few years later. I found Vera easily enough, and she expressed remarkably little surprise at seeing me appear, though one could hardly imagine that many visitors normally arrived at such a destination without some early warning. (The nations of Pakistan – East and West – had been created in 1947, and the major shipping traffic to the sub-continent, which largely comprised P&O and British India (B.I.), the latter a part of the P&O group, had perforce reduced visits to India to occasional stops in Bombay (later Mumbai), though the companies' cargo ships visited some ports with more frequency.)

We sat around the cricket ground enjoying a match for a good while, and I took in the ambience of a fading way of life, not entirely dissimilar to the glimpse of past imperial glories that I had earlier witnessed in Colombo. I was then invited back to the Hayworth's flat, which actually was rather austere, and had tea, ably served, naturally, by a posse of servants. It was all very pleasant, at least as an interlude, but it was not so difficult to see the shadows of the leisurely lifestyle of the closeted world of Somerset Maugham, whose writings I had long enjoyed, and indeed still enjoy.

The pace of life in Budge Budge upon my return to the ship was rather to my fancy, for the discharging of our cargo proceeded at a modest pace, and all was finished by 4pm, at which time all work stopped! This was very unusual on a tanker, and it was difficult to see why we had to wait for the next day; we had discharged all our cargo by then, so our draught was no longer an issue, but wait until 11 am the next day we did. It may, of course, have been on the account of the necessary pilot, for the passage down the Hooghly was, with its shifting bars and unpredictable tides, one of the world's more difficult river transits. In comparison, the Tyne and Plaju (on the Musi River) were characterised by unusually narrow channels, but they had the advantage of at least always presenting the same channels and difficulties.

Unfortunately, it appeared that our next port of call was to be Abadan, a place I had hoped never to see again. We moved slowly down the Bay of Bengal, around Ceylon (after only a short time at sea, I began to see the importance of this island, at least to P&O, for even the Australia-run ships, both passenger and cargo, had to call in every second voyage or so for routine crew changes), and then slowly up the Arabian Sea and through the Strait of Hormuz, the reduced speed arising because Shell seemed not to know what to do with the ship. I was of course hoping to get transferred to another vessel, but this wasn't going to happen in Abadan, and certainly could not happen in Port Elizabeth, where were shortly advised we were now destined to visit.

Although a change of destination was now devoutly to be wished, on this occasion Shell decided to stick with the South Africa plan. Abadan was, of course, as uninspiring as usual, but we quickly left for Port Elizabeth on March 28th, and arrived there on April 12th. I complained mildly about the comparative tedium on a long run such as we experienced, but the 3rd mate told me of an earlier voyage that the ship had experienced from Geelong (in Australia) to Cape Town. This route was 'the wrong way round' because it necessitated sailing into a head-sea, the prevailing incessant wind being strong, westerly, and having a reach all the way round the world, unleavened by any land. *Mantua* had made very heavy weather of it, the Chief Engineer at one point being faced with the probability of running out of fuel and thus possibly needing to consume the cargo; Iles Crozet and Kerguelen represent the only land anywhere near those shipping lanes and are the home only of a few scientists and meteorologists. I ceased complaining.

But I had one useful lesson to learn on the run back up the African Coast. The two senior cadets were old acquaintances of mine from Warsash, both having some five months' seniority to me. The mate's birthday occurred one day after leaving Port Elizabeth, and he held a party at which the two (one having been the Chief Cadet Captain at Warsash, and, perhaps as a consequence, was quite an arrogant young man) razzed him, unnecessarily and at length. I thought it crude and in bad taste, and it obviously displeased the mate. Next day we were collectively called into his office and told that because of our behaviour we were to lose our wine account and shore leave, and that weekends would now be served on the bridge instead of at leisure.

This was, I thought, somewhat harsh retribution, but in the circumstances (and it being a British ship, with mostly ex-Public-School boys as deck officers, wherein the Winchester School motto of 'Manners Maketh Man' – as asserted by my school's headmaster - was almost an article of faith in such a hierarchy) was not unwarranted.

But the very next day the mate decided to 'let bygones be bygones' and told us that the decision to remove privileges and the imposition of weekend work would be reversed. We thought this pleasant news but agreed that this had been the wrong way to handle disciplinary matters and collectively concluded that we had lost some respect for him. It was apparent to us that the structure of a ship-bound society was unique and necessarily called for 'civilised' and consistent discipline. It was also obvious that the acquisition of respect is difficult, but that its loss could be instantaneous and absolute.

The voyage continued without news of our next destination until we berthed in Abadan, where we welcomed the delivery of long-missed mail (the ship-board mail system, an essential lifeline for the crew's sanity, was quite efficient; one's correspondents, especially in tankers, addressed letters to Shell in London, who then, upon determining where a vessel would next berth, mailed to its local agents that mail which it had by then received; it was not necessary to rely upon deliveries to obscure and perhaps mail-less destinations). But the news was this time not good; the loading was to be for Bombay, Gan, Madras and Calcutta, none of which had I the slightest wish to visit or revisit.

But every now and again interesting little scenarios came up, and one such occurred in this uninteresting port. Berthed close to us was a BP tanker, and in the usual spirit of comity in such a moribund place, a couple of cadets came over to visit our ship (*Mantua* was newer than most tankers; it probably looked from the perspective of their senectuous home a vision of comfort and good living). We entertained them in the wardroom, and our conversation moved around to the perspectives that they had of their future careers, most P&O officers (in fact, probably all but 'half-a-mate') seeing tanker service as little but an unfortunate though necessary step towards serving in passenger ships, thus destined to eventually visit a cornucopia of exotic ports. But BP knew of nothing but tankers, some of them being exceedingly small and dowdy coastal vessels; certainly, on that type of ship they got home quite often, but that was, to most of us, much too high a price to pay for that privilege.

Most interesting, however, was the tale of one of our visitors. He hailed from Czechoslovakia and brought with him an interesting viewpoint. Obviously, given the lack of any large body of water in the country (even Hungary merited a navy, Lake Balaton being large enough to need some armed protection) the country was hardly a maritime power. In fact, even when part of the Austro-Hungarian Empire, the two nations were kept away from the southern and nautical part of the Empire because of their antipathy towards the sea, and it was only when I read one of the obscure books in the school library that I had heard of the Battle of Lissa. It turns out that Austria did in fact have a maritime tradition, though Bohemia and Moravia were hardly a part of it.

But his tale was not of his good fortune in getting a job at sea; it was about how we complained about our lives when we had so little about which to cavil. In his country, he said, you can't even think about ideas of freedom, the luxury of choice of food, vacations, careers, indeed practically everything about which he had heard we British moan, usually at great length. (This should not have come as a surprise, at least to me, for in Hong Kong three Russian sailors had visited *Khyber* and marvelled at our quality of life. We were, I recalled, suitably chastened ... but such sentiments have a limited life and soon dissipated during a good dinner.)

We were in Abadan for only a day, thereafter, sailing a short distance to Mina Al-Ahmadi. This is a berth, ostentatiously called a city, adjacent to Kuwait, of which I knew little other than the fact that a family friend had been a British Army officer based in Kuwait in 1961, when a British force had defended the country against the depredations of the Iraqi dictator Abd al-Qarim Qassem. The friend, whom I later met in Sussex, was singularly unimpressed by Kuwait itself, but fortunately he had had little to do when there, the situation being 'saved' by two British aircraft carriers that had provided overwhelming aerial fire-power to the Kuwaiti forces. I recall that all he had been required to do was dig into the sand and await trouble; it failed to materialise.

To me, Kuwait was a desolate place that typified all that I disliked about the Gulf. But I didn't notice, because there at the oil berth was *Malwa*, a Trident Tanker (P&O) vessel. The Captains of the two ships agreed to transfer Young and me from *Mantua* in exchange for two cadets from *Malwa*, bound for UK.

Compared with *Mantua*, *Malwa* was vast, and was a 'black oil' (unrefined) tanker as opposed to a 'white oil' carrier. In appearance, it was also different, having all its accommodation at the stern of the ship. It took us all of an hour to pack our bags and hand over to the new cadets. A new chapter in my life had begun; even the cabin was larger and more luxurious. This again had a purpose; crude oil carriers rarely went to anywhere pleasant. As an example, I knew of no refinery in Ceylon, a result of which was that only the smaller white-oil carriers would go to Colombo, there being no facilities in the country for the bigger crude oil carriers. Almost all of the destinations for these bigger vessels (though they would now be considered quite small) were far from cities and for obvious reasons in deeper waters. Seventeen days later we berthed in Thameshaven. I disembarked.

Himalaya in Columbo

3 Arcadia and Himalaya

Having spent some ten months on tankers with only fourteen days of leave during that time, I was due for a good chunk of time ashore (remember that the working week on a ship was eight or nine hours a day, seven days a week, this routine occasionally interrupted by inactivity whilst awaiting a berth or longshoremen being unavailable, situations that rarely occurred on tankers). Needless to say, I sped home as quickly as possible. Again, nobody else that I knew was off work at that time, and life being somewhat dull, and indeed lonely, in a sleepy Sussex village, it was not long before I thought that maybe the seagoing life was appropriately invigorating after all. It being summer, in fact, David had time off from school, but he had found a job that would augment his savings that would bring home to me that I was perhaps a bit too inured to relative luxury; he had found a hop-picking job in Kent that required 'camp' living, simply because those seeking that sort of work wanted as many paid hours as were available. He had, on the first day of work, been surprised that on a stiflingly hot day how over-dressed were his more experienced co-workers, so out he went in shorts and a T-shirt into the fields. Within minutes he found out how much he was in error; hops are innocuous-looking buds, but actually hide an abundance of savage little burrs. He spent two very uncomfortable days removing the horrible little things but had to spend that time perspiring profusely. I realised that my carping about long hours spent on boring bridge or engine-room watch was not entirely reasonable.

And after six languorous weeks, I was enjoined to report to *Arcadia* at Tilbury (near the mouth of the Thames) for some cruising in the Mediterranean and the North Atlantic. This, I felt, was far more in my style.

The P&O-Orient passenger fleet was large and diverse, and the two companies had for long co-operated in ship design and management. While I was at Warsash they had launched *Canberra* and *Oriana*, by some stretch the world's largest passenger vessels not operating regularly in the North Atlantic. Prior to that *Arcadia, Iberia, Himalaya, Orsova, Orcades, Oronsay* and *Orontes* comprised the largest Australia-trade group of vessels, supported for a few years by the pre-war *Strathaird, Strathnaver, Strathmore, Stratheden* and *Orion*. The Far East was served by *Chusan, Cathay, and Chitral*, these supported by the pre-war *Canton, Corfu* and *Carthage*. It was an impressive fleet, but not one destined to long survive, extinction occurring because of the success of the 707. Prior to the arrival of the two larger ships, *Arcadia* had been the flagship, and was in many ways the epitome of the classic passenger ship design; the five *Straths* (*Strathallan*, commandeered as a troopship, was sunk during the war) were old P&O steamships, originally sporting three impressive funnels, and from whose design there was an almost direct line to *Arcadia* and *Iberia*, but which thereafter abruptly ended with *Canberra*, she and *Oriana* being in their own ways completely novel designs.

Although I had never been on her, I was not unfamiliar with *Arcadia*. An impressive ship, newly painted for summer cruising, she was of 29,734 gross tons, then a fairly standard size for a major passenger ship, today a minnow. These ships were not naturally designed for cruising, as their most profitable use at the time was for the transportation of emigrants from Europe to Australia, for which the Australian government paid P&O a handsome sum. The ships also carried substantial cargo, for which purpose their speed was of some commercial purpose. But generally, the decks were somewhat utilitarian, the pools were small and inconvenient, and the division into first and tourist class gave the one group ample and comfortable room and the other cramped interior cabins and public rooms and little deck space. But as the trade was changing by virtue of Italian and Greek ships carrying large numbers of southern European emigrants, in order to utilise redundant ships, cruising was beginning to become popular (for many decades, cruising had been the preserve of the relatively well-off, and the reverse snobbishness of even the more prosperous working class prevented its members easily accepting what was seen as a rather snooty way to holiday). Nevertheless, for those who chose to see it, the days of this type of ship were numbered. It was only by pure chance of birthdate that I had actually landed on these ships at the right time.

One feature of *Arcadia* was that cadets were not part of its normal complement. It was unclear what purpose we were to serve, as the ship was ordered in a manner that differed entirely from the management of lesser ships. Firstly, the crew was substantially bigger and hierarchy more established. Secondly, everyone had to look smart all the time, and thirdly, one was encouraged to fraternise with the passengers. And, just as advantageously (as it turned out) there was no accommodation available in the officers' quarters; we were obliged to utilise a cabin on a first-class passenger deck. It was immediately apparent that this was likely to prove a substantial social advantage. Of less apparent advantage was the fact one of the other cadets (of which there were six in total) was one Stuart Woodward. He, being a quiet and studious fellow, was very charming, with a sort of amiable insouciance about him that, I soon discovered, mightily attracted the opposite sex. It did not take too long, however, to discover that this demeanour also had, for me, an unexpectedly favourable side.

When I boarded, few crew members were aboard (between trips or cruises passenger ships enjoyed few days in port; they only made money when at sea with passengers aboard and carried little commercial cargo) and I introduced myself to the 4th mate, a reasonable fellow who let me in on a few important details. The most cogent of his advice was that for the deck department this was not the happiest of ships, the mate, Mr Lefevre, being something of a martinet who had a problem with his sense-of-humour-ectomy and enjoyed a negative reputation throughout the fleet. He was not aboard I was pleased to note (as I now knew that to cadets the mate was usually by far the most significant of the officers (Basil was a notable exception) I felt that an introduction could wait). Somewhat confusingly, the big ships also carried a 1st officer, termed the 1st mate, the senior of the watch-keepers.

Arcadia was to complete two cruises before returning to the Australia run. The first comprised calls to Gibraltar, Dubrovnik, Palma and Naples, a selection with which I was quite happy to become familiar, though Naples was the only one where our ship could berth alongside a wharf. The first thing, however, was to become familiar with the boats which we were to supervise, a passenger ship at that time basically having three types of lifeboats, these being two 'crash' boats, perhaps four or more motor-powered covered boats (which were used as shore tenders) and more numerous open lifeboats, often powered by very clumsy hand cranks or simply by oars. All cadets, having been to nautical colleges, knew about the handling of small boats, but the 3rd engineer, being responsible for the motor boats, gave us careful instruction in how not to overuse the gears and engines in his precious charges. We got to know him quite well.

Though putative deck officers, the six of us did not easily fit in with the established hierarchy; while I must have met them, I have no recollection of meeting with the Captain or the Staff Captain. The latter rank was something of an anomaly unique to the big passenger ships. He was a full-fledged Master but was on a daily basis actually in charge of little other than the running of the hotel side of the ship, which overlapped the role of the Chief Purser. He was, in essence, awaiting the death or retirement of other captains, but in the meantime had a pretty cushy job ... provided that he liked glad-handing the passengers and dealing with disciplinary problems (for which he had the assistance of masters-at-arms, usually retired policemen). Not being trained to do such things, few senior officers relished that interim, but apparently necessary, step to ascend to becoming Captain of a major passenger ship.

Once provisioned and with the whole crew aboard, on July 5th, I began to realise how different was this world from that of my recent past. The ship moved to the passenger berth (frankly, like most passenger berths in UK, including the *Queens'* special pier at Southampton, a pretty decrepit structure) and I was ascribed the job of standing guard at the Tourist gangway, presumably to greet those boarding, not an onerous task and rendering some substantial advantages; I got to see that our passengers were by no means all old and grumpy. In fact, some were quite the opposite.

The first day of cruising was as expected. Although it was July, the Bay of Biscay was, as usual, unpleasantly choppy (though not troublesome, *Arcadia* having been only the second of the company's ships to be fitted with stabilisers, and these proved to be a big advance in dampening what could be a very uncomfortable motion), and, typically for the Bay, it poured all day. Nevertheless, the major routine of the late morning was boat drill, an exercise made mandatory by the Board of Trade. It is to be recalled that the idea of improving lifeboat capacity and utility first achieved public notice after the 1912 sinking of *Titanic*, which was fitted with an insufficient number of lifeboats to accommodate all aboard, but which were in any event so difficult to launch that a listing ship in poor weather (which, of course, would usually be the norm) was unlikely to be able to safely get all of its occupants safely into lifeboats. Even then, improvements were limited and regulations ill-thought; while the crew were obliged to practice boat-drill, passengers were not so instructed. In 1915 *Lusitania* (the largest passenger ship then afloat) was torpedoed off the Irish coast. While it happened in bright daylight hours and conditions were good, listing was rapid and the ropes, sheaves and davits proved to be so cumbersome that only a few lifeboats were usable. It is recorded that during a prior lifeboat drill, an alert passenger asked a seaman in charge of the readying of a lifeboat, "It's all right drilling your crew, but why don't you drill your passengers?" to which the response was to tell the captain, advice not followed. Presumably it was felt that passengers should not be disturbed from their amiable routines (reported in 'Dead Wake' by Erik Larson). From 1915 things improved, though no seaman would favour abandoning ship in conditions other than clear days and calm seas (more normal conditions being the foggy night when *Stockholm* sliced into *Andrea Doria*).

On a lighter note, some of us enjoyed lifeboat drills. These exercises, which all passengers were obliged to attend (roll-calls are taken) are designed to familiarise crew and passengers with the route to their assigned lifeboats, and, equally importantly, to instruct passengers in the use and wearing of life-jackets. The latter requirement, we found, often proved particularly difficult for the 18- to 25- year old female passengers, some of whom were all fingers and thumbs when it came to tying or untying knots. We generally found sufficient time to assist; sometimes some expressed complete amazement at our dexterity, on occasion needing help even after the drill!

We arrived at Gibraltar on Monday, at that time under virtual siege by the Spanish (Franco) Government, but still very much a proud part of the Commonwealth. In fact, it was a bit too British; Union Jacks flew everywhere, and the standard fare at the too-British pubs was warm beer and fish and chips. The place seemed prosperous enough, though without the presence of the Navy, it was difficult to see what people would do with themselves, for there was no evident industry and little to draw in any tourists; in fact, it was rather the opposite, as the border with Spain was apparently closed, so that even the mass of north European tourists that came to the Costa Brava could not cross onto the Rock for a visit. It occurred to me that the British Government may have had a hand in encouraging cruise ships to call, because all that I could find to occupy myself was to take the cable-car up to the top of the massive edifice and absorb the very fine view, and there to try to prevent the Barbary apes (in reality not apes but monkeys, presumably named when nobody knew the difference) stealing from me.

The trip across the balmy Mediterranean to Yugoslavia, as it then was, was an almost untrammelled delight. We cadets had to clean up the lifeboats after Gibraltar ferrying, but that job was quickly finished and we were permitted to enjoy some recreation, which is to say, get to know some of the young ladies who occupied first class. Of the passengers, the ship accommodated 675 first- and 735 tourist-class passengers, but the proportion of deck and pool space allotted to the former was very much in their favour. As we cadets also had an entertainment allowance, which was actually quite generous, we were not inhibited in ensuring that we were known to be good persons with whom to dally. And dally we did.

But one aspect of life on board was something of a surprise to me. Being on deck most of the time and enjoying most of the benefits accorded passengers, we were royally treated by the stewards and waiters. Even over just two days at sea, it became rapidly apparent that almost every one of the pursers' crew was demonstrably gay, and it was brought home to me, as indeed it still is, how unique was the attitude in both America and UK towards this lifestyle. I had, of course, been to a British boarding school, where subtle (and very unsubtle) things inferentially showed within society how widespread was the male preference for male company within certain strata of British society, and that, apart from the law, such preferences were largely taken for granted. But the law was at that time rather important. As Noel Coward wrote in 'A Song at Twilight' (1968), "Even when the actual law ceases to exist, there will still be a stigma attached to 'the love that dares not speak its name' in the minds of millions of people for generations to come. It takes more than a few outspoken books, and plays, and speeches in parliament to uproot moral prejudice from the Anglo-Saxon mind." These antediluvian British attitudes subsisted for many years, and it was not until the Sexual Offences Act was introduced in 1967 that gay male sex became a non-criminal offence, but even then, only if committed in private by no more than two people over twenty-one years of age. (The whole iniquitous situation is limned in Chapter 16 of 'John Gielgud' by Sheridan Morley, a stark tale of changing British mores.). Consequently, stewards' departments on British ships were very stable societies, and by common observation notably happy; small wonder, given the alternatives of prison, heavy fines or ostracism.

The first sight of Dubrovnik was spectacular, it being a perfect Mediterranean day with bright sunlight and a seascape for which the Adriatic is so renowned. The harbour had remained fundamentally unchanged since the sixteenth century; it took the brutality of the 1990s collapse of Yugoslavia to bring it all to rubble (though restoration has since been remarkably successful). Our lifeboats were in service until 3am, but such a job was by no means tiring. I even had the opportunity to sample a little slivovitz, a sampling that I did not care to repeat for another twenty or so years … and then by mistake.

A few hours later we were in Naples, a city that resonated with History, Opera and risqué movies. This time we were alongside a berth, although somewhat uncomfortably so in the presence of a substantial part of the US Mediterranean Fleet. As our next port, Palma, was another launch port, we had quite a lot of boat maintenance to complete, but after lunch the mate let us off for the day (he was actually turning out to be much better than reputed, one supposes because he really did not need us to do much apart from maintaining and manning the lifeboats, a far from onerous task). We decided on an exploratory trip ashore and took a bus to see the sights and get a flavour of what should be one of the world's great cities. We quickly decided that 'great' was a misnomer. In part famed for Mount Vesuvius, the very fact of the volcano being there contributes to the city's disorder, for it is Italy's third largest city in population, but has scant land and resources for its people. Further, the southern half of Italy is relatively impoverished; the city had been deeply in debt for most of its recent existence, the genesis for which can traced back to the Unification of Italy in the 1860s, when the Kingdom of Naples ceased to exist and the city lost its international cachet. It did not help that the city lies in an earthquake zone (though Pompeii has long been an attraction) or that during the World War II the city was more heavily bombed than any other Italian city. Many resulting scars were still evident.

Briefly put, our tour amply demonstrated that a recent description of the city as 'the anthill of humanity' was not entirely misplaced. We saw no evidence, of course, of corruption itself or of the Camorra, the Neapolitan version of the Mafia, but the place was home to a great deal of garbage that was simply left to rot where it lay, itself later a scandal of some national importance. Our trip was not improved by the 'beach' which our driver suggested that we visit to conclude our tour; it was simply a pile of bare rock and, to add insult to injury, we had to pay to get onto it.

There were compensations, however. Arriving back on board we collectively repaired to one of the bars and prepared for dinner. It had not really been brought home to me before getting on the ship that there were some advantages to being in our roles on such a ship, a major one being that, without many actual responsibilities, we were in fact very privileged, being entitled to eat in the first-class dining room and enjoy the run of the public rooms in both classes. I had previously examined the differences between the dining choices of the classes, and there was no questioning the quality of the fare from which we could choose. I learned that frogs' legs were more than edible, fillet steak was almost permanently available, and that delicacies like whitebait – which I had never had at home – could easily compensate for scrubbing out lifeboats. And then to repair to the first-class lounge to sample a small brandy (our wine allowance was not mandated only to assist with the entertainment of passengers, though we knew that the mate did occasionally scrutinise such things) and perhaps to engage in small talk with some perfect human being … well, it was difficult to complain about an ostensibly miserable mate.

A slow overnight trip brought us to a very hot Palma, more properly called Palma de Mallorca, a place of which I knew nothing. In fact, few did, as it is the capital of the autonomous Balearic Islands, then under the rule of the fascist Spanish government; only later did it become the popular spot for the young and dissolute. Its location, superb weather and cheap property made it an ideal destination for northern Europeans seeking a Mediterranean vacation.

But for us, it was twelve hours of constant launch operation; of the shore, beach or otherwise, I saw nothing.

This was the effective conclusion of my first cruise, and I certainly had found such a trip much more congenial than any of my prior experiences. But three days later we were berthed in Southampton, this time directly astern of *Canberra*. Although I had seen that vessel before, being so close made it all the more apparent how things were changing in the world of liners. As I have said, one could see a straight developmental line between the elegant *Straths* and *Arcadia*, but it was a leapfrog to *Canberra*. With engine room and funnels located near the stern (though not uniquely so, *Southern Cross* having already demonstrated the virtues of that particular feature) its aluminium superstructure and lack of any interest in cargo, it was self-evidently a wholly new concept, though not one itself, fortunately or otherwise, that was to be so unique for long. As I found out, it was handsome, but a bit flawed.

Naturally I took the opportunity to take a long walk ashore, a necessary exercise even though one could hardly call life on a large liner a cramped existence. I knew Southampton well, of course, so a visit to an old watering hole (one just up the main street had opened in 1150 or so, not as old as some of the places that I had by then visited, but certainly old enough to bring back memories of home) and a couple of hours watching 'Days of Wine and Roses' brought me, at least temporarily, to a life more real than was cleaning lifeboats.

Two days later, after the ritual lifeboat drill, we left the Solent for a cruise in the less than emollient North Atlantic. By then I had realised that one of the essential rituals of passenger-ship life was the Captain's Cocktail Party, to which all off-duty officers were obliged to report. Some loathed the routine of lining up, being introduced to strangers, being given the usual weak drink, and 'entertaining' the mostly boring supplicants. I found, however, that it could be an enlightening interlude; one whisky and ginger ale, thereafter, topped up only with ginger ale, served to loosen the tongue, and the rest was an exercise in finding things of interest to discuss with people with whom, if appropriate, one could meet up again in only an hour or so. It was certainly sometimes a test of endurance, but I quickly found that if all else failed, one could always discuss the guests' children; if that failed, to the back of the receiving line one repaired. And after the line was absorbed, those passengers of interest could be separately approached; after all, we six cadets were distinctive enough, though six was a rather large number to properly exercise one's charms. I did, however, notice that Stuart seemed to embody some characteristics that seemed very interesting to those to whom the rest of us wished to demonstrate our own disarming wisdom.

But one quickly learned to use one's time to good effect, for there were, of course, two of these 'parties', tourist class receiving, the following evening, the same good treatment. It was quickly apparent to me that tourist-class generally comprised a more 'interesting' (and younger) set than did first, though this was not always the case.

I had during the cocktail party espied a young lady who seemed to me more than a little interesting, and the following evening I delayed my departure from the first-class lounge to see if she might appear and I could try out some of my under-utilised wit. I seemed to have arrived at a good time, for there she was, but I was a bit disconcerted to see her coming into the room with a rather sharp-looking young man with whom she was engaged in deep conversation. Fortunately, there was a trio playing a waltz, and when she sat down, I gathered up some courage and asked her for the dance (I had been taught to dance both at school and at Warsash – we were supposed to be gentlemen, after all!) and, to my amazement, she accepted. I was no dancer, despite the lessons, but I knew enough to undertake the basics, and I found that I could dance on gossamer if the moment was right, and she, fortunately, came at the right moment. I was pleased to find that her name was Elaine, but even more pleased when she asked whether I would like to join her and her brother at their table – now I knew why she, the most attractive girl that I had seen on board, had been left alone by all the likely young men that surrounded us. Sometimes fortune does favour the brave!

The next day we arrived in Madeira, one of the most charming and scenic of all the smaller destinations. Reputedly it has one of the finest climates in the world, being at the edge of the Gulf Stream and situated at a latitude where it neither gets too hot nor too cold. And if it does get a bit hot, one can ascend the volcanic hills of which the islands are composed. My luck was in, because only three tenders were needed, the ship being very close to the jetty, and on drawing lots, I managed to be one of those who got the day off. Unlike many such places, the populace seemed not to be intent upon hawking their local specialty, this being Madeira wine, and it occurred to me that this must be one of the world's best places of which to call oneself a citizen. My cup ran over, however, when I found, not quite by coincidence, that Elaine and I had come ashore in the same boat. She was accompanied by her parents and introduced me to them in a most encouraging way.

The following day at sea was something of a follow-up exercise, the weather being calm and the sun hot. The evening encompassed an unusual sport, some sort of dog-racing exercise (with, of course, cut-out wooden dogs) that greatly entertained some of the gambling fraternity, which, I need not add, in those days was in ships quite illegal. My joy was somewhat curtailed by seeing Elaine with another young man, who justifiably seemed very pleased with himself. But this time I did not interrupt the liaison, my confidence level being somewhat straitened by again sensing competition.

Sao Miguel, the main island of The Azores, greeted us in the morning. It was almost a repeat of Madeira, being an autonomous region of Portugal, and with just as delightful a climate. Being the location of the triple junction of the Eurasian, African and North American tectonic plates, it was extremely mountainous and necessitated a long day in the boats; hardly onerous, but not very exciting. The evening was better; I found Elaine alone in the ballroom and we spoke for two hours. Last night's beau was, I discovered, aged 16. I went to bed feeling much the better.

Another short southerly voyage brought us to Tenerife, the centre of the Spanish Canary Islands, another series of volcanic islands. Quite spectacular, they were a popular tourist destination, but did not require much boat-work on our part. In the late afternoon, I decided that a walk ashore with Elaine would be good exercise, and a mere walk turned a nice day into a perfect evening. One of Father's favourite pieces of music was Falla's 'Nights in the Gardens of Spain' – that evening, I thought it the most perfect music ever composed, so much in accord with this earthly paradise was it. I actually thought that I had found a soul-mate; I was, of course, still in the fumbling-troll class of young men, though, like it or not, without the fumbling. Two days later, the two of us attended the tourist Fancy Dress Night (for the first-class to even visit tourist was strictly verboten, but who was to know?) and ended the evening with a rum and coke in my first-class cabin.

The cruise's last port was Corunna. While at school in Folkestone, I habitually spent many hours in its library. It actually had rather a good collection for a school and had a selection of books on military history (some generous benefactor had bequeathed his library to the school), one of which included the story of the Battle of Corunna, when in 1808 Sir John Moore, with a small British army, disrupted Napoleon's plan for the subjugation of the Peninsular. I had always wondered what the place would be like; so small a force, in effect, preventing the conquest of Spain by a quarter of a million men under Europe's most able commander was a feat of arms much beloved of British schoolboys. Unfortunately, this version of the facts was somewhat alternative, the truer story being that an under-equipped and underpaid British (and partially Spanish) army had been asked by a tightwad government to fulfil an impossible task. Almost at once it was entirely outmaneuvered by the French, and then forced to flee precipitously to ships provided for the purpose in the unprotected harbour of Corunna, but leaving behind an accumulation of stores that the French by then needed more than did the British (the French army was required to provision itself, gleaning from the territory conquered what it could, thereby being very mobile, but, as in Russia, very vulnerable). The British also lost more men than the French; British history books had a tendency to grasp a victory from what any other nation would term a defeat, but this was plainly not even a Pyrrhic victory. Moore, killed in action, was subsequently vilified by the very government that had imposed such impractical objectives upon him.

Interesting to see, however, was the topography of the port. Without much by way of defensible hilly terrain, its advantage was that its harbour was surrounded on three sides by water, thereby giving the British substantial advantage; they had all the ships. A good history and geography lesson, though marred by a day of heavy fog.

The last day of a cruise is always a bit of a let-down, but this is even more the case when the day is spent in the Bay of Biscay, though on this occasion it was merely cold and miserable, there being a lot more fog than wind. The evening perked up, however, when the Officers' Wardroom threw a party for officers and their invitees. Needless to say, I invited Elaine and her mother. It was a very pleasant hour or so, being marked, I noted, by Stuart giving me a compliment about the attractiveness of my companion. I could happily preen for an hour or two!

On August 1st, we arrived in Southampton. There I bade farewell to Elaine and commiserated to myself how the path of love had proven far more chaste than I felt it should; I had stolen no more than a peck on the cheek, and for that I could blame only myself. At British schools, one is likely to be and remain completely ignorant of the fair sex; I am sure that the teachers knew very little themselves, most having been to Oxford or Cambridge, where women were for undergraduates rare and distant pleasures … or, indeed, mere visions. It seemed to me, however, that my social life was to be given a second chance, for on that same day Stuart and I were told that next day we were to be transferred to *Himalaya*, berthed immediately astern of *Arcadia*.

Himalaya was slightly older than *Arcadia* and some 2,000 tons smaller. Normally on the Australia run, she was reputedly a happy ship and was not marred by engine or operational problems (some ships were not so lucky, *Iberia*, *Arcadia's* sister, seemed plagued by engine problems, and was scrapped prematurely in 1972 partly because of mechanical unreliability). However, I was happy to join *Himalaya*, especially with four fewer cadets than had impeded my arcadian pleasures, and particularly because it was to undertake a twenty-two-day cruise that embraced all sorts of interesting places, including Athens and Barcelona.

Hours after we transferred to *Himalaya* we paraded on the Boat Deck to be inspected by the usual P&O director, down from London for the occasion, and the Captain. I was delighted to see that the latter was Captain Cowan; he even recognised me! Not quite so effusive was the mate, who, of course, was to have control of our lives for three weeks. He, William Scott Masson, was a formidable man to whom one would, as a callow cadet, mistakenly take an instant dislike, but whose stiff appearance (he wore somewhat pretentious-looking tufts of whiskers on his cheekbones and was possessed of a permanently austere gravitas) was belied by an unassuming authority that engendered a natural respect. (He was subsequently Captain of *Canberra* during the Falklands War in 1982 and was awarded the CBE for his services in that conflict – see 'A Very Strange Way to Go to War' by Andrew Vine). Perhaps fortunately, he was neither familiar with handling cadets' supervision nor with their education and was far from enthusiastic about even having them aboard. For Stuart and me, our job was to run the lifeboats for passengers going ashore in ports at which there was no berth at which to berth, which was fine by us. Fortunately, few of the ports required tendering. And as cadets were normally not needed, the two of us were again, as on *Arcadia*, provided with a first-class cabin deep the ship; which is to say, we were largely out of the control of the officers, whose accommodation was several decks above ours.

Early next morning we were ushered into the mate's presence and told, rather obliquely, that he had no idea what to do with us, this ship not really being suited to the training of cadets (there was little need for us on the bridge, there always being two certificated officers on watch, a helmsman, even if George was actually steering, and usually two look-outs, and for deck-work there was no call, passengers not much wanting to see the greasing of winches while they enjoyed the sun). Therefore, not wanting even to oversee our academic studies, he suggested that we be on call for any miscellaneous shipboard needs, but that otherwise we entertain such passengers as needed help in passing the time. It occurred to us immediately that this was some sort of dream come true; we were on the most exotic of P&O's schedule of cruises, were in first-class cabins, dined in the first-class restaurant, had a wine allowance, and it was even suggested that we socialise as much as we pleased!

The normal rigours of routine came and were enjoyed. Lifeboat drill was largely left to the two of us and the petty officers (it was a British crew at this level, Indian from Serang downwards), and Stuart and I were more than pleased to see that this group of passengers, unlike the *Arcadia's*, had decided that it was good to bring daughters on this trip, and to do so in considerable numbers. The two of us were careful to ensure that their lifejackets were properly secured, because, as always, most of them appeared to be quite cack-handed with knots, loops and their clothing. Such a job was, of course, entirely necessary, for a lifejacket had to be quite tight around the chest, otherwise it could ride up in the water and impede breathing, or indeed it could float up right over the wearer's head and drift away.

One task that the mate decided that we should carry out was pass judgment on some of the tours. In general, passenger tours arranged by local agents were outside P&O's direct control, but to local entrepreneurs they represented a profitable business. As is always the case, those who enjoyed the tours had mixed reactions, some declaring them a rip-off, and others finding them a very comfortable way to see the sights. The mate therefore decided that he could obtain an objective view from otherwise under-employed cadets, subject, of course, to our submitting written reports. We thought this an excellent idea (part of our training was to write English essays for the various tickets, and it would be difficult to think of a more enjoyable use of this obligation).

But first we had to go through the business of the Captain's Cocktail parties. I had by this time by some practice managed to overcome my aversion to whisky, so much favoured on these occasions. The emancipation of the taste for whisky finds no better an expression than that of Winston Churchill; "Nor was this a momentary acquirement," he wrote, "…once one got the knack of it, the very repulsion of the flavour developed an attraction of its own … I have never shrunk when occasion warranted it from the main basic refreshment of the white officer in the East," (cited by William Manchester in "Visions of Glory"). On *Himalaya* the social obligations were far from onerous, for we had on lifeboat drill seen that the passengers included a veritable cornucopia of delight; the absence of the other cadets was itself most fortunate, especially as the mate had made us in part responsible for entertaining lonely passengers.

Therefore, the first evening of dancing was very much an exploratory event. I decided very quickly upon whom to try out my charms, having spotted a particularly attractive young lady sitting with a group of older people. My skill, however, appeared misplaced; upon approaching, I got a very cold shoulder with barely a nod of rejection. I asked one of the younger officers what this was about (for nobody else came over for the entire time while I watched what was happening, and I watched for a considerable time) and was told that that was the McAlpine family, which even I knew was the name of one of Britain's biggest building contractors, and therefore was on the list published for the officers by P&O to alert us of passengers to whom to pay special attention. (I never found out the truth of their identity, but it was a group that seemed to mostly enjoy its own company, so I saw no reason to doubt it. But plainly I was not of the right stuff.)

The evening's dancing did not, however, end there. I discovered another young lady to be much more amenable, but after a few minutes found out that she was twenty-three years old, patently far too old for me. Thereafter a girl actually approached me (a very disarming experience, nobody of the fair sex ever having done that before) but after a few minutes found out that she was the sister of the cadet purser, of whose existence I had until then been totally unaware. She was an extremely nice girl, but as I had already been advised not to even think of cavorting with female ship's staff (most of whom were actually quite young and comely) I thought that she – Penny – might be too close to a liaison *dangereuse*. Despite this rather disappointing evening, I went to bed reasonably satisfied; next day looked like being a long one.

By daybreak we were in Palma, but on this occasion the operation of the boats was left to the petty officers, our task being to ensure that all those who came ashore from the ship were properly attended to as they went on tours or walked around the port. The stay was a long, hot one, being from six until two the following morning. But it was not onerous, my main task later in the day being to operate the crash-boat, always ready for boating accidents or drunken passengers falling off the tenders. Fortunately, nothing of that sort occurred, in fact I note that my main event of the day was that Penny had coincidentally come ashore and that I was even more taken by her obvious charms. But, of course, it could not be. (On these occasions, a day on a barren pier, without any sun-tan lotion, was the norm; like many, I suspect, I paid for that omission later in life.)

Because of the very long preceding day we were given the next day off by the mate – despite his severity, his personality grew on me, though I recall no smile ever disturbing his outward equanimity – and I elected to sit on deck and be ready for passengers who needed competitors in games of deck quoits. Fortunately, there was an extremely nice-looking young lady sunning herself nearby whom, completely by accident, I twice hit with a thrown quoit. Anyone watching would have thought that missing the real target so frequently could not be an accident, but such was my state of personal confidence that I would have found it impossible to plan such a coincidence. I did, however, notice that her friend, sitting beside her, and not quite so comely, was very solicitous towards her. I found later that this seemed to be how they viewed each other all the time, even on the dance-floor that evening; I never got a look-in when I asked for a dance and could only surmise that they found all males as hairy, smelly and noxious as I did. Actually, I always felt that all women should prefer the company of other women to that of men; fortunately for me, only a minority seemed to exhibit that preference.

But all was not lost. I discovered among those enjoying the sun a young lady of perfect design who seemed somewhat bemused by the abundance of sporting, lazing, drinking and social opportunities, and as our task was to help those in such straits, I took in hand the task of helping her to understand how the ship could be enjoyed. She, Anne, resided in Brighton (Basil's hometown) a well-known coastal resort of iniquitous repute in East Sussex that was, from my home, the nearest big city, and to which I had infrequently cycled. Her father, I discovered, was one of that city's leading barristers and unable to join his wife (whom I never located) and daughter on the cruise. We spent a couple of pleasurable hours in conversation.

Evening duties were, however, soon upon us, and the entertainment provided by the ship was the rather puerile 'dog-racing' betting game. Although it allowed for a good deal of socialising, and I won 8 shillings, it was not a gripping sport. At that time there was really no entertainment of the sort that is now found necessary on cruise-ships, the only concession to such needs being two small groups (piano, violin and whatever other itinerant musicians were unable to find better employment) that provided dance and lounge music of the wallpaper sort. I therefore decided to take the evening off and repaired to my cabin. However, when I arrived at the appropriate deck, I was disconcerted and delighted (at the time the two emotions were to me not much different when such things happened!) to find Anne waiting for me in the corridor. So, I invited her into the cabin and offered her a drink. But then I discovered two things of profound importance. The first was that I had not a clue what I was supposed to do next, and the second was that she was only 16. Although we were then in Italian territorial waters, and I had no knowledge of what was legal and what wasn't, these facts put a major crimp on any of my intentions. I did not take too long to draw an embarrassing end to the evening, embarrassment to which Anne seemed immune.

But life had to go on. The next day dawned bright and warm, but the mate had some work for us to do for the greater part of the day, work that I actually found a bit of a relief after the previous day's disappointments. The evening, of course, was occupied in more leisurely activities, which I decided to start with the first-class ballroom event. And there, seemingly awaiting me, was a young lady, all alone and wistful. A vision of blonde perfection, I quickly found her fascinating; she had finished her History 'A' level (as had I two years before) and was looking forward to going to London University (therefore there was no 'age' problem). Carole was her name, and at once it was apparent that she would be a popular young lady, though one little cloud on the horizon was a rather homunculus-like fellow whom she, and a number of other young ladies there that evening, seemed to find unusually compelling. I could see that he had none of the overt charm of Stuart, but that he was equally adept at attracting pretty well anyone that he chose. In fact, as the days passed, I realised what I had not before fully appreciated, which was that England was still very class-ridden and that this ordinary guy had the assurance of his class, and that on this particular cruise there were a lot more passengers 'of his class' than I had experienced before in my life, and that he operated on the basis of literally 'knowing' that he could get what he wanted. Therefore, given his accent, subtle but seemingly evident to all, little stood in his way; I could see that Carole, coming from Bedfordshire, a somewhat ritzy county, felt a magnetism that was quite foreign to me. It is at such times, along with the misplaced consciousness of persons such as Basil, that awareness arises as to the deep divisions in British society; the cricket match between Gentlemen and Players (amateurs v. professionals, in common parlance), so discreet but so profound, had gone the way of the dodo, or, probably more accurately, of the coelacanth. But the chasm, I suggest, survives.

Dubrovnik beckoned. This time there was no need for any arduous work for the two of us as the quartermasters were running the tenders. This unfortunately meant another eight hours on the bleak jetty directing tender traffic that needed no directing, and I had time to think about where we were (this time there wasn't even the odd slivovitz to provide some solace). The thought occurred to me that the geographical position of the Dalmatian Coast was so similar to that of Italy, which lay only a few miles across the Adriatic, that it ought to be similar in other respects. Yet it was not. The country was simply old-fashioned, the city itself being more suitable for a film-set than a place to work, and despite an educated populace and weather that paralleled Italy, the economy was more akin to India than to the West. True, the country was more mountainous, and it was, of course, a communist state, but it seemed that the difference lay in the 'Cockpit of Europe' heterogeneity of its peoples, languages and religions. As David was later to begin his studies at Southampton University, I asked him if he knew of a ready source of knowledge for Balkan enlightenment. Indeed, he said, there is one; a professor of Eastern European history at Southampton recommended 'The Balkans since 1453' by Stavrianos. I later bought the book;

it inclined one to believe that it was fortunate that the country was not in a state of permanent warfare. Such is the luck of geography ... but in a few years, history and tribalism played their allotted destructive roles.

Come the morning, I was on the bridge as we entered Venice; indeed, it is by far the best place from which to enjoy an arrival, for this is without doubt one of the most splendid of port entrances. Created by geographical and defensive needs, the city sits at the head of a lagoon on over 100 islands; its founding has been agreed to have been in about 420 AD, its very existence probably resting upon the desire of ancient inhabitants to flee to a safe place, protected by water, in the face of marauders from the north. For long one of the world's most important cities, its twentieth-century decline in population has been dramatic, in large part because of its one supreme surviving industry is tourism, which requires tour-guides, boatmen and waiters, but few others. In 1963 it had largely recovered economically from the war, and cruise vessels were starting to come regularly; the future looked fairly secure ... except that the city was also slowly sinking.

What also pleased me was that I had been charged with experiencing a tour, and to this I devoted most of my day. And what a day it was! Naturally not all of the sights could be visited, but the abundance of extravagant churches (though one could easily become 'over-churched') and the vitality of the architecture made me realise that the UK, though splendid, was impoverished for the baroque; we went into St. Marks, and while there was no Gabrieli in which to wallow, it was easy to imagine what the ear could have experienced, for there was at least an organ playing (probably Vivaldi, a son of the city). And the lunch which was provided, while certainly not very splendid, was at least a pasta, which at that time I do not recall having ever had on one of the big ships; we enjoyed it in a sort of subterranean grotto, cold, but by then, deliciously so. (Having since revisited the city in 2016, it is easy to see how the problems arising from tourism in a city designed for walking, or 'boating', are exacerbated as crowds get larger as more tourists from all over the world can afford to visit. The painting of buildings, however dishevelled they appear, seems to be forbidden, home repairs appear impossible to have approved by the 'building police'... and still it sinks.) My written report, although I say it myself, was a masterpiece (I naturally wished to enjoy this sort of job everywhere we went!).

The evening was distinctly doleful, virtually all of the passengers seemingly having taken an evening gondola tour (not all tours, unfortunately, required reports). This was of little moment, as it occurred to me that I might be burning the candle at both ends, and early nights were becoming the more called-for. As the next morning saw us still berthed in Venice, I delighted in some more sight-seeing (and an espresso, which by now I was coming to appreciate!), as it became apparent that the mate actually believed that, if not on watches, Sundays were days of rest; I was beginning to like this enlightened, if gruff, man more with each passing day. And as leaving Venice is quite as spectacular as arrival, the day ended with a sunny drink on deck accompanied by this wonderful view and a long talk with Carole, who looked more perfect every time I saw her. However, all was not sunlight and perfection with her; it had begun to dawn on me that some of these qualities, both appearance and speech, verged on the artificial and glib. Being totally unversed in the art of such polite but superficial conversation, I was beginning to think that I was becoming merely a useful companion, substituting for the wily Stuart, though I could not blame him for making use of opportunities. After all of the Venetian ambience, the evening was quiet; a time for contemplation – and some scotch.

It was a fairly routine trip from Venice to Athens (actually Piraeus), a day again spent partly in cleaning boats and assisting passengers in their daily needs. I decided that a bit of time spent in tourist-class would not be wasted, and certainly was aware of a livelier atmosphere there than in first-class. As the deck space was substantially less than that enjoyed by the upper echelons, but there were more passengers in tourist, one felt a good deal more cheek by jowl with passengers. This factor had obvious attendant advantages, one of which was called Jayne.

This young lady, travelling on her own, was a comely young model, evidently from Birmingham (not the most ingratiating of accents) and, I noted, seemed to dislike wearing too much clothing. Actually, everybody else apparently noted the same, but that concerned me little; after a while we made an assignation (a more suitable word than one might at first think) for an evening dance. After dinner, mine being in first-class, there being oddly enough no officers' tables being reserved in tourist, I repaired down to their far less opulent dance-floor and had a couple of dances, but as Jayne stated that she disliked dancing and had a bottle of wine in her cabin, she suggested that that was a far more suitable place to talk than was the dance-floor. She was, of course, correct, but I prefer to draw a veil over the next hour or so, as my sheer ineptitude was once again exposed to me.

Although this cruise had witnessed some notably scenic ports, Piraeus took second place to none. Certainly, it was more sun-ravaged and oddly bleak than the previous two ports, but in terms of history, it surpassed in interest everywhere that we had visited earlier. In the 1960s it was the 'cradle of civilisation'; now, of course, it is much more realistically regarded as the 'cradle of western civilisation', there then being, excepting in the minds of a few of the enlightened, no consideration of the reality of Indian, and especially Chinese, thought and inventions having preceded the rather slow emergence of Western culture and society. However, this was all pretty academic on this day; all of the officers of any significance having gone ashore, my day was spent looking officious at the head of the gangway. And that was all that the job seemed to entail, there being no security concerns and no inspection of boarding cards or similar documents. In fact, it was rather to the contrary, visitors (potential future passengers) actually being 'greeted'. Today those days seem to have been the days of innocence.

The evening was more enlivening. I decided that it was time to see a bit of the city, and I thought to combine two forms of leisure by taking Jayne ashore for a more exotic drink than one partaken in the tourist bar. We hailed a taxi and were taken to a hotel in central Athens where, the driver indicated, one had a view and plenty of 'life'. We ascended to the roof, only five or six floors up, and found ourselves with a wonderful view of the Acropolis. Each armed with a drink, we enjoyed the conviviality and the sheer romantic glamour of it all. There were many reasons to go to sea on passenger ships, but I could discern none better than such an evening! But it did not last. When the bill came, I found that the drinks were about thirty shillings each (together, 30% of my monthly stipend!). To my lasting shame, we crept out without paying. The evening ended thus.

Much less ambitiously, the following day the Staff Captain, the mate and most of the deck officers invited Stuart and me out of a lifeboat trip to a local beach. The Purser laid on an excellent lunch, accompanied by a very good supply of liquid refreshment, and we sped off to a carefully selected location where the great heat (it was over one hundred degrees) was somewhat alleviated. To me, again a good reason for going to sea. Memories of a stifling engine room recede quickly. Such a scenario would cost most people a goodly sum. But pleasure is tiring – I was in my bunk before 10 pm.

The next morning saw us heading for Naples (I had actually seen very little of Athens, but as it was one of the most popular of ports, I anticipated having many more future opportunities to explore at greater leisure). The day was spent in the usual tedious way (entertaining young and lonely female passengers) but the evening was more sybaritic, the nursing staff deciding to throw a party for the junior officers (the nurses were all youthful and comely, so senior officers were notably absent), an occasion to which I was glad to invite Jayne. And a good time was had by all, though I declined to adjourn to her cabin afterwards, as I knew that it was likely that I would again make an ass of myself. Even then, I knew that, though it was frustrating, time was on my side. But there was no point in inviting humiliation.

Furthermore, a bit of luck came my way. The mate, obviously liking my previous work, asked me to join the following day's tour to Pompeii and Mount Vesuvius and to submit a report on the most popular excursion. This was good; but it was made great by the fact that I found that Jayne was also going on the tour. And although I did not know much about the subject, I discovered from a book (probably not the Pilot volume) that Pompeii was world-renowned for its erotic frescoes and statuary. While I knew little or nothing of such things (the

English were still stuck in some sort of time-warp compared with the decadent continentals) it struck me that if Jayne liked that sort of thing, she would probably like this sort of thing. It looked like being a good day.

But it wasn't. When retiring, I missed a scheduled time-change. So, when I awoke for a stimulating day, the tour had gone! Missed by ten minutes, 'despair' did not begin to describe what I felt, later made only the worse by looking at some of the tour brochures; what even *they* showed was well beyond what I thought publicly acceptable (though, truth to tell, erotic art very quickly turns into grotesquery, and here much did so).

We departed in the evening; even the rather romantic image of Capri disappearing astern (for me, accompanied by Scotland's finest product) did little to raise my morale. It certainly did nothing to raise Jayne's.

The voyage to Barcelona, which should have been a pacific interlude, did not prove to be so; we were heading into a westerly wind of unusual ferocity for the Mediterranean, and while the pitching was slight, stabilisers can do nothing in that sort of sea; the dining saloon was almost deserted for dinner. It did not worry me too much; I was told that Jayne was now having a very good time with the 2nd mate (a useless Lothario-type of fellow, in my view) and Stuart was disconsolate to find that Carole was evidently enjoying the attention of the homunculus; la donna e mobile (times two)!

From the sea, Barcelona simply looked like a big city. But we really didn't have eyes for it, for anchored outside the harbour was the magnificent USS *Enterprise*, at that time virtually new (being launched in 1962), the world's first nuclear-powered aircraft carrier and the longest naval vessel ever built. While the world boasted a number of small aircraft carriers of dubious utility (naval minnows such as Brazil and Canada each operated such vessels, though both were without significant navies), and they were therefore not uncommon, this was a singularly impressive ship. One could only assume that it was in a Spanish port because the U.S. was keen to bring that fascist state into NATO, though this objective was not achieved until 1982. The Americans were judicious in their behaviour, however; the pilot told us that the first boats ashore from the ship disgorged 200 military police, charged with maintaining order by asking questions of disorderly crew only after knocking them on the head and bringing them back on board. And this, we knew, unlike the Royal Navy, was a dry ship, so there obviously being, in spite of sobriety, an acute awareness of Spanish sensibilities. Still, there were about 4,000 lusty young men on board, each with a lot more money than most Spaniards were likely to have. And aircraft carriers do not operate like lone wolves; somewhere in the harbour were likely to be at least five (manned) escort warships.

I was pleased to find that Anne and her latest beau had decided to pull together a half dozen or so of our ship's own lusty youth and take a trip ashore, and to this group I was invited. We put ourselves in the hands of a taxi driver (this, we were told, was a city of the honest, presumably because la policia enforced their own inquisitional morality), and he took us to a rowdy night-club.

My enthusiasm for flamenco dancing and associated hi-jinks had never been very great, and this club, half full of U.S. sailors, most of whom did not seem to eschew the local beer, made something of a convert of me, though perhaps not a whole-hearted one. Flamenco was certainly noisy and skilful, our small group exhibiting little British reserve; in fact, Anne seemed to become quite flirty, something to which I took no exception at all, she complementing my inelegant shape exceedingly well. Nobody seemed to get drunk, but that might have had something to do with the four MPs who hovered by the bar. It was a noisy, but surprisingly chaste, long evening out.

The morning saw few activities. Another tour would have served me well, but as Barcelona was a frequent cruise port, I was unworried. However, I was never to return.

The final port was Gibraltar (it did seem that politics may have been involved, for in comparison with the preceding joys of Venice, Piraeus, Naples and Barcelona, this was a place of few pleasures – the Barbary apes may be cute, but only for ten minutes. And there was no shortage of alternative ports, the most obvious being Lisbon, Oporto and Corunna, all of which had unique features that were more exotic than British pubs). But after a cruise of this length, nobody seemed concerned that three days later we berthed in drab Tilbury. Relationships ended – though not all – largely, one supposes, because even on a large ship, everybody lives in close and artificial proximity to all sorts of people, and propinquity does not always breed tolerance.

Although to me the personal experiences of nearly two months of Mediterranean cruising were eye-popping educational and maturing events, it should have been clear to all observers, including me, that we were at the end of an era. While both of the ships were fine examples of 1950's design and function, they were essentially obsolete even as they were being built. No longer would moderately fast ships carrying passengers and cargo to the ends of the earth be in demand, for the air routes were now thoroughly conquered and specialised cargo ships could far more effectively carry the varied products to and from the large container ports that were beginning to be constructed. P&O had foreseen the changes being forced upon international trade, for the company had produced *Canberra* and *Oriana*, but the implications of the changes were not fully realised even with these two vessels, which were magnificently obsolescent even when launched. A further somewhat myopic decision was made when the catastrophic political maelstrom that was the independence of the Belgian Congo reduced the Belgians' need to maintain their new ships *Jadotville* and *Badouinville*; they came on the market in 1961 and P&O grasped the opportunity to replace *Canton, Carthage* and *Corfu* on the Far East service. But, again, much was changing. Such ships were unnecessary; Britain no longer needed to maintain civil servants, bankers and troops in the far reaches of the Empire, a conglomerate that itself was in slow decline.

With changing economic circumstances and even greater political earthquakes, the shipping industry could rarely react to world events as they occurred; almost any vessel took a long time to plan and build. Meanwhile, the world's need to absorb many new technologies and products (who had in 1963 had ever heard of 'rare earths'?) had exponentially increased the sheer volume of shipping that clogged the trade arteries.

For me personally the pattern of life was changing; while I had now experienced a good variety of ships, ports, cargoes and technologies, all in the space of less than two years, the whole nature of training in the deck officer's craft was becoming more specialized and attuned to life's experiences rather than towards a life simply spent 'before the mast'. But in the interim, it was nice to be at home again, this time for what was in reality a very extended time. I was again to go to school.

4 Mid-Apprenticeship Release

A plaint oft heard in the sea-going community was that the educational requirements of the navigating department were so particular that the progress through the indentures, qualifying sea-time for tickets, and the difficulty of the tickets themselves produced a stable of men, and only men, who knew a great deal about very little. This issue did not arise among engineers, who could readily transfer their skills to innumerable branches of their craft, but in the real world the skills required for, say, calculating a ship's list or boxing the compass were little called for, other than for the teaching of those same arcane skills to similar ciphers. In addition, the wastage of trained persons of sea-staff was very high, particularly in a company like P&O, where the average (white!) officer could see at first hand the great opportunities available in Australia, New Zealand, Canada and the US, all of which nations (with some others) were physically less decrepit, were economically- rather than class-conscious societies, and which were actively seeking educated immigrants. To staunch this wastage of the highly-trained, the powers-that-be in the Merchant Navy, in particular Captain Wakeford (of whom more anon) set about broadening the scope of training offered to navigators in particular. With the Government being in the process of creating a number of new universities (mainly the transformation of polytechnics and technical colleges) and upgrading the nation's skills-creating facilities, the whole post-1945 training ethos seemed almost Luddite, especially because it became very apparent in the first half of the 20th century that the technical training of the German artisan and engineering classes was far better than was the British, which was part of the reason for manifestly superior German armaments and innovations during the two European wars.

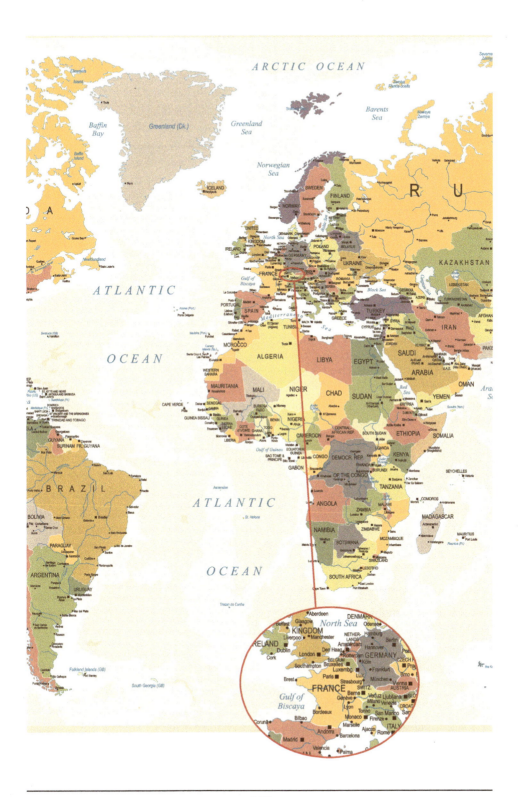

The School of Navigation (Warsash) was created on a very small scale in the 19th century. In the late 1930s Whalley Wakeford, a New Zealand Shipping Company (N.Z.S., later a subsidiary of P&O) navigating officer, took the position of head of the school, became its Captain Superintendent (it being the title preferred for the head of the cadet school, the 'head teacher' of 2nd and 1st mates being a far less grand office), and was successful in transforming it into the leader of the four pre-sea cadet training schools (at least, that was where he ranked the institution). He was an austere man who ruled from afar; when I was a cadet prior to going to sea, he was rarely seen, and then usually to lecture on how to be a gentleman officer. Some of the programmes that he instituted were useful for me at least; we even attended dancing classes, a quite needless exercise for those joining cargo or tanker fleets, but useful for those who intended to be employed by passenger fleets. The latter, of course, were and are far less numerous than the former. The relatively new MAR course was his brainchild and was designed to inculcate into the students more rounded thought and education; it was to be a university equivalent for those who felt that purely nautical training was too limiting for the average young man who wished to advance intellectually as well as nautically. It comprised a six-month course having nautical components (which the Ministry of Transport demanded) but much extra-curricular training as well.

There were about twenty cadets on the course. We were housed in a dormitory-like building that allowed us some freedom, but not a great deal, because we were quite a walk from the village of Warsash, wherein lay the pub and the bus to Southampton. A few of our number had cars, and the primary owner was one M. Reid, a P&O cadet who because of his car, had some prestige. (Though the prestige was to tarnish because it was soon discovered that he owed this largesse to being a victim in a motor vehicle accident, he having sustained some significant internal injuries; the settlement obtained for him a convertible Sunbeam Rapier, a classy car that only came second in the pecking order because another student owned a 1951 MG TD, one of the world's most uncomfortable cars. However, an MG was a thing of beauty to us, and almost everybody coveted it in preference to the Sunbeam.)

This collection of potential savants was under the supervision of Commander Southcott, an amiable Micawber-like figure who was almost ideal for supervising such a group, though we never found out what he had ever commanded; we never saw evidence of any uniform. The remainder of the teaching staff was a very mixed group, though there were enough ancillary activities to make classroom attendance a relative rarity. What I did not like, however, was the twice-a-week parade-ground drill.

My prior life had engendered in me a severe dislike of 'drill'. When I was at school our Combined Cadet Force (CCF) was a putative training ground for the Buffs (The Royal East Kent Regiment). Weekly, we got into army uniforms and paraded about pretending to learn field-craft, signalling and shooting. At the last I happened to be rather good, reaching the school shooting team about two weeks after my first effort (my grouping, I learned, was as good as either of our officers had seen in one so young) but the thing I most disliked was the incessant parading about while being shouted out by Regimental Sergeant-Major Dowsing, and the school Head Boy, who was our Company Sergeant-Major (and eventually went to Sandhurst). Dowsing was actually a good man; he had fought in Italy while a Regular, and taught us PE, but he above all reflected what many in our type of school did not acknowledge, which was that it was his rank that had made the Army so formidable (Major Lampard, the CCF's senior officer, was reputed to have managed during the war only to shoot down one of our own aircraft). It was evident even to the boys that the officers patronised the rough-hewn Dowsing (whom we respected) and that he in turn thought the officers a bunch of prigs, a category well known to most of the pupils (who were pretty priggish themselves).

When at Warsash I had found, not to my entire surprise, that we had to again learn drill. But Army and Navy drill, even the handling of rifles, was markedly different; the army favoured much foot-raising and stamping. In the Navy, the motions were smoother and swifter; basically, without the stamping. Our guide was a Chief Petty Officer (CPO) whom we called Nelson; he had lost an eye in the War, and, again, while disliking the drill, we all respected him. He was tough and knew his business.

After settling in, we soon got down to the business of finding out what we were there to learn. At the top of the tree was Whalley. He, I felt, would not be of much moment to us; he liked pontificating, but was harmless enough. Immediately beneath him was Captain Stewart, a formidable and very severe man whom I had once seen smile, but with whom I had sailed on the School's schooner and observed to be a first-class seaman and ship's commander. He, however, mainly concerned himself the cadets yet to go to sea; as expected, he was not much seen by MAR students.

Next day, we had our interviews. These were conducted by the disparate staff; Captain Percy and Commanders McKillop and Peter Ward. I knew them all; the first was an elderly waffler who had earlier taught ship construction and could easily be parodied with his Geordie accent, but he knew his stuff and was a good teacher, cordial and very knowledgeable. Mr McKillop was a different cup of tea, and the denouement of his first lecture to us was instructive. We were sitting around, chatting, when in he came, glared at us and declared, "I am going back out and will return. I expect you all to stand up when I come back". We looked around and needed no real discussion; we were no longer schoolboys and remained seated. He returned to silence. He was not happy but knew that there was nothing that he could do; his paymasters were now the big shipping companies. And finally, I was delighted to see the estimable Peter Ward, a very pleasant man who commanded by respect and had greatly assisted my tuition when I had earlier been at Warsash; he had offered personal help, particularly because I had no previous sailing or boating expertise, which many of the new cadets already had.

My interview comprised my being told that we were to face both a Liberal Arts and a professional development curriculum. I wasn't too sure what 'liberal arts' encompassed, but I first of all declared that drill was a waste of time; nobody prances around on ships in hobnailed boots, and in my two years at sea I had seen maybe two salutes in the entire time – the Merchant Marine just wasn't the Royal Navy. "There's going to be drill," I was told, but of explanation there was none. I also declared that I saw no need for much tuition, as I was aware that my brother was going to get a good education, and I thought that this opportunity to learn good new stuff overrode all other considerations. Besides which, nobody had ever said that the tickets were mammoth intellectual exercises ... I had seen enough stupidity, even with my limited knowledge, to know that much of what we were to be taught was just embellished common sense. I could not see why we could not be taught ethics, economics and some practical medicine (as I had witnessed, accidents happen at sea, and ships were often at least four days from a port which boasted a hospital). But my comments seemed to fall upon stony ground; the Ministry set the educational component, I was told, so I saw that, despite its being a new type of course, it was already quite hidebound. To allay my concerns, I was told that a thesis was to be written; some reassurance, I supposed.

The first day of lectures did somewhat encourage me, despite the 'stand up' farce. We experienced a new man for General Studies and English. This was Dr Broomhall, who had nothing of seagoing experience but was a pure academic, apparently with a Ph.D. from Skopje University. He spoke five languages (presumably a selection of Balkan tongues, though one could not imagine Macedonian – from a 'country' of only two million or so souls – being of great international value), was charged with teaching us English and, in general, an understanding of life, debating, philosophy and ancillary 'intellectual' pursuits; frankly, just what I hoped to gain from the course. David was apparently learning something of the concept of an epistocracy, and I thought that here was someone who could make me equally learned; unfortunately, I hoped in vain. But though he had a somewhat effete and academic demeanour, he was plainly a man of considerable acumen and, without any effort on his part, worthy of respect; there was no unruliness in his classes, and he presented a laudable sensibility towards understanding other cultures. He respected all things Balkan, a region quite outside the scope of British education, which for obvious reasons paid great obeisance to Asia but almost ignored historical Thrace and its unique ethnic complexity.

But we were also there to learn our craft, brought home to us by the immediate need to get some rowing experience. For that tuition the school was equipped with a few gigs (often called Captains' Gigs, as the Captains' transportation was their primary task in the days of sail) but which now are for more mundane use, including learning how to row. This 'skill', rapidly learned, was familiar to me, as those same boats were used to train all cadets. But it was not exercise that I enjoyed, for it was hard, created blisters, and was far less efficient than using a motor boat. But rowing was on the curriculum!

The first rowing exercise was therefore something of a 'trial to be borne'. Our task (eight rowers could be accommodated) was to row across the Solent up to, and under the lee of, tankers berthed at Fawley oil terminal, one of Britain's biggest oil ports and sited opposite Warsash. On the very day that we rowed over, under Nelson's command, berthed in a conspicuous place was *Manhattan*, a virtually new behemoth of a tanker that shortly thereafter achieved fame by being, because of its special elongated bow, the first, and indeed only, tanker to brave the Northwest passage from the US east coast to Prudhoe Bay, Alaska, bringing back from that there one token barrel of crude oil. (The vessel was at that time at 105,000 tons perhaps the world's largest tanker, but that was a record not to last; *Ardshiel*, by no means the world's largest in 1974, weighed in at 214,085 tons).

To a degree it seems strange how world economic, climatic and political changes have affected the whole world oil supply, particularly in the Arctic. Oil no longer needs to be taken from Alaska eastwards (a topic that I will later address), that passage being almost ice-free, future ice-breakers will likely be submarine rather than surface vessels, and in 1969 political disagreements between Canada, Russia (soon to be a much-reduced political force) and the US caused Canadian Prime Minister Trudeau to assert Canadian Arctic sovereignty, apparently successfully.

Back in the classroom, we settled down to lectures, which I had begun to enjoy. Other activities included a quiz, a debate on a Chunnel or a Bridge (I seconded advocating the Tunnel with a brilliant argument, but which failed to carry the day), and attending a long and fascinating economics talk by a lecturer from the London School of Economics, coincidentally at the time that Mick Jagger was attending that august institution. (Many adults then considered such reprobates to have IQ's too low to be measured, but Jagger had qualifications very similar to my brother's, who could have got into any University. Again, in my mind, a class reaction – Jagger's lack of 'proper diction' and louche appearance condemned him to, well, condemnation.)

I was very happy at this time to receive from Carole a long and quite affectionate, but rather anodyne, letter, though I was not at all sure that it was generated by my urbane wit or by the fact that she had gone off someone else.

But I also felt a bit depressed in the girlfriend stakes, because I found that David had landed a job at a Sussex boarding 'prep school' (which means boys up to the age of 14) as a history and judo (by that time he had a black belt) teacher. The iniquity of this fact was that he had only three 'A' levels, and as yet, of course, no degree, but the school (which shall remain unnamed) was one of the most expensive in the county and I was quite sure that had parents known that one so educationally unqualified (though his teaching abilities were actually outstanding) was teaching their beloveds, there would have been hell to pay. But from that perspective the situation was rather particular, for the owner and headmaster (for whom my parents' friend, Mrs O'Leary, was secretary) was a Lloyd's Name, a status characterised by two seminal facts. The first was that one could make scads of money, for (mainly shipping) insurance premiums were very high and the insurers were only rarely called upon to pay claims. The second fact was equally significant; if there were a claim, Names are liable up to the entire extent of their wealth; in recent years many of the very wealthy have been bankrupted by asbestosis claims, which have amounted to billions and will likely long continue.

This excursion into Names serves only to underline why David was able to obtain such a job; his services were cheaply bought. To the headmaster, this was important, because he annually hired six Danish girls to look after the school's domestic needs; in return they received a minor stipend and English tuition, the latter in part provided by David. He, of course, could not have been happier; by chance, all the girls were, he said, good-looking and, to put it bluntly, had been brought up with what might be termed a Scandinavian morality, this in an age when films made in those northern nations displayed things then shown UK only in 'certain cinemas'. And here was I living at times in the lap of luxury, but which was devoid of other personal activities about which I seemed able only to dream. It seemed unfair; but I am not sure to whom.

One activity in which I enjoyed myself was Dinner with Captain Wakeford and Pearl, his wife. This was a 'training dinner' at which one was to learn how to use a knife and fork. I had been to one two years earlier, as a cadet, and knew that the food was good, but the conversation stilted (though now there was wine, which helped!). We had to borrow boat cloaks for the occasion, a smart addition to the usual uniform, and, if we were lucky, there would be an interesting guest. But there wasn't; the special guest was the Bishop of Southampton, about whom, and of whose conversation, I recall nothing.

Fortunately, I was quite accustomed to long dinner conversations. Our family had for years got together on festive occasions with the O'Leary family, which comprised Mr (John, an RAF pilot during the war, a financial analyst by the 1960's, an arch-conservative Catholic with little real understanding of the political world, and a man whose hobbies included beer consumption and the standard opera fare), Mrs (Paddy, a highly intelligent lady of great vivacity, whose first husband, a fighter pilot, had been killed in the war), their daughter Jacqueline (two years older than me, a very darkly attractive and intelligent young lady who went to school in a convent and excelled in everything that she tried) and a much younger Michael, the son of John and Paddy, a rather forlorn young man, probably gay, but confused, I think because his father dearly wanted him to enter the Catholic priesthood, probably against any of Michael's personal preferences, but who as a young man of some sixteen years later came to a tragic and rather mysterious early death. Into this mix my parents, of substantially more liberal views, encouraged David and me to express views of our own and not be afraid to express them with polite force. Thus, when Whalley began to ask us to give some background, I somewhat blithely declared my preference for history as an intellectual discipline (because I had that 'A' level, a qualification that very few as young as I had obtained, but which for which I had sat because of a superb teacher who had taught both of us, and who simply believed that anybody with drive could pass a two-year course in one; both David and I found him to be quite correct) but I was then delighted to hear Whalley declare this to have been an excellent choice of personal interest. I was home-free when he found that I also favoured Sibelius symphonies (about which he was obviously completely ignorant) and that I knew how to properly use a knife and fork and the order in which to use the Waterford. From Pearl, apparently permanently ailing, we heard nothing; she looked elderly and uninterested in discussion. In the style of 'Downton Abbey' she disappeared early from the table and we men(!) were left to pass the port decanter (encased in a pristine silver wheeled vessel with 'from N.Z.S. to the School of Navigation' emblazoned thereon) to the left (in order to leave the right to grasp our swords). Discourse became somewhat less erudite from that point onwards. It was, somewhat like the Captains' cocktail parties, a prissy, old-fashioned sort of evening with desultory but interesting conversation; I thoroughly enjoyed it.

    I had decided that I would choose for the subject of my 'thesis' an essay on the Russo-Finnish War of 1939. I chose it because after the war my father had bought the nine- volumes of 'The Second World War' by Sir John Hammerton, and these contained the tale, and pictures, of a war of which few seemed knowledgeable. And, of course, it was redolent of Sibelius' music. Moreover, the Finnish Embassy in London provided me with all sorts of good leads when I wrote to them to ask what I could find that would enlarge the feeble stuff in the school's library. After the dinner with Whalley I felt that, if needed, I could get an accolade or two from that powerful corner.

    One of life's most momentous events in a young man's life then happened; I passed my driving test. And this naturally leads to the next important step; the obtaining of a car! On November 16th, I realised that the need for a vehicle had suddenly become that much the greater; the school had an Open Day and Jacqueline came down to enjoy the festivities (she lived at home in Horsham,

West Sussex, thus only a short journey) but I had to borrow another student's car to drive her to and from Southampton. My search ended on November 22nd, when two other cadets and I found a magnificent old 1946 Austin 12. It cost ten pounds, and with repairs and a battery we had to spend the princely sum of seven pounds apiece to render it roadworthy.

The Tank – 1946 Austin 12

It was easy enough to arrange insurance over the phone and we drove the car to the agent's house. Immediately upon arrival, he told us the shattering news that President Kennedy had a few minutes ago been assassinated in Dallas. The world had changed, but in what manner was little understood in UK, guns and their misuse being reserved to the 'uncivilised' parts of the world.

But life went on, as it had to. The next day, a Saturday, was the MAR dance. Jacqueline came (as so often with 'family friends' we enjoyed a platonic friendship, having known each other since we had been seven or eight, she and David being two years older and younger than me respectively) and we dallied in Southampton because *Oriana* was in port and we had the opportunity to go aboard this splendid ship; it was quite a lot larger than any of those ships which I knew, but had all sorts of novel facets, not the least of which was its elegant appearance; I rather hoped that one day I might serve for a good while on such a vessel. The dance was a considerable success, but, as it had to be, very chaste, and I drove Jacqueline home in what had now been christened The Tank. I stayed the night, the next day being the occasion for a visit David's new workplace, only a short distance away. We met three of the Danes; David's permanent half-smile was instantly explained.

I quickly returned to business at Warsash, or, more accurately, Whale Island, Portsmouth. This site, more particularly known as HMS *Excellent*, is the Navy's gunnery school, and it was for that purpose that we were there for a few days (it was but a short distance from Warsash). We were soon told that we would be under the command of one Lieutenant Tricky; when met, it was evident that he would be a hard task-master, for he was an officer who had risen from the ranks into the officer class.

It is worth explaining the perception that the RN had of itself. It had always been the Senior Service, and many more sovereigns and dukes had served in its ranks than in the Army, let alone in the Air Force. It was difficult to be accepted into the Naval College (Dartmouth), and there was a decided preference for those with the right accent and bearing. The perception that had been inculcated into me was that in order of precedence, there was the RN, then P&O (four of us cadets on the course were from that company) and lastly, the riff-raff of the Merchant Navy. The Wavy Navy (RNR, so named because their stripes, while of the same ranks as the other 'navies', were differentiated by having wavy rather than straight stripes) didn't really rank, members being too few in number. The RN, being very conscious of its majesty, kept out lesser beings, the exception to this rule being those exceptional sailors from the ranks who exhibited 'the right stuff'. And Lieutenant Tricky had the right stuff in abundance (smart, a good instructor, technically more knowledgeable than those who had never maintained, cleaned or had to take apart a Bofors Gun, and with an officer-like bearing) but he was plainly an outsider – his accent immediately relegated him to the ranks of a social interloper. We were invited into the Mess (the communal dining room, where treasures of war – some going back to the Armada – sporting trophies, there being a very important annual Navy/Army rugby match, and alcohol were kept for both display and consumption), but it was apparent that he was not one of the gang of lascivious young men who constituted the bulk of the officer corps; he moved in a much smaller and less noisome group than did the majority. But, it should also be noted, the Navy never knew what could happen; in the 1870s to 1918 period there emerged from an obscure and poor family living in Ceylon Britain's second most famous Admiral (after Nelson), the short, ugly and obstreperous Jackie Fisher, who from all the wrong beginnings created the Navy of the First World War, whose ascendancy was never seriously challenged by Germany's High Seas Fleet.

The training on the first day comprised being out on the rifle shooting range with .303's at 200 and 500 yards. This was hardly very testing, as we were shooting with only slightly more modern rifles than those with which I had shot at school. By itself this was a bit of a surprise, because at school the Belgian-designed FN had begun to be used by the Army, and we had been given a few of these rifles to fire two years before this exercise, a gun at once better but more complex than the antique Lee-Enfields which we were now given. We thought that this was because rifle-shooting is hardly at the top of the Navy's agenda, whereas it was all that the Army was about.

Following this pleasant morning we were given instruction on loading anti-aircraft guns, principally the Bofors. Again, we thought this somewhat strange as the Oerlikon had seemingly overtaken that weapon for naval defence, but it didn't much matter to us; we had no expectation that this expertise would be called upon in the nuclear age. (Little did we appreciate how things would work out – the next time that such knowledge was needed was in the Falklands, when such weapons were a principal form of armament.)

But next day was heavier going. We were to begin with a practical exercise in firing big guns. We soon found out how such an unlikely exercise was to be carried out within Portsmouth Harbor, when we were ushered into a large and smelly warehouse, wherein was a platform mounted on gimbals, and upon which resided a full Bofors gun, evidently with ammunition and all the appurtenances of war. This we were apparently going to fire (thankfully with blanks) in a simulation of an aerial attack upon a destroyer. We were shown how to manipulate this devilish thing, and then a crew of four of us was placed upon the platform, again being shown how to operate it. We were told that a simulated search-lighted aircraft was to pass 'overhead' and the all we had to do was 'load', then shoot it down. The lights were turned way down, and the platform began to roll in a most nauseating manner (that was why the simulation was a destroyer, a battleship obviously being a far more stable platform!), almost immediately after which a tiny little aircraft appeared on the ceiling. Hitting it proved quite impossible, so difficult was the wheeled mechanism for rotating the gun and aiming the gun, and so tiny the target. Then it got worse – suddenly we were doused with sheets of water, again to simulate what it would be like as a gunner on a real ship (at once, we knew why we had been issued with oilskins, one of man's least comfortable outfits). Despite firing off hundreds of rounds, we had missed all of the target aircraft; had it been live ammunition, we would probably have devastated Portsmouth! This fatuous exercise enormously entertained Tricky, especially because most of us were very seasick!

But it was not over. We were then directed to an adjacent building in which a complex machine-gun type of weapon was replaced by a 6-inch gun. Now, a 6-inch gun was pretty small, being the prime weapon of British light cruisers, but to us it looked enormous, even though a large part of the barrel had been cut off. (The largest guns of all were those of the World War II Japanese battleships *Yamato* and *Musashi* which were equipped with 18.1-inch guns, a size difficult to conceive.) Fortunately, we were not required to fire this horrible thing, merely to know how it worked (and not under a hose, an experience none of us wished to repeat).

The remainder of the day was, of course, anti-climactic. A lecture on how to operate a ship in warfare was given to us by a very erudite Lieutenant-Commander, but the idea of how to operate in the nuclear age seemed a bit skipped-over; we were instructed, for example, to put white-painted screens over windows and portholes to deflect some of the blast effect of a nuclear attack, but I failed to see how we were to be so prepared; on the ships on which I had sailed, no such screens were in evidence, and it seemed to me unlikely that the Soviets would give us a warning that would allow a ship's carpenter to suddenly manufacture several hundred of them. But I understood; Britain was often ready to fight the last war, but never that which we were to face (except for Agincourt!).

For the most part, all this new learning was quite academic; the likelihood of having to know how to load a Bofors, for example, was very limited. But strange things can happen; I believe, though not with certainty, that Martin Reed, later (in 1982) mate on *Canberra* in the Falklands, was on this same course. Naturally, he would not have had to fire such a gun in anger, but it is a precept of command almost anywhere that those in charge, while not needing to be expert in all aspects of a discipline, should know the basics. Perhaps that is why cadets at some time have to clean out paint lockers!

There were, of course, other things to learn. The rather peculiarly named Efficient Deck Hand Certificate seemed easy enough to obtain (what it allowed one to do I never really ascertained), the Certificate of Efficiency as a Life boatman seemed to be of obvious utility (by then I had, of course, spent many hours, not always unpleasantly, in a lifeboat) and a Radar Certificate, which, given the pace of progress, was obsolete virtually from the day that it was granted, all served to fill up pages in my Discharge Book (which is a record of qualifications, service in vessels, and an alternative type of Passport for Seamen).

More importantly, the year was coming to an end. Part of the MAR exposure to the real world was a period of overseas acculturation. The group of cadets previous to ours had 'enjoyed' a week in Bruges, a Belgian town full of all sorts of interesting historical stuff, but which Mr Ward told me, perhaps rather too truthfully, was a bit on the dull side. We were therefore much gratified to learn, shortly before going home for Christmas, that our life-enhancing experience in January was to be spent in the ski-resort of Leysin in the canton of Vaud, Switzerland. Without knowing anything about it, even we knew we were onto something much better than a city primarily known for making lace, which would not have been a turn-on for a bunch of randy nineteen-year-old youths.

Another Christmas at home was a bonus indeed for those accustomed to being at sea. I was very pleased to have the use of the Tank for the duration, for as usual my family spent the holiday with the O'Learys. Though enjoyable was the company of Jacqueline (who was by then engaged to be married to a fellow whom we considered a Loser), the holiday was made much better by a Boxing Day party at their house when I was introduced to a young lady named Sue, a local 'friend'. This young lady, slight but shapely, was very bubbly in a nicely suggestive manner. In fact, on one evening when we went out to a pub and Jacqueline drove the Tank, four of us found ourselves in the back seat with her (it was a big and very comfortable vehicle), I gratefully found that she rather enjoyed intimacy. Then, upon telling her my name, I found that she was best school-friends with Anne, who had actually talked to Sue about me! This was all good information that deserved room in my memory banks, especially the fact that this must be some 'school'!

Shortly after returning to my studies – if they can be so called – I received a nice long letter from Carole. Although she seemed to follow drab letters that said nothing with others that were quite effusive, the latter were quite memorable. From this missive I learned for the first time that she was now at Finishing School in Gstaad (I had never known anyone who had been to Finishing School and thought it only an anachronism beloved of romantic fiction writers), which town by careful research I found was only twenty-three miles from Leysin. That interesting fact cannot have occurred by chance; destiny, I thought, was playing a game with me.

A few days later we arrived in Leysin. We were pleased to see that the accommodation was a hostel that was comfortable, warm and located within a short walk from the T-bar, which was all that the resort boasted. But what pleased us far more was the fact that we were not the only guests; in fact, there was a whole class of girls from a teachers' training school in Portsmouth (one presumes that male teachers went to teachers' training, but they weren't here! We were overjoyed to see that this looked like ten days of unalloyed pleasure and leisure … oh, and a bit of skiing). Although the rooms for boys and girls were divided, there was no evidence of any senior advisers on either side of the divide, and while I believe that Commander Southcott was there, I never recall seeing either him nor a chaperone for the nubiles.

The days of skiing were effected with ski equipment that would now be laughable. Skis were common to all, the generic boots were similarly uniform, and the bindings occupied about two minutes to adjust. The T-bars took a bit of work to utilise with ease, and the hills were by no means too steep for novices to enjoy (not one person in either group, it would seem, had ever before even thought of taking a skiing vacation), but quite quickly it was evident that skiing was by no means what primarily interested both sides of the gender divide. The issue, though it was not much of one, was that there was no privacy whatsoever, but it became apparent to me that it was not a problem because all of the Lotharios who boasted of their prowess were actually sexual neophytes, as practiced in the ways of carnality as was I. There was also no excess drinking that I ever saw, and none of us was in possession of sufficient funds to actively go out and seek bacchanalian pleasures elsewhere. Which is not to say that things were not tiring, for although we were all quite fit and young, skiing exercised parts of the body which were unaccustomed to such rigours, and the evenings were devoted to much socialising (when the alcohol was limited to jugs of gluehwein, a spicy concoction that I then, and have since, found tends to be very cloying after a glass or two. It is difficult to conceive actually getting intoxicated on the stuff, and I never saw anybody try).

I decided one day that it was necessary to take the promised trip to Gstaad and see whether there were glimmers of hope with Carole. This journey I undertook by hitching, a means of transport that I had used occasionally in England and found a good way to get around. But this was not so in Switzerland, the Swiss apparently liking to keep themselves to themselves even more than does the Englishman. Having phoned beforehand (no easy task in German, I having failed 'O' level German) I met her for a coffee and found her to be even more gorgeous than I remembered. But the discussion was short and not very sweet; even I realised at that point that I wasn't exactly a catch, although I tried to be at my amusing best. I had actually reached the stage in life when I could assess people reasonably well, at least I thought I had; the numerous ships' personnel, officers, crew, hangers-on, fellow cadets and passengers met at cocktail parties and similar events, all required sometimes rapid evaluation. It therefore dawned upon me that Carole and I were simply not on the same wavelength, even though she could converse easily on virtually any subject (she could even talk about 'Eugene Onegin', the first opera that I had attended in London, and do so with intelligence). It all seemed a bit 'coached' however, and, for me, palpably insincere. However, as a young man much taken by feminine pulchritude, it was not easy to forego possibilities that had not yet actually been foreclosed; the flame of hope was not to be entirely extinguished.

But all was not yet lost, there still being plenty of interesting people of both sexes with whom to converse over the gluehwein. A couple of evenings later, while sitting resting my sore muscles, I espied, some ten feet down the table, a most interesting looking young lady whom I had not seen before. There was no time for introductions, the table by then being a hotly competitive environment, so I moved down beside her as quickly as I could. This girl, with a lovely smile, a strong face, but not one that one would call attractive in any conventional sense, I took to immediately.

Author with Heidi

She, Heidi, was talkative, humorous and, I found, had come down from Stuttgart for a couple of days' recreation. She was German by birth and upbringing, but her English was flawless. I knew little about Stuttgart, other than that it had had a strategic and economic significance due to its central position in Germany and had been cruelly treated by combat in both the Thirty Years' War and World War II. But my ignorance mattered little, as she was obviously well-educated and seemed to have an interest in everything that interested me. She was also, as I found out, a very good skier.

For the rest of the evening I was frankly entranced. I believe that the gluewein gradually became wein, and therefore our conversation became more and more interesting as the evening wore on. Suitably, I believe that it even snowed 'romantically' while we were sitting there. (We were, of course, surrounded by quite a good number of snuggling couples, which was itself all to the good, as I rapidly discovered that Heidi was not at all bad herself at snuggling … in fact, she was quite excellent at it!)

Her visit was short, she being in Leysin for just the weekend, and off she drove on the next evening. I did, however, feel that this was a life-changing encounter; even a couple of my companions complimented me; praise indeed (most cadets, I found, were cynics).

The following day the trip was over, undoubtedly one of the signal episodes of my life to that date. But another interesting interlude came up only three days after our return. This was a visit for our group to the Royal Naval College at Dartmouth, which was just a day's drive from Southampton. This was to be significant; we knew that the Senior Service looked down upon us; it was our job to enlighten them (in just three days).

We were accommodated in a rather plush barracks, and the lectures that we received were given by highly professional officers who imparted their knowledge with a notably good description of reality, largely because in 1964 we were at the tail-end of the careers of a number of Naval officers, many of whom had seen active service in the War, and who had been selected to teach their craft to the up-and-coming midshipmen with whom we were consorting. There was still something of an antique air to the lectures, however, because the battleship was still regarded by many as the quintessence of the mighty warship, whereas the reality of the day was that the aircraft carrier was now the reigning queen of war at sea (though submariners had begun to be the cutting edge of mature navies, their presence, by their very nature, had to remain quite undemonstrative, the complete antithesis of the *Enterprise*). Thus, lectures would be about the Battle of Matapan (between the Italian and British Mediterranean fleets), rather than about the decisive Battle of Midway, where aircraft from two US aircraft carriers sank four Japanese carriers without the ships ever seeing each other. We, of course, were directed more to convoy requirements than to fleet manoeuvres, though how a convoy could protect itself from aerial atomic attack seemed to be a topic to be skirted; logic would seem to dictate that for ships to be widely separated would in such circumstances avail them better than grouping together for protection. Again, however, I felt that we were being prepared to fight the last war.

We were later privileged to witness Divisions, a smart word for a parade, of the trainee Naval officers. Actually, we more than witnessed Divisions; we joined the drill itself (miraculously Nelson had appeared at the College to ensure that we looked our best and drilled with some degree of equality), but it has to be said that we were a rather shabby bunch compared to these well-drilled professionals. (Not that this fact changed my view as to the value of our being drilled, for I could envisage no situation in which executing a superb 'about-turn' could have had any role whatsoever on *Khyber* or *Mantua*.) They also seemed to have a lot of swords, which made the drill that much the more impressive (and, incidentally, antiquated); we had no such glamorous tools (though I learned a short time later from the company magazine that there was a 'P&O sword' with which we could have gained some dignity in face of the rather stuck-up RN cadets) but I knew nothing of this at the time. (It should be noted that, although not coincident, RN 'midshipmen' were roughly at the same level as we 'cadets', though the latter rank was of more recent provenance. Many will have read 'Midshipman Hornblower'; that rank had serious leadership responsibilities.)

The second day at Dartmouth was devoted to more lectures on varied subjects related to some arcane matters, the topic du jour at the time being radar and its value and future. Fortunately, this required much indoor work (late February was not the time to go out for a row or a sail). A newish radar had been developed which delighted in the term 'True Motion Radar' of which, of course, the Navy had the very latest equipment (only later would modernity come to Warsash). This technology would not to the non-mariner seem very revolutionary, but its principle tenet was to put the ship not at the centre of the screen, but wherever one wished it to be and to allow other vessels to stay in position relative to the ship, which moved at its assigned speed across the screen. It took time and work to become accustomed to it, but its immediate effect was to render my Radar Certificate obsolete. In fact, it was a substantial advance in navigational tools; but to a degree it was no big advance relative to the avoidance of the radar-assisted collision. And some senior officers never became inured to its advantages.

This was useful training, but in its own way, so was the evening. This was the occasion of the Midshipmen's Mess entertaining us for a Mess Dinner, full regalia included. Upon entering the imposing Refectory, however, I was disconcerted to find that my worthy companions had elected me to give to give thanks to the Mess for their hospitality and entertainment. There being, seemingly, several hundred of them and less than thirty of us, this seemed a major undertaking ...

but definitely not one to be shirked (I earlier referred to Mr Mallard, whose sound advice, though not said in so many words, was that almost every challenge, once faced, could be overcome; he was not only referring to climbing a rope without the assistance of one's feet). I also remembered that I had a few months earlier heard Martin Luther King's 'I had a dream' speech, which, Churchill notwithstanding, I thought the greatest peroration that I had ever heard, recorded or otherwise. Therefore, I thought that in the absence of a joke, which I did not have to hand, a short, deliberately delivered and simple message would serve me best. I was emboldened by the midshipman whom I had to follow; he did not set a high bar. And indeed, I was fortunate; I went on a bit too long, but this I realised when the buns being hurled had become ill-aimed spoons; I could see knives soon becoming the missiles of choice. Therefore, I sat down (there was no dais, my perch being atop my chair), not a moment too soon. My companions, who had thrust this upon me, seemed very pleased; again, an accolade much appreciated.

Back in Warsash, our education proceeded with a visit to Winchester Assizes. This was the sort of 'liberal arts' that I had sought. Mother had long been interested in the Law generally, but I had had little experience of it in operation, though we had discussed it frequently with respect to some of the great advocates of the day, including Norman Birkett (who physically resembled her father) and Sir Hartley Shawcross, the British Prosecutor at the Nuremberg Tribunal. One day at the Assizes hardly provides one with insight into the process, but after watching a parade of poor souls who seemed to want little more than adjournments, and counsel whose eloquence seemed little better than mine, I realised that the law was not very magical once one knew what one was about. Indeed, thinking about it later, I realised that what I had witnessed was not much different from the descriptions of the courtroom in 'Pickwick Papers' (I had yet to read 'Bleak House'). What I saw seemed little different from the processes of Dickens' time.

The next day, however, important matters again began to obtrude; I received a letter from Carole that, not unexpectedly, sort of sat on the fence. I noted, "I don't seem to be getting anywhere and I don't know how to get anywhere," but, again, young lust does not easily give up the forlorn chase. By coincidence, the next day I received one from Heidi, which I note I referred to as 'marvellous' and with which my literary style would be 'stretched' – and this from a girl whose first language was German! So, as a relief from all these stresses, one of the co-owners of The Tank (Don McGill, a very good fellow) and I decided the next Sunday to drive to Brighton and visit Anne, whom, I discovered, had an American girl staying with her. We drove there (although it seems now to be a very straight coastal road, at that time it was an obstacle course; the journey lasted over two hours. Now it would last less than half that time) and drank coffee. But I could see the relationship hitting the rocks very soon! It did; I never saw her again.

The journey back to Hampshire, however, was a very sorry affair. A major problem with The Tank was the water pump; when the engine was running, it operated satisfactorily. But if the car was left standing, the water would drain away down to the level of the pump itself, so on any journey, if one stopped, one had to have a container of water to return the water level up to the pump. I had forgotten this important fact (it was a minor repair actually, costing about fifteen pounds, but funds were always tight) and had brought no water. The Tank gave its last sigh on the Chichester By-Pass. We had to abandon it and I never saw it again; periodically, the lesson about 'false economy' has to be relearned. We returned to Warsash at about 2 am after a succession of short hitches, and, sad to report, we were contacted by the police shortly thereafter because of "a car registered in your name on the Chichester By-Pass that has to be removed". Two days later, a scrap merchant paid us three pounds to take it away; I am sure that he made a bit of money out of it. (Despite this tragedy, we actually did quite well with that car. One had to go to the lowest gear to get it up even the slightest hill, but as I have said, it was very comfortable and built to last.)

Don and I decided to commiserate with a visit to the Warsash Pub, a cheery place that prospered with all the local students. After my first rum and blackcurrant (a sweetness that quickly palls!) I found myself sitting next to a young lady of very considerable personal attractions, two in particular. By the second drink, we were in good shape; she (Eleanor/Elly) invited me to her home, a two-minute walk away. There I met her sister, a similar magnificence who ignored us completely and left the couch to us. I liked the fact that no parents were apparent!

Apart from a little such sordid behaviour as that with this pneumatic young lady, with whom I was, however, notably unsuccessful, our 'education' had to go on. One of Captain Stewart's friends had instituted a series of lunches which were to teach us manners (again!) and some social graces and enjoy an afternoon of recorded music; it was made quite clear that it would not be of the Mick Jagger variety. Equally, it was made clear to us (four cadets comprised a suitably-sized group) that the food would be excellent. (The food at the school was actually good, if repetitive, so a change of this sort boded well.) Now, however, we had to go there (part way to Portsmouth) by bus; one quickly misses the convenience of a car once it is lost.

I am pleased to say that the afternoon was very enjoyable. Our host was obviously an ex-Merchant Navy Captain, one who had plainly seen over sixty-five summers but was only superficially a gruff old martinet; once he realised that we would be happy to hear about his seagoing tales, he opened up as if in his ship's wardroom. Lunch was preceded by a good local beer, and the main course (it was coming up to Easter) was an excellent baked ham. Thereafter, we sat down for music, and he selected the First Act of 'Cosi Fan Tutte', a Mozart opera that to me was rather boring, conversational rather than dramatic. However, and here was the lesson for the day, he liked to hear his music at suitable volume. He had good equipment, but mono, stereo not being in general use at that time, and a single very high-quality speaker. His idea of 'suitable' was 'high', a volume that my parents did not much favour, and I only then realised that records could, and should, create a concert hall in the home; I never thereafter looked with pleasure upon the sotto voce. (A cognac would have made it an unsurpassed afternoon, but it was not offered.)

The next week was occupied in learning something about fire-fighting, one of the least pleasant parts of the whole course. To put on heavy protective clothing and a gas mask and then to drag a hose into a smoke-filled building was a very nasty task – and we knew the shape of the building, that it would not collapse, and that the smoke and flames could be turned off almost instantaneously; all did little to reassure. All we could know was that a real fire in any confined quarters would be very dangerous. Cargo holds were not so bad; at least they had remote CO_2 protection.

The final act of the course was, I am pleased to note, the awarding to me of the prize (a book) for the best thesis. This, I am also pleased to say, followed the Upper School History Prize that I had won at Cranbrook in 1959, and 'The Defeat of the Spanish Armada' which was awarded to me as a cadet at Warsash in 1961 for my essay on the subject of Juan Sebastian de Elcano, the man who took over from Ferdinand Magellan after he was killed in the Philippines at the Battle of Mactan (we live in a circular world; he very nearly lost his life when his fleet discovered the pleasures of Cebu, where unmarried girls wore no clothing, manifestly a recipe for disaster with a Portuguese crew of men who had for months been cooped up in smelly and rotting ships).

So, the MAR was finished. What now was in store for me?

Oriana at Hayman Island

5 Oriana, Comorin and 2nd Mates' Ticket

I was assigned to *Oriana*. If there were one ship that I could have chosen, this would have been it, though *Canberra* would have been equally desirable, if only because the latter was the fleet flagship.

A quick consultation with my fellow cadets persuaded me that I had been given the best of all of the choices available for that time of the year; one of them had been appointed to *Ballarat* (and while I wanted to go to Australia, it took but moments to appreciate that my way of going Down Under was likely to be infinitely more comfortable), and another to *Surat*, similar to, but certainly better than, *Khyber*, on the Far East service (though it would doubtless actually reach Formosa). And I still had ten days or so of 'leave' to enjoy, although it has to be said that leave was now an even more lonely existence; I had difficulty seeing how that substantial disadvantage could be overcome. I needed a car.

On May 1st, 1964, I joined *Oriana* in Southampton.

It was being refurbished, repaired and getting a lick of paint, so there was only a skeleton crew aboard. And this was a good way to get to know a ship, for any deck officer had to know how to get around the ship, essentially in smoke, murk or darkness, without the assistance of lighting (there were, of course, all sorts of such emergency features, but having already been on a ship that had essentially completely died in the middle of the Indian Ocean, I was not so sanguine as to think that everything would work as it should). Additionally, it was in dry-dock

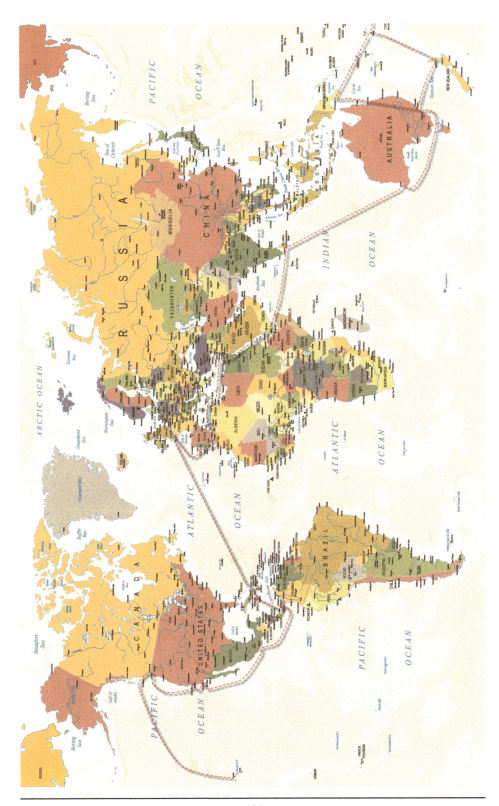

127

having its anti-fouling paint refreshed and some repairs effected to the propellers. It was also interesting to properly see the hull, because this ship incorporated transverse thrusters (propellers). This feature was not entirely unique (*Canberra* had them, though of a quite different design) but in 1964 such thrusters were unusual and a useful maneuvering feature.

Although there were few personnel on board, I learned from those who were aboard that there was more than the ships' nomenclature that differentiated the combined companies.

Oriana propeller change

They had effectively merged only some two years before, but Orient Line had long been a small but very elite entity, whereas P&O could be said to have been far larger but much more prosaic. Orient operated only four to six ships at a time, but all were very fine examples of maritime design and technology; it had nothing resembling *Khyber* or *Mantua*, the workhorses of the shipping world. And with this difference Orient Line affected a different hull-colour, older-style uniforms, and an unwillingness to train cadets; I was therefore accommodated in a very pleasant cabin near the bridge that had earlier acted as a spare officer's cabin (there was to be another cadet sailing with me, but he was enjoying a leisurely leave). I was also pleased with the voyage that we were to undertake; it was to be through Suez to Australia, a two-week cruise from Sydney, and an eastward return home via Panama.

On May 13th everybody arrived on board. My companion cadet, Mr Carveth, seemed a reasonable enough fellow, and I was interested to see that Commodore Edgecombe was to take over command, a man with a strangely mixed reputation, but very much an 'Orient man'. The mate (under whose aegis we would operate) was Mr McGowan, whom, I very soon discovered, flourished under the rubric 'Black Mac'. He was a man of powerful but low-key presence, but despite a rather fearsome reputation and a dour demeanour, was actually a humorous and very efficient officer. A little way beneath him was the second mate, Malcolm Rushan, another rather dour but pleasant enough personality who, I discerned, was probably the one from whom I was likely to learn the most; apparently even the Commodore respected him – a fairly select group.

The next day the passengers arrived. *Oriana* differed from the earlier passenger ships in one minor but telling way; it had accommodation for 638 first-class passengers as opposed to 675 on *Arcadia*, but 1,496 tourist-class as opposed to 735. Plainly, immigrant passengers (though they were now more Italian and Greek than British) were of growing importance, but the premier and more expensive traveller remained worth P&O's cultivation. This we cadets could easily see as we kept watch on the gangways; we agreed that this looked like a dull voyage, first- class being rather elderly and infirm, tourist being of middle-age and with younger – rather too young - children.

In the evening of the 14th we left for Australia. Next morning I was on the 8 to 12 watch, but with an even lesser role than I had had before on the big ships, there now being an excess of officers, including a 1st mate who was the senior watch-keeper, and a Staff Captain who seemed to have his eyes on the top job (rather unsurprisingly, for the Commodore was quite overweight and ungainly, a relative rarity in seamen, and to me seemed to be in a permanent bad mood … probably anxious for retirement, I thought) and spent an inordinate amount of time on the bridge. But my main observation of the day was that we were traversing the Bay of Biscay at an amazing speed, the vessel's service speed being twenty-seven knots, which it was able to maintain with ease. My second observation was at lifeboat drill; our initial view of the passenger list was correct; socially, this was likely to be a dull voyage indeed.

But maybe not. On this ship, with so many more passengers, the coterie of officers was much larger than I had earlier experienced. The higher ranks, 2nd mate and above, had their own passenger tables, but we hoi polloi sat together at larger tables at the unfashionable end of the restaurant. And more passengers meant that sitting among our number was a good number of FAPs, three of whom were noteworthy. Foremost was one of two two-stripers (they could go up to three stripes), a gorgeous blonde who kept much to herself (I was told that she was the Commodore's secretary, having to spend quite a lot of time 'assisting' him in his cabin), the other was Judith Smythe, a tall and severe lady but with much charm, and lastly one Carole Orchard (known, of course, as Cherry Orchard), an attractive and guileless young beauty.

But enough of leisure and pleasure; the same strictures about fraternisation applied throughout the whole fleet (though perhaps not at the highest levels, although it was hard to see this crusty Commodore being of much interest to the comeliest FAP of all).

Early next morning we were in Gibraltar, but for only two hours. Again, even though we took aboard a few passengers and a few people disembarked (presumably travel agents who 'required' promotional events), it hardly seemed worthwhile for the ship to visit this unrewarding port unless there were political motives. The next leg of the voyage, to Naples, was undertaken at a lesser speed, and, I think, the eight-hour stop there had no greater a motive than to break up the voyage (our next sequence of ports was distinctly drab) and the Italians had enough passenger ships going to Australia to render fruitless P&O's attempt to include transporting their emigrants. Personally, I had seen enough of Naples, with its unfortunate experience, not to again go ashore.

I was still re-orientating myself with the ship's speed as we steamed towards Suez, at which we arrived two days later. The routine was as normal, but noticeably there were far more bum-boats surrounding the ship than I had ever before seen, and, of course, they were selling hundreds of pyramids, mummies, camel-stools and Tutankhamen busts than seemed possible. However, I mused, this was a feel-good and harmless transfer of wealth to a society that needed all the help it could get. But, I noted, we then had a good dinner; trout, pheasant and strawberries. Although the previous life wasn't so bad, I appreciated at least twice a day how little I yearned to get back to a tanker.

The difference between steaming from Suez to Aden at fifteen knots on *Khyber* and twenty-seven on *Oriana* was manifest; the world had shrunk. And now that

Black Mac had decided that we were surplus on the bridge and were on 'day-work', mainly lifeboat maintenance (*Oriana* had twenty) other things changed. The evenings were now clear, but this was not much of a social advantage; there was little to be had (though this was not entirely true, for I enjoyed a pleasant evening with Cherry, but this was her first voyage and her naivety so disarming that I felt 'the rule' to be warranted).

We were quickly through Aden and fully bunkered, it being a very expensive proposition in virtually every other port that we expected to visit during the voyage, with the possible exception of the less costly Los Angeles. Arrival in Colombo late in the evening of May 27th was a bit like a home-coming for me. But it was on that day that Nehru died, and 'arrival' was oddly ambivalent. During the 1960s, the triumvirate of India, Yugoslavia, the short-lived U.A.R. and some other states had formed a loose assemblage of 'Non-Aligned Nations' (though India was the only member of the UN that voted with Russia respecting the invasion of Hungary; in reality, the assemblage was 'loose' indeed). As a consequence of the removal from the world scene of such a seminal figure, Colombo on that day was witness to much personal anguish, many of the crew included. By one of life's unforeseen coincidences, on our list of 'Important Passengers' appeared the name of Sir Harry Brittain (born in 1873). This austere gentleman, who was listed inaccurately as the founder of the Royal Commonwealth Society, was plainly a very eminent man, but for precisely what reason was difficult to disentangle; he had been to all the right schools and university, had practiced law in London for one week (!), became an eminent journalist, worked for years in establishing good working relationships with American journalistic societies, and incorporated or founded many obscure societies (who now knows of the Yorkshire Society, the Inter-Parliamentary Union or the Incorporated Sales Managers Association? I suggest that even their members would not claim those groups to be currently of any real moment … if they still have any members!). I believe that the Indian High Commission on this day found a role for him in the memorial of a great man, but to that ceremony I was not privy. I never met Sir Harry personally, but saw him around the First-Class Lounge, a cadaverous old fellow who looked as though he appreciated the verity that each day did not count for much until such time as each day became one's pre-occupation. However, he had longevity, shedding the mortal coil when 100 years of age.

But again, as I have said so often, life had to go on. Although the next day saw the ship crossing The Line (with its attendant High-Jinks for the young at heart, though I had by this time crossed that particular Rubicon twelve times) with soap-suds, champagne and rum playing their central role, I was perforce available when boat-drill duty for the new passengers arose, a suddenly interesting job for there, in tourist and among a group of noisy and uninteresting passengers, was a young lady, perhaps of twenty years.

Sandra Taylor was a comely young lady, but above all was a friendly, bubbly, personality. The securing of the life-jacket she seemed to find immensely diverting (as did I), even without any dubious help on my part. A little discussion revealed that she was travelling with her Mother to a new life in New South Wales, that she knew nobody on board, and, yes, would with pleasure join me for a pre-dinner drink by the pool. As we were by that time speeding gracefully over the equator in a calm sea and with a light breeze, this looked like an idyllic evening under the stars.

So it proved. I discovered that her father was British and her mother Sinhalese, and that she was a trainee psychiatric nurse who was looking forward to a future in Australia that was simply not on the cards in Ceylon (I never found out anything about her father, other than gleaning from her demeanour that he was an educated man). Not beautiful, but pleasingly presentable, she spoke well and had a gracious self-confidence that I found disarming; in one short afternoon, this trip was suddenly looking a lot better! At the first opportunity (the next evening at tourist Island-Night, always a better evening in tourist- than in first-class) I enjoyed her company again, and she seemed to enjoy mine.

Four days later we berthed in Fremantle and, again, the virtues of a bigger ship with the most modern stabilisers was apparent; the weather was unpleasant with a strong westerly wind (as is usually the case to the south and west of Western Australia) but there was little point in going ashore, this being a short stop for the purposes of disembarking some passengers, and, truth to tell, it looked an uninteresting place, though we were told that Perth, a very short distance inland, was far more vital. Some ports inherently seem interesting, of course, and the sheer remoteness of these two cities from other significant conurbations probably merited exploration, bearing in mind that there was then virtually none of the resource-based wealth that later produced a far more prosperous local economy, but I knew that I would be back (besides which, I didn't mind; I had received a most welcome and lucid letter from Heidi).

The run across the Australian Bight was accomplished with expedition, much assisted by the usual strong westerly wind; it generated one of those seas into which one was pleased not to be heading, but could be dangerous to small vessels because of 'pooping' (a sea or wave-form that ran along with a ship and whose water could overwhelm the deck as it slowly overtook a vessel). On June 5th, at the beginning of winter, we arrived in Melbourne. For the first time on this voyage I took the opportunity to go ashore and see the sights; this city had for me neither reputation nor profile. Nor was my ignorance much altered by an afternoon's walk; I noted no particular features nor much of interest other than that it seemed an expensive sort of place, hardly surprising perhaps as it was at the southern end of a very large country and long railway (though Tasmania, completely unknown to anybody of my acquaintance, was a good deal further south); my conclusion, perhaps oddly, was that it resembled Woolwich, largely on account of the building styles, which is to say, dull and stolid. We sailed that evening, the remnant of which I spent canoodling enjoyably with Sandra.

We arrived in Sydney amidst pouring rain in the early evening of the following day. It was not hard to see that this was perhaps the finest harbour I had yet visited. Immediately obvious was the magnificence of the Sydney Harbour Bridge, at that time the world's tallest steel arch bridge. Beyond it lay the business end of the port (where rude commerce ruled and cargo ships berthed) but we went alongside the splendid Ocean Terminal almost directly under the bridge, opposite which was sited the nearly-completed Sydney Opera House (the world is not that large; the unique shell design of the roof was tested at Southampton University), itself constructed upon pilings which had supported a tram terminal. The Terminal itself was without doubt the finest that I had yet seen. Of those ports that I had visited, undoubtedly the most magnificent from the sea was Cape Town (though the harbour was commonplace), but I began to see that there was a reason why so many P&O officers who had left England for finer economic opportunities had so often chosen New South Wales; it looked dynamic and prosperous, quite different from the rather drab and uninviting Melbourne.

That evening I went ashore briefly with Sandra, King's Cross being close and recommended by my compadres as a place for a drink, some life, and a view of the more ribald side of Australian civilisation. I bade her farewell, not at all sure whether we would ever again get together, but definitely feeling some considerable warmth towards her, a positive soul who faced a challenging but promising life.

Next morning the passengers disembarked, but as we were due to leave Sydney the following day, a busy twenty-four hours followed for the hotel side of the ship's complement as they discharged the old baggage and brought aboard the new passengers' appurtenances. I took the opportunity to see a little more of the city and took a short harbour cruise; my appreciation of a splendid port only increased.

On the 8th, we began our cruise, a rather beguiling mixture of the exotic and the very exotic. But firstly, there was the usual routine of lifeboat drill and Captain's Cocktail party to be endured. I noted that the Commodore did not seem enthusiastic about these events, and except for the unusual company-mandated Specials (such as Sir Harry, now disembarked) left the glad-handing to the Staff Captain. But upon lining up, especially in tourist-class, I noted that this cruise was not one so much to be endured as enjoyed; I had never seen such an assemblage of young ladies, most of whom seemed to be travelling in small tribes, parents nowhere in evidence. First-class was pretty good, but tourist was simply amazing. I went to bed that night full of hope and expectation.

In the morning, we were anchored off Hayman Island, a developing 'resort' just off the coast of Queensland. This was a port where the crew was not permitted ashore, there being insufficient tender space for anyone but passengers; in this enticing-looking place nobody was likely to voluntarily remain aboard if given the choice! So I sauntered on deck to enjoy a book, the winter being cool in Sydney, but nicely temperate in our new latitude.

The constant issue bedevilling passenger ships arose from the fact that they had to have engines, and that meant that they could make a great deal of smoke if fuel and air were not mixed in precisely the right proportions. In order to prevent this occasional but unwanted shower of soot over the deck and the passengers, *Canberra* had its funnels at the stern of the ship, a solution indeed, but one giving rise to its own problems. *Oriana* had another smoke-dispersal technique, this being large indentations in the superstructure immediately abaft the bridge that forced the air flowing past the ship into the hollow and upwards, this draft forcing the smoke from the funnel (the aft funnel – the 'flower pot' - was a dummy) high into the air and away from the decks. This bonus deck space became a sort of reserved officers' relaxation deck, and on this occasion, there being few passengers aboard, most of the FAPs and junior officers assembled for a touch of camaraderie. In this number was Cherry, who unsurprisingly displayed extremely well, and Judith Smythe, accompanied by another and rather colourless FAP who seemed constantly to be by her side, Judith evidencing no interest in any of the officers at all. I was surprised to see that the pleasant but rather standoffish Judith possessed a body that surpassed all my understanding, perfectly sculpted and perfectly tanned. To my eternal discredit, my early, and indeed continuing, thought was, what a waste! I certainly could not have made any move (rank had a role to fulfil even in an enclosed society like this) but nevertheless, given my earlier *Himalaya* observations, it did seem a shame. I read barely a paragraph.

The evening was not so great either. There was no question that Australia is a largely outdoors sort of country, and this shows in the athleticism of Australians generally, men and women alike – witness the disproportionate number of sports in which they lead the world. However, in a restricted environment, even on a large ship as was *Oriana*, their differing mores became very apparent to us supposed 'gentlemen'. All the girls, and there were a great many of them, looked superb, but acted just as their male counterparts did. That is to say, they drank just as much beer, swore just as roundly, would arm-wrestle all comers, and despised you if you happened to open a door for one of them. Ultimately, we cadets began to feel that our personae had become effete, and possibly gay, in their collective eyes. And the boys seemed quite keen on showing their manliness by, for example, smashing cans of Foster's against their foreheads, an endeavour for which I could see no use apart from for those entertaining careers as gladiators. But I found that there was a saving grace; her name was Margaret.

This young lady, exceptionally pretty (a description that I dislike, but it carries the right connotations) I found alone by the dance-floor. She hailed from

Melbourne (this, I thought, was significant, for inhabitants of Victoria seemed a bit less 'outdoorsy' than New South Wales residents) and was, and this was not difficult to guess, a model. I thought it strange to find her so alone, but I realised that Australians, too, found some of their number boorish; she actually liked to have a door opened for her, a habit that to others marked me out as an oddball. We enjoyed a couple of evenings together; the cruise was fulfilling its promise.

On Saturday, we anchored off Honiara, a place that I was looking forward to visiting. It is the capital of the Solomon Islands, and in particular the largest town (by no means a city) on Guadalcanal. On my 13th birthday my parents had given me a requested present; Fuller's 3-volume Decisive Battles of the Western World (yes, I had strange predilections even when young) and in which there is a full explication of the War in the Pacific, with particular reference to the battles of Midway and Leyte Gulf. One of the major theatres of the naval war was Papua New Guinea and the Coral Sea, and in particular on Guadalcanal, from where the Japanese planned, among other things, to isolate Australia (a bizarre notion, given Japan's limited resources by 1943) from its Asia Co-Prosperity Sphere. From August 1942 until January 1943 the Americans landed on Guadalcanal and eventually forced the Japanese to abandon their garrison on Papua-New Guinea, the culminating event being the battle of the Bismarck Sea, in which some twelve of sixteen Japanese ships were sunk by US aircraft. All this had occurred in a remote and impoverished part of the world about which I knew nothing and wished to see something, for it was not an arena frequented by cruise ships, or in fact by any ships at all. But what I could see was instructive, one easily being able to envision how difficult control of the area would be without substantial forces, both naval and aerial (I had absorbed enough history to wonder what weird mind-set characterised Japan's thinking about attacking the United States at all. One comparison alone tells all of the facts that one needs to know; during the war Japan produced or converted from other hulls eighteen aircraft carriers, but in that same period the US produced 124 carriers of all types. Even the United Kingdom produced over forty). It was instructive to sail through these waters in which so much natural perfection was witness to so much pointless violence and waste; underneath these tropical waters lay tens of thousands of tons of wartime waste, ships, planes, and guns, and thousands of people who in the ordinary course would have been citizens of the world. But still we fight!

The perspective of the futility of the Pacific war was somehow brought into further focus by our final port, Suva, on Vitilevu, Fiji. This island paradise lies some 1,000 miles to the east of the Solomons, yet going there barely brought us into the orbit of the Pacific; the conquest of the Fijian archipelago was, even at the height of its military successes, well beyond Japan's military capabilities. Hubris does not cover it; pride or overconfidence are not tautologies for stupidity.

I was fortunate enough to be asked by Black Mac upon arrival if I would be able to monitor one of the tours; there were some spare tickets available. As always, I gladly took the opportunity and off we went in a naturally air-conditioned (by which I mean it had no windows) cranky old bus. Lunch was at the Beachcomber Hotel – one of the Islands' premier spots, but whose food was oddly characterised by being the antithesis of what I conceived as Pacific fare (fish, perhaps pork, lots of fruit, and perhaps rice-based). Instead we received fruit, yes, but chicken and other meat whose dubious origins eluded me. However, I was hardly one to complain, the hotel being the epitome of my concept of a Pacific Paradise, at least while we were permitted to sit and watch the waves lapping the beach. Unfortunately, we then moved on around the island's perimeter road, stopping at another hotel for drinks and folk dancing. The drinks were somewhat specialised, comprising a peculiar watery mixture in which a bunch of a grass-like stuff was, literally, hand-washed, and the resulting product was then poured out into halved coconut shells, one of which was given to each guest with expressions of lip-smacking delectation. I found the potion quite disgusting, rather as I suspected washing-up water might taste. This concoction was termed Kava, which I vowed never again to touch, and never did. There followed an hour or so (it seemed to be about three hours, my rumbling stomach by this point rendering each passing minute the equivalent of five) of folk dancing, of which I was never an enthusiast. But the people seemed to enjoy it, so my tour Report was positive; all had worked hard.

It was a short two idyllic days back to Sydney. The weather was good, the food, freshly brought aboard from the Pacific, more exotic and imaginative than usual for a few short days, the work light (there never being much shipping in the South Pacific), and the company quite delightful. I very nearly messed this up, however; it was not permitted to bring passengers up to one's cabin for intimate purposes, but this was a rule difficult to enforce, because one could entertain passengers if it was appropriate (to whom?) at any time for, say, a game of chess, and to cavort with crew members always 'enhanced' the team spirit ... and some crew members were very much people to be personally entertained. My mistake was to choose the wrong time to entice Margaret from the dance floor, and to make a bee-line for my cabin over the open deck; the 2nd Engineer was having a quick smoke by the ship's rail while I was en route, caught me red-handed and sent me to escort her back to the rear portion of the ship. This was embarrassing but no more than that; we went down into the accommodation and took one of the twenty or so routes that brought us back to our objective; dallying in my cabin for a few hours. The cruise ended thusly; twelve days of fun, learning and leisure.

Oriana took the best berth in the harbour, of course, but in port at the same time was *Orcades*, a vessel some seven months older than *Himalaya*. An old friend from Warsash, Scott-Turner, came over to see us, and by coincidence Don McGill (of Tank notoriety) was in Sydney on Blue Star Line's (a cargo-ship company with impeccable ships, but offering a rather uniform career, which is to say with very little route variation, no large vessels and no tanker experience) *Rhodesia Star*. We went to a local bar (the 'Oceana') close to King's Cross and saw the night out with a somewhat salacious floor-show.

We had such a good time – though the morning on the gangway was heavy-going as I watched various members of the crew coming aboard obviously having been to places far more salacious than anything that we had witnessed – that we decided to have a repeat performance the following afternoon. During our walk-about to find a suitable watering-hole, we happened upon a large crowd milling around outside a hotel, and thinking that something interesting was going on, moseyed over to see what it was. And as we approached the crowd, out of the hotel walked The Beatles! I would like to say that we walked over and shook hands with Ringo … but we didn't. (Had we done so, I suspect that we would have risked being torn apart). Times were, of course, different (tickets for their Adelaide concert were (up to!) $3.70 per seat), but the clamour and the crowds were well up to the mania exploding across the world. After that, anything would have been an anti-climax, but I can only recall from my notes that we drowned our sorrows in 'a dive of much lewdness'; if I could be more explicit, I would be.

Two days later, somewhat tired, but much in love with Australia, its weather, its culture, its vigour and a good number of its *citoyennes*, we sailed away to the mid-way point of our voyage around the world; New Zealand, in particular Auckland.

The Tasman Sea, which divides Australia from New Zealand, lies within a notorious weather system. Partially protected from the ferocious Southern Ocean by Tasmania and the southern extremity of Australia, it is subject to extremes of wind and storms. The cyclone, as it is called in the south-west Pacific, is a phenomenon which ships, even the largest, endeavour to avoid; by observing the barometer, the mariner (bearing in mind that in the southern hemisphere the cyclone spins anti-clockwise because of the Coriolis effect, which also directs the bathwater down the drain) can often avoid the cyclone's effects, but the direction a system takes is difficult to predict with accuracy.

The run to Auckland, however, provided no drama of this sort. We spent twenty-four hours there, and I walked around a city-centre that was pleasant if not very stimulating. The country's population being less than three million, and the economy being based upon little other than farming, millions of sheep especially, the nation seemed like some sort of economically-parlous temperate paradise, even the local accent being a much toned-down version of the Australian twang ('Strine', as wags termed it). Leaving there for Suva (where I chose to remain aboard, no more free tours being offered … perhaps fortunately), where we enjoyed Saturday, we departed from there to enjoy another Saturday as we crossed the International Date Line en route to Hawaii.

Despite the fact that the Hawaiian Islands were once very nearly part of the British Empire (the islands accepted the British dominium, such as it was) but only formally accepted close friendship and the Union Jack. Additionally, Captain Cook, the most famed of British explorer-mariners. and George Vancouver, one of Cook's crew members, endeavoured to bring peace to the islands' warring inhabitants, but which efforts resulted only in the death of Cook. These facts, plus the sheer distance from the UK, made Hawaii a virtually unknown quantity to the British.

I looked forward to arrival in Honolulu, therefore, with pleasurable anticipation. But there was little to excite the senses. The town around the terminal was surprisingly tawdry, there was little to buy other than trinkets of little value, and although I caught sight of Waikiki beach, it did not seem to me to be of any particular merit. It did have the weather, though, for the warm temperature was leavened by pleasant breezes. Despite its fame or notoriety, whichever one prefers, I did not much care if I were to visit again. Particularly irksome was local radio; there was little enough news and music available aboard at the best of times, but the poverty of the US stations was particularly apparent if compared with the ABC and NZBC just left behind. I reflected that the US stations, motivated by the profit motive, tried to please everybody but pleased nobody.

The trip to Vancouver, the single longest stretch of ocean travel in the voyage, began a bit more pleasantly, as I discovered a very amiable young lady whom I had not previously noted. However, for some reason she found me not quite so charming, so I arrived in Vancouver alone and unloved. Poetic justice, I suppose.

The West Coast of North America offered interesting ports and much activity. Firstly, we were to visit Vancouver and Seattle, the latter for the first time. To enter these two ports requires a longer pilotage than I had experienced anywhere, far longer than Budge Budge and half again as long as the Suez Canal. Upon entering the Strait of Juan de Fuca, the passage goes on for several hours, one turns to port, and several hours later reaches Vancouver; if one goes on for an hour or so from that turning point, one turns to starboard and eventually reaches Seattle. To say that these are two of the best protected harbours in the world is to state the obvious. But the pleasures of the USA were to be ennobled from there by our visiting San Francisco and Los Angeles, a section of the voyage which I thought potentially its most interesting.

But first to Vancouver, a port entered through a narrow headland gap, topped by the impressive Lions Gate Bridge, under which the mast just managed to slide. The harbour itself was long and wide and overhung by mountains to the north and to the west a valley of narrowing width that eventually took one to the Rockies. It was a scenic harbour, really second to none; I have to put it on a par with Cape Town and Sydney. Our berth was something of a letdown, being an elderly cargo warehouse spruced up for the occasion with bunting and flags. Immediately adjacent to it sat the Marine Building, then the tallest building in the Empire, and in walking ashore I observed a nicely laid-out city, but with some curious features (such as pubs – though in England most would qualify only as rather shabby bars – having separate entrances for 'men' and 'women and escorts') and singularly ugly busses. A few passengers boarded and we sailed for Seattle.

Seattle was a very different proposition. A port more spread-out than Vancouver, one quickly realised that it played a different geographical role from that Canadian port. Vancouver was the end of the rail line across the country, the coast north of the city being sparsely inhabited because of the mountainous topography. In many respects Vancouver is quite remote, the nearest city of any size, other than Seattle, being Calgary, over 650 miles away to the east over the Rockies. Seattle, on the other hand, is not only an important industrial city (the home of Boeing for example, and is a well-known intellectual hothouse) but it also provided air and sea access to Alaska, the largest state in the United States, purchased in 1867 for about 2 cents an acre, and which had been admitted to the union only in 1959. Alaska being politically and physically isolated from the contiguous states by western Canada, Seattle was a major transportation centre, which by 1964 had become of considerable economic importance to the US; the discovery of gold had created a maelstrom of activity from the 1890s, later to be supplanted by commodities, in particular lumber and, as referred to earlier, the discovery of oil on the state's north slope. This concentration on trade and commerce to the north was apparent in the number and newness of bulk carriers and ferries that monopolised the wharves and slipways of this industrious harbour; there were even small passenger ships engaged in Alaska cruises!

But of immediate significance was the fact that the day had been designated '*Oriana* Day'. Though not an insignificant passenger port, *Oriana* was by all measures the largest passenger ship to visit to that time, and it must be said that the civic authorities had made much of our arrival. Whether or not the Terminal was inferior or superior to that of Vancouver could not easily be seen, so festooned with people, banners and flags was it. The effort to welcome even extended to the officers; I was fortunate enough to be offered the day out with the representatives of the local tug company, who bundled us into taxis and took us around the city and over the longest floating bridge in the world (how true that representation was I did not know; I had not even heard of any other such bridge). We witnessed a city facing the future with a high degree of confidence, for less than two years before our arrival the Seattle World's Fair had been a striking success; friends of our parents – the Daveys – had attended because of the propinquity of Vancouver, where their daughter and son-in-law resided, he being Canadian and working for Canadian National Railways (CNR) and having been sent to UK to see how a small country could efficiently manage such a complex rail system as was Britain's. She (Gog, the English having a curious propensity for creating pithy and meaningless names for each other) had declared Seattle to be unsurpassed in facilities, cleanliness and the friendliness of its people. After an excellent lunch, accompanied by, I vaguely recall, some Washington wine (good, indifferent or bad mattered not one whit), I returned to the ship to be placed on gangways for the afternoon; it passed in a sufficiently pleasant haze.

One of an officer's pleasures (though I was not yet one) was the ability to meet some interesting passengers. On the way to San Francisco I found myself sitting over a scotch with an English couple who had embarked in Colombo and stayed in Sydney during the short cruise from there. Though not really elderly, they were certainly not spring chickens, and they told an interesting tale. The husband had retired, and then, like many at such a stage in life, had decided that they had not seen enough of the world. They therefore entrained for Paris, and upon deciding that that city was a bit ordinary, elected to catch a train to Poland, itself at that time an adventurous step by itself, the Iron Curtain showing little sign of any rusting away. Warsaw they enjoyed, so, fearing little, they took the train to Moscow. This, a drab and desperately cold city in every sense of the word, they much disliked, and took the Trans-Siberian Railway to ... wherever. The trip, they said, was interesting in some ways but tedious, the scenery, traversed at excessively slow speed, was boring (hundreds of miles of birch forests, impoverished villages and populated by people of almost bovine disposition) and the food execrable (very much as was the view of Fitzroy Maclean, described in 'Eastern Approaches', published by Jonathan Cape in 1949, as he described a very similar journey). Their expectation was to reach Vladivostok, but in Ulan Bator they found their welcome much worse than cold; they were ejected from the train and obliged to hand over all of their belongings. All but their valuable hoard of photographs was eventually returned, but they decided that adventure was good only to a point; they had had enough discomfort. With some difficulty, they travelled by train down to Bombay and Ceylon, and sought passage on *Oriana*. I could only feel humbled.

But we did not always meet these unusual people. On the 'important people' list in effect while en route down the west coast was Ramon Navarro, a fabled actor of the silent screen. Born Jose Samaniego in 1899, he entered the film world in 1917 and made his first talkie in 1929, his romantic image beginning with his 'revealing clothing' in *'Ben Hur'* (1925). His twin problems – presumably related – were homosexuality and alcoholism. All that we knew on *Oriana* was that his steward reported that he ate alone in his cabin and spent his entire time drinking and watching TV. We never saw him, at least to our knowledge. (He was murdered in 1968 by two boys, who stole $20 from him, were convicted, and then released in the mid-1970s; presumably because of the opprobrium of the US view of 'sexual deviance'.)

San Francisco is, of course, one of the more fabled of the world's ports (and not always in a good way, its exposure to earthquakes being one of the most potent of its symbols) and one of the best-protected from the violence of the oceans. In fact, its entrance, between two headlands, with the Golden Gate Bridge linking them, is very similar to the gateway to Sydney, though the bay, almost dominated by Alcatraz, is too large and commercial to have any residual beauty. Nonetheless, I was pleased to see that the berth allotted to us was in the centre of activity, the cable-cars being just a short walk away from the Fisherman's Wharf conglomeration. The city itself was quite spectacular, more so than Sydney but for the prominence there of the Harbour Bridge. We arrived on a very cold day, but in part because of the frequency of dense fog off the coast, this unwanted cold was apparently quite common. Suffice it to say that for the thirty-six hours that we occupied our berth, I was able to see a good deal of the city by carefully choosing the cable-car rides, and incidentally have a demonstration of the evanescence of 'fame'; 'Scranton for President' signs were everywhere, but who now would recall the name? I had already learned that judicious use of public transport was often the best way to see the layout, delights and dregs of any city. But, strangely or otherwise, I noted that I was primarily aware of, and disappointed by, the fact that nobody was sending letters to me; I had expected letters from home, Carole, Heidi, Sandra and Margaret. I was apparently forgotten!

Los Angeles (more particularly, San Pedro) is as unimpressive a port as is Rotterdam. Both are completely without scenic interest, it is difficult to see where the ship's destination is to be when entering port, its layout apparently having no pattern, and berths were miles from the centre of the City (if indeed there is any 'centre'; walking is unknown, the bus system can hardly be termed a system, and, it being July, it was unconscionably hot). However, I was not one to complain, Black Mac deciding that it was time for another tour report, this one on Disneyland in Anaheim.

The bus departed early, as it was some distance to travel. But it was an instructive journey; this plainly was a large city, but I was struck by the fact that the neighbourhoods through which we travelled showed distinct signs of poverty. Most of the houses were small and almost shanty-built, many of wooden construction and generally in poor shape. In comparing them with housing around, say, British ports, they looked distinctly 'temporary'; British row houses around the London docks, Newcastle or Southampton, for example, were old and bleak, but they had been solidly built and, indeed, if they had a particular problem, it was that they were constructed to last for a hundred years or more; they looked permanent but grim. I had actually been inside some of those dwellings in East London (owned by various persons living in Woolwich) and they were as small and glum inside as they appeared from their grubby tiny front 'gardens'. What seemed to be the equivalent in Los Angeles, admittedly in a far more benign climate, was of a far more impermanent order; many didn't even look professionally built.

But I was not there to criticise the American way of life, even that witnessed from a bus speeding through the less desirable environs of a great and growing city. What was far more to the point was Disneyland itself.

Built only some ten years before my visit, the manner in which this paean to pleasure operated was a revelation. I have to admit that I had never been to a British parallel to Disneyland (not that there was a true equivalent, Butlin's Holiday Camps perhaps being the only pleasure-palaces that catered to a similar segment of society), but I was completely taken aback by the sheer efficiency of the operation. There were thousands of visitors, but if a queue was necessary, it was always moving quickly, the staff were abundantly polite and attentive, the food was well prepared and fresh (if, in taste and imagination, pretty dreadful) and the attractions themselves ingenious and spectacularly maintained. Given the fact that I was visiting from a ship, an entity that sought to provide some of the same thrills to its younger clientele, in retrospect it seems odd that I did not foresee that many of the deftness of the whole operation could well be transposed to a cruise ship designed for the young in spirit, and, of course, to the young themselves. Furthermore, it was, to my eyes at least, supremely affordable to the ordinary family. Quite plainly, in this particular line of business, the Americans were miles ahead of anyone else in the world.

Upon my return to the ship, I sat down at one of the deck bars to enjoy a cooling beer. I was not long left alone, however, for Lou, one of my favourite stewards, came over to me with a rather attractive young lady and introduced Paula to me. He said that she was a very charming girl who had been a passenger on a previous voyage and that I might like to meet her. His meaning was plain, he himself patently having absolutely no interest in good-looking young ladies, though as a person I knew him to be a very charming young man. He couldn't sit with us of course, and I was thus left with this all-American girl with blonde locks, a wonderful (probably manufactured) smile, and lovely legs. She was attending college in Pasadena (though I did not know how broad was the definition of 'college' in the US, there not really being a similar educational structure in UK) so I assumed a degree of intelligence, and she certainly had a bouncy, melodious voice to which I could happily listen all afternoon. The time slipped by most agreeably (it was also cheap, she not wanting any alcohol, choosing instead a Coke, which I believed, and still believe, to be a disgustingly sweet concoction that, I was led to believe, dissolved all the verdigris on coins if they were exposed to a few minutes of immersion). This little talk improved my mood immensely, lending a glow to Disney and Southern California.

My subsequent report to Black Mac was entirely favourable; whether it could have been a better tour I did not consider, it having shown me much about American efficiency that was to long stay with me. Even the depressing run back to the ship did not impinge on my consciousness of well-oiled Southern Californian commerce.

It was a two-day voyage to Acapulco, but the time was not entirely wasted; the Captain's cocktail party brought forth a rather charming Sally, small but perfect, again hailing from Los Angeles. I dallied a bit with her, but after a while considered her too limited an intellect, my critical faculties now being very well honed, or so I stupidly thought (she liked Coke as well, this being to me too much a sign of advanced naivety; it was an immediate signal of unsuitability).

Acapulco constituted an anchorage, with the tendering being carried out by local boats. Therefore, there was not a great deal for us to do, and a bunch of us, radio officers, engineers, deck cadets and FAPs put together a smorgasbord of shipboard delights and took a lifeboat tour of the Bay and its beaches. It would have been difficult for us to say anything other than that this was a perfect day, with great food, a hot sun with cooling breezes, good beer and a bevy of comfortable young ladies. Particularly of note was, of course, the fact that we were being paid for this 'work'. The evening I designed to top the entertainment by having Sally up to my cabin for a drink, but for some unknown reason after half an hour or so of mostly talk, she suddenly recalled a pressing engagement elsewhere on the ship. Such was my life.

July 17th found us anchored in Balboa, the southern end of the Panama Canal (curiously, when one traverses the Canal from West to East, topology dictates that one is actually steaming East to West). Far more complex a canal than Suez, this was about half its length and included five or six locks. I had been through locks before (particularly in the London Royal Docks) but never witnessed anything quite as efficient as the system employed in Panama. Firstly, they were very big locks, more than capable of handling big ships such as *Oriana*, secondly, there was no fiddling about with ropes and ship's winches, the locomotion being supplied by tractors (eight or ten of them, and called Mules) that simply pulled one through without any risk of scratching the corn-coloured hull paintwork, and, thirdly, once inside the lock, the gates quickly closed and in just a few minutes the water level was up or down as the case demanded (the ship was actually traversing sub-tropical lakes high within the isthmus' mountain range; the backbone of Panama). The use of time was obviously a significant component of the operation, for many ships were waiting at each terminal. The efficiency was mind-numbing in comparison with every other lock that I had experienced.

But my mind was not entirely on the job. I had earlier come across two girls who were on their first overseas trip to Europe, Scandinavia in particular. Named Karen and Vicki, they came from Vancouver, were good-looking in an unostentatious way, were elegant in a manner that Americans were not (at least in my experience) and mature (which is to say I was two years younger than they were). Norway was a primary destination (Karen being of that parentage) and England was to be a passing pleasure. They gave absolutely no evidence of interest in men, a feature that, in my competitive mind, made them doubly attractive. Enjoyment of the Canal transit was much enhanced.

Leaving Central America behind, we made our way with all due speed to Kingston, Jamaica. Coming from London, where the transport system was almost entirely staffed by Jamaicans, I felt fairly comfortable with the Jamaican sensibility, but after a day watching the gangways (here, there *was* a security problem, for there were many in that impoverished island who desperately wanted to get to the fabled English cities and what was thought to be economic security) I realised that Kingston was not a happy city, and that the visible 'wealth' of the nation existed along the north coast, where the hotels resembled forts into which relatively wealthy tourists were herded en masse. Nevertheless, the country itself was well-off relative to the other Caribbean nations (except for Trinidad and Tobago, where oil was king). I saw a little of the city first-hand, for that evening a very pleasant couple invited me ashore as company for their young daughter, the purpose being for them to experience genuine calypso at first hand in a nearby night club. It was a very pleasant evening, the family being very good company, the ridiculous drinks with palm trees and straw umbrellas notwithstanding. On the way there and back, however, I noted that the taxi driver securely locked our doors and carefully avoided, whenever possible, stopping at red lights. This looked like a violent city, and everything that I knew of it disinclined me to step ashore on my own.

Two days of comparative rest ensued, during which time I dallied somewhat with Sally and wrote to Paula to determine if she was a good future candidate for my personal ministrations (geographically I thought that she would be, because every time a ship were on the US West coast, it would inevitably bunker in Los Angeles; other than the Persian Gulf and its surroundings, nowhere else was in the fuel-price competition). I had also become more aware of the 2nd mates' exam that was looming in a few months, and this obviously required a good deal of studying. The visit to Bermuda, pleasurable to contemplate, was a damp squib; an anchorage at an island of transparent perfection, and home to many of the rich and famous, there was no opportunity for crew to go ashore. It looked perfect; I never saw it again.

Though notorious in its own wild way, a crossing of the North Atlantic could be relatively calm; even if windy, it was usually a westerly wind, which meant that the smoke from the funnel would have a tendency to go straight up, discharging its soot straight down onto the pristine decks. The decks were, of course, cleaned every morning, and in my new enthusiasm for learning, I made the acquaintance of the ship's sail maker, for as cadets we had to learn flag etiquette, storage and manufacture. I had never heard of a ship's Sail maker before (indeed, I knew of no others, he being an old salt of some hundred years' experience) but I understood him to have been with Orient Line since joining as a teenager, and from then on basically lived on its ships. There were obviously no sails to make, but there was a call for canvas repairs (lifeboat coverings and the like). Few calls for flags though, especially for India or Ceylon!

The last few days of any voyage always seem interminable; this was no exception. I seemed to spend a lot of time with Sally, whom I decided was pleasant but a bit of a flibbertigibbet; she was very keen to be with me on the rather flaccid Calypso Night, but a subsequent visit to my cabin resulted in talk and very little else, and by that time I rather felt myself to be beyond touchy-feely.

Two days later we berthed in Le Havre. Oddly enough, this was in reality the most 'foreign' port on the voyage, even after a trip that encompassed some unusual spots. For a start, relations between the two nations were frosty, as they long had been (Churchill is often quoted as saying, "The hardest cross I have to bear is the Cross of Lorraine", almost certainly words of another wrongly ascribed to him, but pithily apposite), the locals had no desire to communicate in English, and de Gaulle was pressing hard to exclude UK from European affairs; he wished to divorce France from the Anglo-American hegemony, and was doing so by exerting his political endeavours towards French rapprochement with Germany. Secondly, it hardly seemed worthwhile to stop in France; there were virtually no passengers leaving the ship, and cargo was of little moment (one could only conclude that the destination had historical justification; when *Arcadia* and others were operating as originally planned, each could have held several thousand tons of meat and dairy, but *Oriana* simply wasn't in that trade).

But this was all quite insignificant in relation to things that really mattered. Late in the evening I bumped into Karen, fortuitously, or so I thought, and she invited me to a midnight liaison in her cabin. Naturally I was not going to refuse such an offer and was delighted to see upon entry that Vicki was nowhere to be seen. However, this was plainly not to be a smooch or a sexual dalliance; she evidently wished to become better acquainted. I realised after a fairly brief talk that I had been a complete ass, misread obvious signs, and completely 'missed the boat'. This was an intelligent girl, had worthwhile opinions on almost everything, though her predilection for poetry was not one that I shared, and with whose company the voyage from Vancouver could have been far more enjoyable. All I could do was exchange UK addresses and leave her cabin feeling quite the fool (an emotion with which I was becoming all too familiar).

The vagaries of the mail were such that I received in Le Havre a letter from David, a bit silly as we were due in Southampton the following morning. He had little to report other than that he had hitched up with a certain Louise. This girl I knew, but vaguely; our respective mothers had many years before been great friends and the two of them had given birth on the same day, one to David, the other to Louise. The families had grown apart, and we had last seen them some ten years before; of Louise I had no recollection. However, he reported her to be rather nice; more to the point, she lived close to the Docks. Of this I made a note; in the interim I had a pleasing day off at home.

I re-joined the ship and two days later we sped past Gibraltar, the inspection (which is to say, lifeboat drill) having yielded nothing of interest; it looked like being a dull cruise. But in the evening things perked up with a pleasing young lady called Anne. She already had two 'A' levels, and thus was obviously possessed of a good mind, but unfortunately had two rather too attentive parents; she was blonde and pretty (again, a poor word, but suitable) and I could see problems – there was a good number of young men, but this was the only girl that I had located – quite apart from a hawk-eyed father.

Next day, the first port – Cannes. This was a tendered port, but there was only a short distance to the shore and there were lots of boats available, so I took a walk ashore. I have earlier remarked upon the unfriendliness of the French towards all things British, but this coldness appeared not to infect Provence. Maybe it was the heat (this was August 4th) maybe the bon vivant atmosphere, maybe the vacationing foreigners, but there was nothing unwelcoming about this paradise. Perhaps it was also because it was difficult to discern even the English tourist when adequate clothing seemed optional. My experience of such bronzed pulchritude being so limited, I spent my whole time just traversing the promenade; absurd, but time well spent.

To Palma the next day, where I managed to persuade Anne to accompany me to the beach (coincidentally, this was one day short of one full year since I had last visited this port) and she unfortunately was exposed to too much sun. 'Unfortunate' because I found out later that evening that her parents were well-advised to be cautious with her; she knew a lot more about 'social interaction' than I did; but I could not even get to the touchy-feely stage with that wretched 'tan'. And the following days were little better; plainly the parental eye had seen something in me that invited suspicion and she was watched from a distance, but very effectively.

Our final port was Lisbon, with no better resulting a personal 'interaction', though I did get a brief opportunity to see something of the city; at that time Portugal was becoming internationally isolated because of the independence movements started in Angola and Mozambique, its main African colonies. Guerrilla wars began in 1964 and continued for over twelve years, conflicts the nation could ill afford.

The voyage to Southampton revealed nothing more to me of my social life, but I had to make some decisions respecting the sitting for my Ticket. This had to be arranged with P&O as my Articles were drawing to a close and I had some leave due. The preparation for taking the ticket could occupy as long or as short a time as one wished, but the conventional way was to go back to school (and I chose Warsash) and reside there for the duration of the course. There was little that was optional, and thus I was rather thankful that I had experience on both tankers and cargo ships. In fact, variety was still to come; in the days following my return I was told that my next appointment was to be senior cadet on *Comorin*, a somewhat drab choice, but one with some good features.

The intervening days between the two appointments I spent alone at home, the family being away on vacation, a rare event. Actually, 'alone' was not quite true, as I had been able to arrange with Karen to come down to the countryside with me for a few days (I didn't know her friend Vicki very well, but she seemed to be amazingly diplomatic, rarely needing to be together with her close companion). The days were actually spent very innocently and pleasantly, for although she had not been to university and had no intention of doing so, it not being part of her family's personae, she had read widely and well, and despite our very different upbringings, we got on unusually well. But some canoodling, I was to find out, was all that I could expect; I found that I didn't mind!

One of the pleasures of living in South-East England was that London was a mere train-ride away (though actually getting to the station was the hardest part; two wheezing busses a day came to our part of the village, an introverted community that hardly saw the need to know much of the outside world) and the summer saw the appearance of the Promenade Concerts at the Royal Albert Hall, in London, only one hour away. David and I used to go with some frequency when living in Woolwich, but my being at sea had greatly curtailed such opportunities. Late in August I journeyed up and enjoyed a program that nowadays I believe would be considered too long for public consumption; 'Mozartiana', Rachmaninov's '3rd Piano Concerto', Arnold's '2nd Symphony' (unknown to me, but after which I was not concerned about re-acquaintance), Debussy's 'Prelude a l'apres-midi d'un faune', and 'The Sorcerer's Apprentice'. Very nice, but for the first time I became aware of the size of the place (it held about 5,000 souls) and the resulting cavernous and opaque sound (the BBC broadcast the Proms every evening during the summer, and I was quite unaware of how much better the aural spectrum was through the ether rather than heard in this vast cave; it was a better venue for boxing matches!).

On September 7th I joined *Comorin* in London. This was one of three ships, the others being *Cathay* and *Chitral*, both referred to earlier, comprising a trio providing monthly passenger and cargo service from London to the Far East.

Comorin at sea

Comorin was the odd ship out, being the renamed and re-painted *Singapore*, a 1950s black-funnelled vessel with updated but similar features to *Khyber*. It carried a dozen passengers, or rather, could do so, because those civil servants, bankers and the like who were destined for the eastern postings preferred to go in first-class, air-conditioned and fast ships rather than be bored in a converted freighter; cargo, of course, wasn't fussy. Thus, passengers on this ship were rare but welcome. *Comorin* was to be the last of the old ships to be 'modernised' prior to P&O realising that they were no longer viable economic units. But they for a while they provided a tri-monthly service to Hong Kong.

It was a sign of the fading utility of this type of ship, however, that while I joined on September 7th, we waited until the 18th before sailing from London for the Netherlands, all that down-time being expensively occupied in paying the ship's expenses while it earned nothing. Even then, we spent three rather tedious days in Rotterdam loading miscellaneous machinery and manufactured goods, followed by arrival in Genoa on September 29th, at this stage a port holding little of interest for me. We had, as I recall, three passengers, one a young lady whom I approached and by whom I was immediately rebuffed; all to the good, in fact, because of the exams that loomed ominously. I suddenly found a bit more time to brush up on chart-work, celestial navigation (I was not a mathematician, but fortunately enjoyed spherical trigonometry) and ship construction. The atmosphere on board was really quite congenial; the Captain's wife was accompanying him (usually a good factor to calm what could be the savage breast of the man in command) the mate seemed to enjoy life, and we even had an officers' quiz night, which I, with the R/O as partner, was happy to win. (This, I found out, was not much to do with me; on the second such occasion I was paired with the Captain's wife, and the R/O again walked off with the prize. He was a walking encyclopaedia; a bit of a bore, but a thoughtful companion.)

Without incident, we reached Colombo in mid-October, and I was mightily pleased to learn that a letter from Heidi had arrived at home (again, it is difficult to over-emphasise the importance of mail in a mariner's life) because I had my 21st birthday coming up almost simultaneously with our scheduled return to UK, and I ardently wished her to figure in those plans. Colombo, of course, was Colombo, completely unchanged from two years ago (even the derelict ship at anchor in the harbour was still there, only more rusted) but now, I am pleased to say, no longer in semi-famine (the Colombo Plan, originally a Commonwealth creation in 1950, had successfully brought many poorer parts of its components up to current developmental standards, agriculture included).

Simultaneously I was pleased to learn that one of the perks available to seagoing staff had worked out very well. Occasionally there were voyages that were under-subscribed and made available to the families of those at sea. The information provided to us some months ago was that a trip to Trinidad and back had become available for $100 per person for the voyage outwards from Southampton on *Oronsay* and back from Port of Spain on *Himalaya*. I thought that my parents would like to go, and Mother accepted with alacrity (Father had a bit of an old-fashioned 'work must come first' ethic and decided that he would stay at home to work … this meant that he had to buy and refrigerate twenty Fray Bentos steak and kidney pies for the duration. This was totally unnecessary, for our next-door neighbour was a French lady who was a Cordon Bleu cook, and Mother had specifically asked her if she could occasionally help; the problem was that the husband was a boring 'old-colonel' type who grunted his way through life, and she was not so much garrulous as a motor-mouth with much to say about absolutely nothing. Father chose to eat pies alone for those consecutive evenings rather than put up with his gloom and her prattle; I couldn't blame him). I received a letter stating that Mother had had a wonderful trip, having met interesting people, including officers.

The consequences of a converted freighter replacing a ship that carried 250 passengers and little freight were that the full Far East route could not now be accomplished; we took six long days to discharge a small amount of cargo in Penang, Swettenham, and Singapore, our passengers departed, and we made for

Manila. My contact with the real world came through a letter from Heidi (she declared that she had been subject to 'emotional troubles', but hoped that I still liked her) and Paula, whose letter was gushy; I had written to her, informing her of my literary and musical preferences; she answered that, "She liked everything". I knew from this that, firstly, I really wanted Heidi to my 21st, and secondly, that all was over with Paula; one who likes 'everything' either knows nothing about anything (an airhead) or is a polymath. I knew no polymaths, but I was pretty sure that she wasn't one. Pity, a contact in LA would have been nice.

It was something of a relief to arrive in the civilisation that was Hong Kong, a very rough passage from Manila making me realise that the South China Sea could sometimes be anything but benign (it is subject to two monsoons, both of which could be severe, but neither usually bore comparison with the Arabian Sea SW monsoon). But the time off was welcome (Hong Kong cargo-handling being left almost entirely to the local companies; Mr Ah Fat seemed on all occasions to be in charge of our gangs. He was large and imposing, unusual for the Chinese, perhaps because he came from northern China, where the staple diet was more wheat- than rice-based) none of the supervisors much appreciating officers interfering with their skilful discharging and loading. I also took a ride north and stood on the hills overlooking Communist China, elected not to buy a copy of Mao's Little Red Book, and enjoyed some local food (Chinese cooking was high on my list of favoured styles – British had come crashing down some time before!). We departed Hong Kong at midnight, the late time being because of the sudden illness of the Captain; this was only a slight inconvenience, on P&O vessels the mate always, and the 2nd mate usually, being master mariners, so a sick Captain could be flown to wherever was appropriate upon recovery. The important point was that I was suddenly the (uncertificated) 4th mate, unimportant in fact, but good for my morale.

Singapore was usually a fairly dull port, which sounds unlikely, but the trauma of that state's relationship with Malaysia rendered this a very difficult political time for that nation, which comprised Malaya, Singapore, North Borneo and Sarawak. Malaysia was created from these separate Commonwealth members in September 1963, but the relationships were fraught with mistrust, culminating in 1964 with race riots (we were there in November 1964). The issues, racial inequity, preference for Malays, a quiescent Communist uprising, economic uncertainties and the contribution of each state to the economy were of little concern to most of the world (with troubles in Africa, the Middle East, Cyprus and the like – not to mention Vietnam), but reading 'The Straits Times' one could conclude that Malaysia's problems were the world's most pressing dilemma. Ashore, one was only too aware of submerged tensions.

But Singapore was not entirely dull; one of the officers was acquainted with a nurse stationed in Singapore at the British Military Hospital (the Alexandra

Hospital) and he prevailed upon her to bring aboard a group of nurses for a party. While they could not be called a group of lovelies, they were young women, all that was really required. *Comorin* being a twelve-passenger hybrid (more than that required the vessel to carry a doctor) it was equipped with better passenger rooms than one might expect; we occupied the comfortable lounge, and though there was no pianist, quartet or anything of that nature, dancing of a sort was arranged, and I actually had a pleasing evening in the company of one Julie. And as the Chief Steward was as unhappy as the rest of us with the lack of the feminine touch, he put on some small eats that were surpassingly good; we had never seen that sort of repast before, and never saw it again, and wondered how it appeared so fortuitously. It did occur to me, however, that these ladies represented something that I had not earlier considered; when there is a garrison, in any location, its pointy end, the troops/sailors, represent a small portion of the establishment. Given the expense of Empire, the global economic pressures exerted upon UK, and that Harold Wilson, the new Socialist Prime Minister, was primarily an economist interested in mundanities such as the balance of payments, and who avoided any material support for the US in Vietnam by undertaking the maintenance of armed forces bases east of Suez, it was evident that the need for British troops in Malaysia was political and not military. Further, that when the US prevailed in Vietnam (sic!), the British military presence would disappear.

Of course, events distorted the reality of political and Commonwealth plans as predicted in 1964, in particular the sustained dynamism of a vibrant Singapore economy, which was not really then foreseeable because the nation possessed no natural resources, other perhaps than its geography. The world's failure to appreciate that the intellectual and economic skills of its leaders and inhabitants more than compensated for those deficiencies was not unreasonable, given that comparisons with Indonesia, Thailand, Vietnam, Laos and Cambodia all later attested to the vigour of the Singapore experiment. At some political cost, human capital soon demonstrated its value, a lesson largely ignored by those slower economies.

Upon these matters we did not much dwell, particularly as far as I was concerned, for we were now on the way home, where we expected to arrive on my 21st – and I had already discovered that the schedule was very likely to be maintained, unlike with *Khyber* and the tankers. We were to visit Swettenham and Penang, but these were to be the last loading ports of my time as a cadet, and with rubber being the primary cargo, our supervisory role was limited. I did learn, however, from my brother's letter that he had suddenly begun to use the word 'love' and even marriage, far too prematurely in my opinion, though perhaps, upon consideration, not so bad a decision, for if we went out together to a party, he usually got the first partner-pick, leaving me in his wake.

But other events had supervened. We had heard of an incident in the Gulf of Tonkin, just a day or two's sailing north of where *Comorin* had been plying its trade. This contretemps, evidently an attack launched upon a US destroyer by North Vietnamese gunboats, seems in retrospect to have been a set-piece casus bello that those of us who thought about it believed to be very odd, even at the time. It may be recalled that the US Navy reported two attacks upon USS *Maddox*, attacks which resulted in a single bullet-hole being found on the destroyer, and little apparent damage to the gunboats. This 'battle' seemed so unlikely as to be risible; I had seen enough US warships in Naples, Barcelona, and the UK to know that US warships were well-armed and their crews highly trained. The North's navy, on the other hand, was tiny and comprised mainly motor gun-boats, vessels quite incapable of taking on a modern destroyer with heavy guns, aerial support and great manoeuvrability. It would seem that even now the actual events have not been fully revealed, but this 'action' permitted the US to escalate the War and, eventually, suffer a fate reminiscent of Dien Bien Phu. Perhaps it was 'the fog of war', but it seemed more a signal of the perfidy of the United States. Harold Wilson was right to keep out of the mess.

A straight and rapid run across the Indian Ocean, as usual, ended in Aden. However, this charmless place had further deteriorated; an uprising against British rule had escalated, perhaps partly on account of neighboring Oman's civil war, a conflict arising because of its senescent ruler's antipathy to anything that he thought modernising occurring in his antiquated land (he reigned under a decrepit British suzerainty), or, more likely, because of the Nasser's virulent pan-Arabist policies. There had recently been sporadic unrest in Aden, particularly in 'The Crater', and as a consequence all members of the crew were prohibited from going ashore (no great loss, it should be said). Parenthetically, it seems in retrospect absurd for Britain to even bother with the 'hold onto the empire' sensibility, Aden having lost all strategic importance to the Commonwealth with the independence of South Asia. Indeed, though the situation got worse (as will appear), British tenacity rapidly dissipated, much to the detriment of those Aden-nationalists who sought independence, for envelopment by Yemen was the all-too-foreseeable consequence. Indeed, the Law of Unintended Consequences operated after escalation of the unrest in the following months; why is there no comparable Law of Foreseeable Consequences?

My much more mundane concern when we arrived in Suez (which is a virtually unvisited port other than for anchoring to await a suitable convoy) was mail. Unfortunately, and probably because we were ahead of our posted schedule, a problem unknown to *Khyber*, there was none there for me, and having sent a 'reminder' to Heidi about my 21st, I was anxious to see if my plans accorded with hers; perhaps I would perforce have to spend the evening with the ever-reliable Jacqueline ... actually, a pleasing prospect.

The penultimate port was Le Havre. It was its usual drab self (although it being December 4th the chances of it being anything else were, well, remote).

However, I did receive two letters from Heidi, though on the subject of the birthday celebration on December 19th "…seems to be coming over…" (she was then living in Geneva) was as much as I could glean. This, however, was but a passing distraction; two days later, I was in the train bound for Tunbridge Wells, my Articles assigned to P&O, and I was free until January 4th, when I was due back at Warsash for the two- or three-month course.

The sojourn in Sussex seemed delightfully long, and it being the Christmas season, there was a lot more activity in the village and town than was the norm. I also learned that Mother had had a great time on the voyage to and from Trinidad. In fact, she had met a delightful couple of Australians, and had invited them down to the country to meet me shortly after my return, and a few days later they came down for the day. They were a mother and her daughter, Christine, a young lady who seemed nice enough, but was a bit ungainly and wore her hair, most noticeably, in a fringe that almost covered her eyes; rather peculiar, I thought. They lived on the north shore of Sydney harbour, so I dutifully took their address and phone number; for some reason I was confident that P&O would want me back (this did not happen automatically; I knew a newly certificated P&O officer who found that the company had no vacancies when he applied to return to its employ, and he suddenly had to find work on a scruffy coastal Shell tanker; he was lucky to be recalled to P&O after plying the grimy northern English routes for less than six months) and it would be nice to have such a conveniently located friend in a port to which I expected to return at some time in the near future.

The further news on that trip was that she had met a couple who knew me personally and became well acquainted with Mother (she was a very easy person to talk to, even with those for whom she did not much care) and this common thread gave them some common ground. But I was amazed to find out that this 'friend of mine' was Judith Smythe … and that she was travelling with her long-term boyfriend! So, firstly, she was not 'a waste', and secondly, that female officers followed the same shipboard ethos as we did. This was a major blow to my belief that I was proficient at reading people; patently she was a very subtle lady who had fooled us all.

I actually did do a bit of studying, but that did not represent all of my activities. The main event, my 21st, was part wonderful, part fiasco. (I should point out that Jacqueline was to be married on January 2nd, and we were in part celebrating my birthday at this belated time because of conflicting dates, my course beginning on January 4th.)

Father had arranged to have a dinner/dance in the main hotel in Brighton (actually, I believe it to have been the hotel in which Margaret Thatcher was bombed by the IRA, and some of her ministers killed, a few years later). I had reminded Heidi by telegram of the date and even the trains by which she could most conveniently join us, and on the afternoon in question I awaited her arrival at London's Victoria Station. I waited for three or four Continental train arrivals, until, in fact, there was the minimal time for me to arrive in Brighton with sufficient time to change. She did not arrive.

Disconsolately, I boarded the Express to Brighton and made the Dinner just on time. My mood was not of the highest order, but I knew that because Father had made such efforts to arrange everything, I had to put my best foot forward. Fortunately, this turned out to be not at all difficult; Jacqueline was indeed there, unaccompanied, and wearing a gold dress that fitted marvellously what had always been a notable figure, and we actually enjoyed a superb partnership for the evening. As a measure of what could go wrong, however, one can always be thrown a 'curve-ball'; the sommelier was very pleased to bring out the red wine "straight from the fridge", as he put it, thereby generating a minor apoplectic fit from Father, who was, of course, in the wine trade himself. New bottles were found, but for such a classy place, this was a strange error; even if one wants chilled red wine (not itself a mortal sin), that choice is surely sufficiently unusual for it to merit enquiry. Nevertheless, it was an evening to remember, both for the event itself and for the company. Meanwhile, back home, David and I had been to a local party or two and found that in the village there were now a number of eligible young ladies. He had briefly enjoyed the ministrations of one Judith, but the brevity arose from the fact that he was now securely anchored, and, strangely, because Judith sought to have with him a brief and chaste affair.

The big change in my life was, however, the purchase of a car. I visited a number of dubious dealers to research what I wanted, and quickly found that my preferences (Jaguar XK, Rapier, Daimler Dart) were all too expensive, the cheap ones (bug-eyed Austins and MGs, MG TDs and TCs too small and innocuous) and the middle-ground (MGAs, Healeys and Triumphs) within purchase-ability. I finally found a sleazy fellow in East London who had the perfect red MGA Twin-Cam. Its body was in great shape, and it was very handsome. As I knew nobody with any real knowledge of the car business, I decided that this was the best that I would be able to buy, and on December 30th plunked down my one hundred and seventy pounds; I was sure that my social life was suddenly on the upward curve. I immediately took Judith for a ride, and she much admired my new masculinity, or at least I thought that that was what she was thinking.

Christmas passed, and I cut a dashing figure at the Jacqueline wedding, which, although I believed him a lucky man (I thought him something of 'a stiff upper lip above a loose flabby chin', but that view was not unclouded by some elements of jealousy) I actually quite enjoyed. That was in part because the groom had in his party a distant relative, Stephanie, a girl of considerable beauty. But I found things not as easy as anticipated, as I had never really considered the magnetic effect of a uniform (though Mother had told me to remember its advantages, and about which I little thought until I was in 'civvies' and found myself rebuffed). On this occasion my charm, exercised so effectively on *Oriana*, was completely wasted, Stephanie obviously being gay … or equipped with ill-tuned antennae.

An MGA is not the easiest of cars to drive, certainly in comparison with the Tank, but it certainly made one feel good. I sped down to Warsash ('sped' is not really a good word, because although it looked streamlined and sexy, it was by no measure a fast vehicle, and every now and again a gear problem arose that necessitated a change on engine revolutions alone). There I registered and found my room, a neat little cabin ideal for studying and located within an easy walk to the pub in the village.

I settled down to studies, which I attended as religiously as possible (a practice not followed by every student; I had never been a night-owl) besides which I was glad to be familiar with a number of the tutors, warts and all. I even enjoyed being in class.

The status of the students was one of 'unemployed' so we could obtain unemployment income (actually a reasonable emolument) from the Employment Office in Fareham, a pleasant country town that fortunately boasted a good garage, with whose mechanics I soon established far too friendly a relationship. I also found that the bunch of students with whom I had coincidentally landed were quite well-known to me (hardly surprising in retrospect – we were beginning and ending our apprenticeships almost simultaneously) and that, in the eyes of the instructors we had, it seemed, suddenly morphed into 'officers and gentlemen'. I did, however, discover that one could take the exams over and over again until one passed, no obloquy arising because of past failures. I forthwith registered with the Ministry of Transport office in Southampton to sit the exam beginning on February 1st, the earliest available date.

We also had some interesting stuff to absorb. In 1965 one could validly say that there operated a form of anarchy on the high seas. International Collision Regulations had been in force in some form for centuries (and still featured sailing vessels' differing abilities and lighting), but in restricted waters (the English Channel, Malacca Straits, South China Sea, Straits of Hormuz etc.) the size, speed and sheer numbers of ships had rendered them obsolescent. IMO (at that time 'IMCO', the International Maritime Consultative Organization) was endeavouring to create control mechanisms in the danger spots by instituting 'traffic lanes' (Traffic Separation Schemes (TSSs)) and mandatory short-wave communications with 'traffic managers' ashore. Naturally, resistance to change or rationalisation was huge; linguistic, 'not necessary' and plain dogmatic arguments were more common than agreement that something had to be done. A group of academics, ship-owners and geographers came down to Warsash and we students were able to sit in on a major discussion about how all of this was to be planned, disseminated, and given practical implementation. It was obviously of great international importance, but symptomatic of the problematic nature of international negotiations was the fact that the first formal steps to these ends were not introduced until as late as 1970. Soon, of course, it was, "How did we manage without these traffic rules?" (Naturally, Whalley stepped up to the plate to be admired, but although he himself was plainly obsolescent, one had to commend the manner in which <u>his</u> Warsash had taken its place at what was considered UK's leading maritime training institution.)

One advantage of my location was its closeness to Southampton University. David and his girlfriend Tina had settled into 'group living' in which a number of disparate individuals had rooms that adjoined central facilities, and the access being so easy, I much enjoyed periodically going over to cook a chicken or two for the group (I have to say, with respect, that their cooking was far less impressive than their learning; one student of Greek extraction favoured for a snack above all else a raw garlic sandwich. I was always able to keep a sufficient distance from him – apart from this habit, though, he was a good fellow). It did bother me a bit, however, that my brother was discussing Montesquieu, of whom I had barely heard, while I was learning how many lights a tug needed to exhibit. Not that there was anything wrong with that, but once learned it did not have much of a future in the sense of rewarding intellectual flights of fancy.

This issue was of concern to me, of course, because I could see that I was following the trail of knowing more and more about less and less. My exposure to the sea thus far had been very favourable, with the major caveat that it was difficult to find any senior personnel who did not regret their international 'vagrancy'. I had made the endeavour at some self-education by investing in a number of Pelican books ('Ethics' by Nowell-Smith, 'Anarchism' by George Woodcock, 'A History of British Trade Unionism' by Henry Pelling and 'Keynes and After' by Michael Stewart, for example, but was distressed to find that I couldn't even *understand* 'Ethics' despite re-reading and much cogitation) but it was obvious to me that learning was not gained just by reading. I was young enough to soak up more disciplines, but not while in a typhoon in the Pacific!

There were other matters to attend to, however. On a whim, I thought that a nice evening out would be good for me. I recalled that Elly had lived in Warsash when I was on MAR, and perhaps I should give her a call. I found her at home, and I was gratified to find that she remembered me! We met at the pub, and I found her in splendid form, perhaps even more splendiferous after a year of further maturity. After my usual rum and blackcurrant (a pretty disgusting drink, but at the time I thought it quite sophisticated) she invited me home, and we repeated, but with more vigour, the exercises that we had practiced twelve months earlier. I was disconcerted to find that while certain touching was not only allowed, but encouraged, she was also wearing something resembling a chastity belt, a rock-hard creation that resisted all my subtle and not-so-subtle ministrations. She was quite amused at this, unquestionably because this was evidently not the first such occasion upon which this had occurred (or not occurred, as the case might be) and we parted with a laugh.

Two days later I was in the Ministry's office for the first day of the exam. It started off with Seamanship (which included an oral exam by a rather mean-looking little man whom, I thought, had probably had an argument with somebody earlier that day), and concluded with Chart-work. This was a good deal easier than I anticipated, my having only to recite Rule 18 (the longest, but somehow the most 'poetic', of them all). I did not look forward to the next day, however, as it included Maths and Navigation. However, I am glad to say that the questions were not really difficult and with the final day, including the essay question, I returned to Warsash reasonably confident.

The response was commendably quick. On February 4th, I received notice that I had passed the Ticket. Coincidentally, on the way to pick up the document, I bumped into Peter Ward. He recognised me with, "I didn't know you were here!". I responded that I had been there since the New Year but that day had been told of my having passed 2nd mates. "But it's a three-month course!" he said. Upon my saying that I had been 'fairly' diligent in my correspondence course, he lamented that so few took that opportunity while at sea. I felt quite chuffed and told him that I expected to see him in a couple of years for my 1st mates. We parted on the best of jocular terms.

Chitral in port

6 Chitral, Salsette and Cannanore

I decided that I would apply to P&O for a job, as I had determined to my own satisfaction, that there was no more suitable a company for me. Firstly, however, I had to find out about Heidi, for whom I still carried a burning torch. On February 6th, I therefore purchased a ticket to entrain for Geneva, but this was preceded by an unfortunate accident in the MGA; I was driving on a country road with high hedges and sharp turns, and as usual the road was about as wide as the car itself. In turning a bend too quickly, I was met by a very solid hedge. The left-hand side of the car was badly dented, obviously an unexpected and unpleasant expense that I really did not need. I still wonder whether getting the ticket, writing to Heidi to tell her that I was about to arrive, and the accident were connected; they probably were.

Three days later I entrained for Geneva, but have no recollection of the trip, including the cross-Channel passage (the idea of there being a Channel bridge or Chunnel seemed to have died a natural death). Arrival in Geneva revealed a delightful city, mountains and lake providing a perfect scene, and the place as clean as a whistle. It took but an hour to find her address, and I knocked on her door.

The door partially opened, and there she was, looking, I thought, a bit wan. I mumbled something, she said she had received no letters or telegrams, and that we should meet in a coffee bar down the street in a couple of hours. Without seeing anything, I sensed a presence behind her in the flat, and away I went. I probably need not add that she did not show up; the torch was quenched. I stayed overnight in a sleazy hotel, the pleasures and elegance of Geneva quite lost to me and boarded the train the next morning.

Life, of course, had to continue; one probably learns more from such experiences than from even the most pleasurable revelations, Nietzsche notwithstanding.

Back in England, and deciding that I needed a brief change of scenery, I took an enjoyable drive up to Father's cousin's home in Suffolk, a delightful little bit of antiquity that was part of Lord Somerleyton's estate and for whom my 'uncle' worked as a gamekeeper/carpenter/groundsman. This was really a scene from the past; only a few years before our family had spent a week in their cottage, and the manner in which the estate looked after its employees could be partly gleaned from the fact that there was an outside toilet (straight into a cesspit) and no running water (there was a communal pump on the adjacent village green). By 1965 things had been modernised, but not by much. Anyway, this did not much bother me, as they were good company and he was a Jack of all Trades (he was an actual 'Uncle Jack') and able to explain to me a few of the intricacies of the MGA, not all of which were welcome news. I drove it around the area, saw the Broads in greater detail, and visited Oulton Broad and Lowestoft, all the while becoming more acquainted with the interstices of this car. Worryingly it had a tendency to stall for no reason and to re-start only after a hammer blow upon the battery, which was uncomfortably located below and behind the driver's seat.

Driving back to Sussex, I diverted to London, headed for Leadenhall Street, and applied for a job with P&O's Marine Superintendent (this was the position at the head of all seagoing staff, usually a retired senior Captain or Commodore). I did not know my august interviewer, but his questions were desultory, I was sent downstairs for a medical, and twenty-five pounds later (for the medical, I believe) I was back with P&O-Orient Lines. I celebrated by deciding to spend the evening with Anne, of *Oriana* and Palma history, whom I knew to be in London – and without her father! – and we went to the play "Who's Afraid of Virginia Woolf?" By this time I was actually quite familiar with London theatres; when we had lived in Woolwich, David and I went to quite a number of plays on Jacqueline's behalf, as when a trainee nurse at Guys Hospital she frequently received gifts of surplus tickets (naturally, these were not the 'hot sellers'), which she forwarded to us if she could not use them. Anne and I went to the original 1964 production with Uta Hagen and Arthur Hill, one that was thereafter seared into my consciousness but not with particular pleasure; Albee's supposed subplot of the state of the union was quite lost to me in light of the real vitriol that I saw as being the play's only substantive message, and I neither enjoyed the language nor the emotional violence of what was designed to entertain; the purpose, I naively thought, of the theatre. But I much enjoyed the evening generally and was pleased to find that Anne had read about the play beforehand and was able happily to discuss it over fish and chips at Flanagan's Restaurant (next to the London Coliseum and a favourite of mine); I rather liked a thinker! (I also liked a girl who appreciated her food (skate and chips); Mother had advised me to be cautious about picky eaters and those with untidy handbags. This advice that I tried to follow whenever I could see inside the latter!

This vacation lasted until March 1st, at which time I joined *Oriana* in Southampton as Dock Staff 4th mate. These larger vessels necessarily required a substantial amount of periodic maintenance, and Southampton could conveniently accommodate the largest of ships, the dry-docks in that port having been created in time to handle the two *Queens*. The ship's exterior was sand-blasted and re-painted (changed from Orient line's corn-colour to P&O's vibrant white) the interior paintwork was re-visited, and the engines received some loving care, none of which required anything from the deck department, so I was quite footloose and fancy-free. I was able to entertain David and Tina once or twice to dinner (again, first-class, though with a more limited menu) and even had Elly over for an enjoyable evening of food and frolic (though she still favoured industrial-strength underwear). On the anniversary of the demise of The Tank, or close to that date, I was obliged to drive over to Fareham to discuss brake issues with my favourite mechanic, who advised me that my MGA might have been a bit of a mistake. It appears that MG had decided to create a more glamorous MGA to compete with Triumph, which enterprise had enjoyed considerable success in the US, the great target of this specifically British type of small sports car. The MGA itself was quite successful, but the Twin-Cam was too complex and ambitious for its time (innovation was not British car manufacturers' strong point) and although lovely to look at, the model had proved unreliable in too many respects. It had therefore been manufactured for less than two years, a fact that the salesman for some reason forgot to tell me.

Two weeks on *Oriana* in dry-dock were by no means onerous, but nor was it very stimulating, Elly notwithstanding. It was followed by a week's Defence course in London (held partly on board HMS *Belfast*, a World War II light cruiser (with real 6" guns!) which was permanently moored close to Tower Bridge and administered by the Imperial War Museum), a suitable locale for learning yet more about how we were to handle ships in the event of nuclear war; I recall neither learning anything new nor of value.

I did, however, learn that my next appointment was to be 4th mate on *Oronsay*, a handsome passenger vessel of some 28,000 tons built in 1951 and which was permanently on the Australia run; by no means an unwelcome assignment. It was made the better, however, by my starting on May 19th (a bit late really, but that gave me more time for saving to buy the necessary blue mess dress that was needed for formal occasions for all officers, and which to this point I had not needed to purchase) with a Mediterranean cruise. By coincidence I received at about the same time a letter from Karen, who was in Norway, indicating that she expected to be in Venice on the same day as *Oronsay* was scheduled to be there. I wrote quickly to make the date, especially because at that time she had for a time a 'permanent' European address.

All was not over with temporary assignments, however; I had another dock staff appointment to *Baradine*, a black-hulled cargo carrier designated for the Australia run, and was for two weeks berthed in the Royal Docks. As noted earlier, P&O retained a highly competent group of cargo supervisors, and gangs that knew precisely what they were doing. The dock duty was therefore more boring than anything else, and furthermore did not count as sea-time needed to accumulate before I could sit for my 1st mates. I therefore looked forward to this posting with a lack of enthusiasm. Even the location of the docks on the north side of the Thames was against the any enjoyment, Woolwich, East Ham, Ilford and Dagenham having very little to excite the senses.

On April 8th, I joined *Baradine* (much like an un-modernised *Comorin* but infinitely better than *Khyber*). It was a mark of my ennui that it was not until April 24th that David's comments about Louise suddenly came back to me. I had her address and phone number, so a brief call to her house elicited from her mother a dinner invitation. Though Mottingham meant nothing to me, I decided to go there by bus (the MGA was again playing up). Crossing over the Thames to Woolwich I found that bus connections were easy, and I soon arrived to a nice detached house and was greeted by her mother and introduced to her father (an avuncular pipe-smoker) and her young brother, a charming young fellow of about 8 who was deep in a discussion with his father about local politics (all this while we were awaiting Louise's arrival – she evidently knew how to make an entrance, for I myself, because of some tactical dawdling, had effected my arrival at precisely the appointed hour). Ten minutes elapsed before she descended, and my first reaction was, well, I was tongue-tied. She was not conventionally 'beautiful', but appeared very fit, charming and possessed of the sexiest imaginable voice.

Dinner was delightful, though I have no idea what we ate! It transpired that Louise was working for a London company that was engaged in research in the North Sea for oil, and 1965 was by coincidence a rather crucial year. In September oil deposits were found in the West Sole Field, to be shortly followed by the collapse of an oil rig with substantial loss of life. Of course, discoveries of this sort do not simply occur spontaneously; exploration was envisaged by the UK Continental Shelf Act in May 1964, and for some time Louise had been engaged in research with this company (BP? - I never found out). It was known by April that there was huge potential in the North Sea; it took me some considerable time to realise that this fact was probably why the *Manhattan* voyage was a one-off deal; its time had passed even before it happened.

Pretty interesting stuff, but there was more. Her great enthusiasm (others spoke, but I didn't hear very much) was horses, one of which she owned and which was stabled a few miles away. This accounted for her physical elegance, for my experience with the horsey set (of which I knew only one, namely Jacqueline, but on a much smaller scale (she had never owned a horse) told me that those who ride perforce have good posture). I myself was not a fan of anything equine, having been once on an elderly nag which was intent only on grazing, and I found myself quite unable to exert any control at all. It was my one and only such experience.

I made my departure reasonably quickly, as one never wants to overstay such an occasion, but I did extract a promise from her that she would come over to the ship for dinner the following evening. And so it was; I took the bus over again and we walked through the dank and grim tunnel beneath the Thames (which was much quicker, if decidedly less pleasant, than the ferries).

We dined (the skeleton crew still included seven officers and, of course, the entire deck, engine and steward's complement) and repaired to my cabin for fun and frolic.

Unfortunately, Louise had a lot more fun than did I. My ineptitude knew few bounds, and it was not even an occasion for apologies; I discovered that what I thought would come as nature intended did not do so, at least to me. What I was doing proved to be quite hard work, and I seemed to have a knack for attaining the wrong target (euphemism is sometimes called for). It certainly wasn't her fault; she possessed a perfect body and, what with the riding, quite superb thighs. It was perhaps fortunate for me that I had a very patient partner; that little or nothing actually happened seemed not to bother her at all, in fact she found it amusing (the alert reader might recall that this type of response was not entirely unknown to me). Unfortunately, I did not expect to see her for a while, *Oronsay* being based in either Southampton or Tilbury.

The next day I left for home. But on that day, my life changed again; I was to be appointed to *Chitral*, based in the King George Dock, opposite *Baradine's* old berth!

Chitral, named after a city and river located in Pakistan, had recently (February 1961) been bought by P&O from Compagnie Maritime Belge, the main cargo/passenger company providing service between Belgium and The Congo. Belgium had sought an empire in the nineteenth century when it was 'fashionable' – in the worst sense of the word – to do so, but so limited was this agglomeration that its possessions (the Congo, Ruanda-Urundi (sic) and a small concession in China) that 'Empire' was plainly an inappropriate Belgian concept; they were known only as 'the colonies'. (Some riverine/riparian states become known as "The..." (such as Gambia and Congo) because their riverine existence, which was more of a raison d'etre than any 'name'; this structure somehow found a more appropriate role in the English language. Time affected this nomenclature, 'Congo' being vast and ungovernable, the country soon became divided; to what end, and with what names, is even now difficult to say). But when the divestiture of empires became de rigueur for the colonial powers, Belgium rapidly became the pariah of such overlords, the personal reign of Leopold II having been so brutish and rapacious (black labourers who disobeyed their Belgian supervisors could simply have a hand or foot cut off by a machete in retribution) that there was no amicable hand-over; the Belgians had to leave their possessions in a hurry. Consequently, three ships, *Jadotville*, *Badouinville* and *Thysville* came onto the passenger/cargo ships' market. P&O had the three old clunkers (*Carthage*, *Canton* and *Canton*) to replace, and the *Jadotville* and *Badouinville* (respectively renamed *Chitral* (13,821 gross tons) and *Cathay* (13,808 gross tons)) did so (*Comorin* was the third such replacement, but that was a vessel of an entirely different order).

When joining, national maritime preferences were immediately apparent. The electrical system differed from British ships (different voltage, wattage and plugs, thereby necessitating a quick trip to the Chief Electrician to ensure that important things – like my tape recorder – were usable) the lifeboat gear was strange, and many signs were still in Flemish. But on the whole, this was a very neat and comfortable little ship (not that it was 'little' in any real sense, but it was designed for only 300 passengers, and P&O had elected to make accommodation somewhere between first- and tourist-class). It was also Chinese-crewed, with which crewing I had had only good experience. Just as importantly, I occupied a nicely located cabin on the starboard side beneath the bridge; I did not feel that I was disadvantaged in any way by being required to occupy this role rather than become a smaller cog in the larger machine that was *Oronsay*.

Upon joining I introduced myself to the 2nd mate, David Miller. He seemed a reasonable fellow, although he immediately loaded upon me the fire-watch job, wherein I was obliged to go around the ship on a timed route and turn a key in a hand-held clock at all the designated stations. In this way, the whole ship was regularly checked for fire and other observable problems. A tedious job, and one which I thought the helmsmen should have done (in dock, they had nothing else to do!). But I learned the ship's layout. I need hardly add that this fortunate turn of events seemed a message from on High that Louise and I were fated to meet up again. So it proved. I was not on a regular watch, so I could plan my time off by cultivating our relationship, and *Chitral* was a far better ship upon which to eat and canoodle than *Baradine*. I also met the horse … and her boy-friend. As one might expect, the latter was quite a surprise, but he was a nice enough fellow, and, I think, was introduced to me to keep me on my toes (a bit of a loose-minded chap, I thought, but I never found out what he did). We also had a few *very* nice evenings on board, the most notable occasion being when I had actually located, close to my own, her essential lady-parts, but in the midst of that most exciting part we were startled by a knock on the door by Mr Miller, advising me, in no uncertain terms, that the time for my fire-rounds had arrived. This profound event therefore was not a consummation about to which boast for the rest of my life, but it was not at all bad! (This was the closest that I came to being caught in flagrante delicto – the pun is intentional.)

I improved my technique over the next few evenings in this important respect, and on May 13th we sailed for Rotterdam. Our Captain was a very nice man, Captain Nowell, whom, I thought, was the sort of skipper that I might thereafter try to emulate. Loading the usual manufactured products in the Netherlands, we soon arrived in Southampton to take on passengers, and I quickly realised that this was probably to be a rather dull voyage, our passengers consisting almost entirely of civil servants and the retired. Moreover, our trip was only to go so far as Manila and then to head back home.

I received the not unexpected, but disconcerting, news in Port Said that Karen had arrived in Venice and been a bit upset about my not being on *Oronsay* (I had tried the poste restante business, but it had apparently not worked all that well for me). 'Bit upset' did not really express it; she was pretty miffed. While this I could understand, I could see a Karen/Louise problem arising upon my return, for I could only expect a day or two off when we returned to UK. Some planning was needed.

Nor did I get much mail enlightenment in Malaysia; I began to wonder whether the promise made to Louise about ordering a cheongsam for her in Hong Kong should be fulfilled; I knew of nobody else for whom such a dress would be so entirely suited.

I also found that useful information could be gained from some knowledgeable literature; in 1963 Ian Fleming had published a book, not really a travelogue, called 'Thrilling Cities' which referenced some places about which I needed further advice. These cities included Hong Kong, Honolulu, Los Angeles, Hamburg, Naples and Geneva (a far racier place than I had discerned!). This was a useful little tome, for his descriptions were a lot more interesting than those that I would have ascribed to those places, although this was probably because my budget was never likely to rise to the level of that given Fleming by the 'Sunday Times'. Nevertheless, the book was far more interesting than the Pilot Books were ever likely to prove to even to the most chaste of travellers. My appetite was somewhat whetted by other cities that I had not visited, but which I certainly hoped to see, Tokyo, New York and Monte Carlo particularly. It was also conveniently current, the opinions arising from his world-wide trips made in 1959 and 1960.

In Manila I did my usual walk ashore, for while it was a chaotic city and ridiculously full of people, cars and jeepneys, it possessed a vitality that only Hong Kong, at least in my experience, exhibited. Again, ridiculously hot in mid-summer, but just the sort of walk that prepared one adequately upon one's return for a beer by the ship's pool. However, I did receive a letter from Louise. Though not a particularly good literary effort (patently, this was not her strength), I was glad to receive it and know that the boy-friend was probably by now a broken reed. And it also permitted me to press ahead, in Hong Kong, with one of the numerous traders that boarded the ship to sell anything that could be manufactured in a couple of days. And the cheongsam that she had requested required only a couple of hours, so it was ordered … and arrived only hours later! One of the main pleasures of Hong Kong arose because it is, at bottom, so small. One can walk around its central part very easily, a type of funicular railway takes one rapidly to the peak, and the view from there at night was, even then, quite spectacular. On the other side of the island was Repulse Bay, a fine sandy beach in what for a good portion of the year could have held itself out to be a semi-tropical resort. In short, I was beginning to see why Hong Kong was a favoured port of so many experienced old tars. (All was not necessarily as splendid as it seemed, however, for there were, it could easily be noted, a good number of typhoon shelters around the harbour. And in such crowded waters – there were few berths alongside solid piers or jetties – even a modest typhoon or tropical storm could wreak frightful damage to vessels and homes alike.)

Singapore greeted me with a telephone call from one of Gog's nephews, who had for some years been a local harbour pilot. He had been told by her that I was on my way and suggested that we go ashore for the afternoon. Bob Hammond was a bluff sort of fellow with whom it would be difficult not to get along, and he picked me up for the ride to the local Swimming Club. Before arriving there, however, he took me for a bit of a drive around the island, and I had to confess that it was a far nicer place than I had anticipated. Not large, but by the same token not over-populated (as, even then, Hong Kong, with only 3 million people, appeared to be), it looked to be a very pleasing city to live. Of course, the 'Malaysia Problem' remained unresolved, but Lee Kuan Yew (with a double-first in law from Cambridge - and possessed of an iron will) had become Prime Minister in 1965, a position that he held until 1990. After this he remained the nation's **éminence** grise until his death in 2015. During lunch (over a superb T-bone steak, albeit an odd choice in a nation with an overwhelmingly Chinese population) we touched upon all of the local political, economic and shipping issues, but my overall impression was that being a servant of the British Empire, provided one had the right sort of education or standing, was a rather desirable destiny; the weather was lovely, the beer was good, and the ambiance suited me very well. We parted at sundown, vowing to get together again in three months' time (the next voyage, I was glad to note, encompassed Japan).

In Port Swettenham, I was interested to note, we embarked some passengers, including a trio of young ladies, unrelated but all in the 16 to 20 range. This trip therefore looked as though it might well improve, though the Captain's cocktail reception (which I missed, the 4th mate having to keep the 8 to 12) did not give me the opportunity to practice the old charm. But two days later, with seven days of crossing the Indian Ocean, there seemed to be plenty of chances. Of the three of them, one was blonde, curly-haired and rather vacuous, the second seemed highly nervous about life and was socially ill-at-ease, and the third a shy, dark-haired young lady of rather profound good looks. Her name was Susan, with an interesting tale to tell. By profound, I mean to imply that she had lovely eyes and a charming smile, did not much take to talking, but possessed a quiet intelligence.

I learned that she and her parents were on their way to her father's retirement in England. He, a large and impressive man (he had an imperious but by no means unpleasant manner; his persona was authoritarian and somewhat taciturn), had just retired from a Malay rubber plantation that he had operated (though I do not think that he owned it), evidently successfully. Susan's mother was a nice lady, but largely silent. I noted at once that this was a very reserved family, and it occurred to me that while father would be able to master most social situations, his wife and daughter had probably been 'in the colonies' largely by themselves, another example of an ex-pat life-style that looked more enjoyable than it probably was. It was noticeable, however, that Susan, though quite small, as was her mother, was always beautifully, if conservatively, dressed, even to the extent of a one-piece bathing suit. She was, however, very curvaceous; the overall impression was of a reserved and shy English rose.

On a ship like *Chitral*, however, there was not going to be much close socialising with Susan. For a start, there were few places to sit quietly and talk – when Belgian, the ship's voyages down to The Congo were not much longer than we were experiencing in crossing the Indian Ocean, therefore few public amenities were needed. But just as significantly, I felt that this family had something of the Somerset Maugham sensibility – in plantation life, the managers kept to their own families and friends, did not cavort with the natives, and Father ruled the roost. The family contentedly existed as a small and concise unit, by circumstances perhaps a bit introverted, but not the poorer for it.

That the vessel was built for a very specific route did have other consequences. Firstly, it did not have great bunker capacity, and on the South-East Asia run, few ports offered bunker fuel at reasonable prices. Secondly, there was no need for substantial potable water storage; it was easily obtainable both in Antwerp and Kinshasa. Finally, the ship was ill-designed for leisured passengers. The result was that as we were approaching Aden, a significant stability problem arose, partly because the swimming pool was high on the superstructure and almost directly astern of the bridge. One could feel that the ship was becoming 'tender', which is to say that when it rolled, it was reluctant to return to the vertical (this is the opposite of 'stiff', when excess bottom weight made for an uncomfortable 'righting' lever, a jerky and disconcerting feeling for those on board). Thus, when I came onto the bridge at 8am, David Miller advised me that he had ordered the engineers to empty the pool so that we wouldn't have to concern ourselves with stability until we bunkered in Aden. This instruction, given as the sun was rising in the hottest and calmest part of the voyage, was obviously not going to be too popular with passengers – but we didn't want to tell them that this was needed just in case the ship decided to roll over!

We proceeded with some grumbling passengers, but before long we berthed in Aden ... only for the whole ship's company and passengers to be prohibited from going ashore (of course, they weren't missing much, but they didn't all know that) because the British army had been obliged to take over the administration of the whole city.

Seven days later we were in Naples and all flooded ashore (at least, most did so, not having left the ship since Singapore, twenty days before), an exodus that I did not join. Overriding the schedule and cargo issues was the threat of a UK seamen's strike, and the possibility not only of Britain's ports going out in sympathy, but of there being in addition some civil unrest or even a general strike. There was no question that British seamen had a raw deal (a mandated 56-hour week was proposed as a law) but how this would affect P&O was unknown; the company had NUS British seamen, but they were very much in a minority, and more practically, the vast majority of the NUS members were at any time away at sea, thus rendering their vote fractured, uninformed and subject to very real employer pressures. (In the final event, in 1965 the strike was a damp squib, but it was a lingering problem that eventually had to be resolved.)

The leave on this occasion was short, but not uneventful. I found out that Susan's home was in Waveney (a few miles from Somerleyton), went to an excellent Prom with Louise, enjoyed steak and kidney pudding at home (Mother's was undoubtedly the best!) and overdone roast beef (not Mother's best), and received letters from all and sundry, Sandra included, from whom I had expected nothing ... and to my relief got the MGA to start (being away for so long revealed another problem with this, and indeed any, car).

By the time I re-joined *Chitral* in London I was therefore almost entirely broke, but this did not much matter as cargo had been loaded, and embarkation of passengers took place in Southampton, from where the next destination was Naples – I could therefore only spend my funds on board, which is to say, on beer and wine.

A mid-voyage change of route occurred, however. Because the situation in

Aden had gone from bad to worse, and the British garrison had been substantially reinforced (it was not like the British to recognise that their 'best-by' date was upon them) to deal with the violent unrest, the ship was diverted to Djibouti, on the tip of The Horn of Africa.

I knew nobody who had ever been to Djibouti; more cogently, I had never met anybody who had the least desire to go there. This place was one mote of the French Empire, ill-located, virtually without resources, and perpetually hot as hell, its only real purposes lying in its strategic position, its value to Ethiopia as a port (especially after Eritrea gained its independence), and as a place to bunker at low cost. In this instance, the heat being well over 100 degrees, I saw no stampede ashore from those on board.

However, as we had been diverted from Aden, we had a certain amount of cargo to tranship. The larger part of this cargo was Martini & Rossi Vermouth from Naples, unfortunately in two separate holds. As the gangs knew what they were to be unloading, virtually every individual brought with him his cargo hook. These wicked-looking instruments, designed primarily for lifting soft or flexible cargo up and lifting it onto a pallet, were extremely efficient, when brought up sharply under a box of any beverage (and they weren't interested in Pepsi), in releasing cascades of alcohol into small tin cups that by chance were stowed in their *lungis*. Ostensibly in charge of cargo, we deck officers remonstrated with the supervisors about this outright theft, but to no avail … the deck ran red with booze, but there was naught that we could do (certainly pointing out Muslim disapproval of alcohol was not going to win us any friends). Other cargo, including Vespas, was treated in an equally cavalier way. We left in the late afternoon, quite sure that others had enjoyed this cargo once it was ashore. A long Damage Report was delivered to London for the insurers.

Another quick stop in Colombo (it cannot be said that familiarity was breeding much love) was followed by short stops in the Malaysian ports, but it was becoming apparent that the volume of cargo loaded was declining voyage by voyage, perhaps partly because these ships had become too slow for shippers, who lost more money the longer delivery of goods took. However, after the usual interesting stop in Hong Kong, new adventures began for me.

Arrival in Yokohama was naturally something to which I had long been looking forward and I was lucky to be able to exchange some time ashore with the 3rd mate. I boarded a train bound for Tokyo (noting on the way the 'Suntory, Genuine Scotch Whisky' factory) and was overwhelmed by the impressions. My first feeling was of 'too many people'; I was somewhat accustomed to London crowds, but here there seemed to be so many more people, all very busy. The lights were bright, the streets cleaner than I had ever seen elsewhere, and the shops overloaded with goods, in particular music stores being full of DG LPs;

I had no idea that such music would be so popular in a city with a culture so different from that with which I was familiar. I also noted that, while I knew that US forces occupied much of the country, the only concession to English was the station signage – all other signage was absolutely foreign to me. I also could not help but notice that in general the people in the street were very (indeed, excessively) polite.

Yokohama occupied us for a couple of pleasing days, cargo being mechanical and industrial goods, and the ship so well run by the shore-side personnel that the officers' tasks were commendably mild. Our next port, just down the coast, was Shimizu, at that time primarily known as the putative home of Honda, more a motor-cycle manufacturer than one of cars (Uncle Jack, of Somerleyton, was a bike aficionado and had a love affair with his aged and leaky BSA; he thought it terrible that these Japanese bikes had ignition keys – a bike should be started with your foot! – a trendy innovation that could not last), and many of which were loaded carefully without the need for any instruction. So, I took a little trip down the coast.

Among the officers there were two FAPs, the senior one being Cora, an intelligent and pleasant lady who liked Brahms and Rachmaninov. We decided together to see something of the countryside during a break between noon and 1800, found our way to Shimizu station and sought travel guidance. As in Tokyo, however, signs in English were absent, so we eventually found someone who told us that we could really only go as far as Shizuoka, wherever that was, and we then elected to go on what we hoped was The Bullet (the LEX, the Limited Express, rather than the SEX, the Super Express, the latter's first stop being Kobe). I still do not know whether we were actually on The Bullet of worldwide fame, but everything was comfortable, immaculate, and fast. Takeoff was so smooth that I did not actually know that we were moving until I looked outside and saw the roseate slopes of Mount Fuji on our inland side, a sight that will always remain with me. I had thought Malay Railways better than anything that I had seen in England, but this train operated even more miraculously, more like a silent aircraft than a mere train. Again, the losing side in the War, with infrastructure virtually obliterated, had been faced with a rail tabula rasa and had no alternative but to completely reconstruct with the most modern technology available. Britain had rebuilt over the damaged and decrepit; the country had much to lament.

Shizuoka was a nice little village, at least so it seemed in its own Japanese way, and full of light and late afternoon activity. We decided to have a meal and were greatly encouraged by the 'menu', comprising plaster models of all of the choices, these highlighted in a window display. We thought this a splendid idea, having never seen it before. We therefore entered, and were royally entertained, though beer was about all that we could request, none of the other pictured libations being in the least familiar to us. There was a bit of a delay, however, which in the waiter's broken English was ascribed to somebody having to run up the street to find another restaurant that could provide a fork for Cora to use (I was not much better, but had used chopsticks on other occasions, so to me they were clumsy, especially with mushrooms and peas, but by no means unusable). We both (clumsily) enjoyed the repast.

We boarded the train back and ensured finding its port-side seating. The month being September and the sky only a little cloudy, the view of Mount Fuji with the setting sun behind it was breath-taking. And I was pleased to find myself sitting opposite a dapper Japanese gentleman who expressed much delight at recognising my Aquascutum coat.

The next morning another quick trip down the coast saw us in Kobe. This was a city of an altogether different order, spread over the horizon, full of ships and belching smoke from all its orifices. This was more of the industrial Japan that was then emerging, but as I had taken a few loans of watch-keeping time in the two earlier ports, it was my turn to stay on board during the day; I therefore passed a quiet eight hours. The evening, however, was not quite so dull. The 3rd mate told me of a massage parlour where I might experience untold delight, and to that emporium we repaired. After having myself scrubbed raw and being almost scalded, a very well-muscled young lady then *twice* walked up and down my backbone. I felt no erotic urge, just mild to not-so-mild pain.

En voyage south to Hong Kong I discovered that we had taken aboard quite a few passengers, one of whom was a nice young Swiss lass named Agnes, whom I believe was travelling with a family as a child-minder, though I never saw the child (this ship was not big enough to engage a Children's Hostess). I rather took to her, but in a chaste way, for she had a natural innocence about her that was quite disarming. We stopped in Singapore after Hong Kong, and there I was royally entertained by the Hammonds and their delightful young family, but I had difficulty in seeing how I could repay their hospitality (his job was piloting ships, and therefore frequently eating on them; it would be rather absurd to invite them back for a meal on the ship). And that evening I thought that it would be nice to have Agnes in my cabin for whatever transpired, but she really was 'an innocent abroad'; nothing at all transpired, but I enjoyed her company (she came from Vaud, so at least there was some commonality).

Our trip back to Europe included Djibouti for bunkering, but for nothing else. The problem was that there was really no alternative to visiting the horrible place, not because there were no other ports around, but it was simply that at that time oil was a Gulf and Saudi monopoly. However, on this occasion, having learned from the experience of the previous voyage, the pool remained open, more machinery having been loaded in Japan in the ship's lower hold, thus avoiding 'tenderness'.

The remainder of the voyage was uneventful, in part, one supposes, because we stopped at no ports before arrival in London. This may sound a bit dull, but there was a good mix of both crew and passengers and the days and evenings passed quite enjoyably; it was a calm, prosperous and socially satisfactory voyage.

While on leave I saw Karen for a few very pleasant days, and on November 6th, David, Tina and I saw her leave on Cunard's *Carmania* for Canada. Ours had been a good relationship; whether it had substance was a question that much exercised me.

The voyage that then commenced was at first without incident, other than the quick stop in Djibouti for bunkering (and a good number of crestfallen Djiboutis must have seen us steam away with much regret; we did not discharge one ounce of cargo). Just as importantly, I later enjoyed my first taste of sweet and sour crab at a delightful open-air restaurant in Singapore with the Hammonds. Unquestionably, the Chinese could cook.

Transit of the South China Sea towards and beyond Hong Kong was accompanied by poor weather (it was in mid-December, so it was not unexpected, but approaching Japan it further deteriorated, visibility being poor, the winds force six to eight, and with heavy rain; in fact, a minor typhoon). This was so much the case that eventually the Captain decided to take the ship further out into the Pacific than was normal, simply because we frankly did not know where we were! Before long we were pitching and rolling uncomfortably (the ship had no stabilisers), and I recall a time when all of the watch-keepers were on the bridge seeking some guidance from the gods. But the only viable system was Radio Direction Finding (RDF), which I had never seen utilised before (and I found out why – it was completely inaccurate unless prior to use it had been carefully calibrated, and ours had never received any attention at all.) The dense cloud precluded sights, so we simply headed West and watched the radar; fortunately, the water was very deep, and the only land anywhere near us was Japan; all we needed to do was find it! And eventually we did, but precisely where we were located was not easy to discover. So strong had the wind been that the dead-reckoning position was of little assistance; it took half an hour of poring over suitable charts to correlate these to the radar image. Eventually we found ourselves, but a very considerable way north of where we expected to be. Passengers were not informed of this minor drama.

This time I altered things about a bit and took some extra watch time in Tokyo, thereby giving me a little more flexibility in Kobe. Like Osaka, Kobe was known primarily for industry and commerce. Therefore, I elected to see something more of historical Japan, namely Kyoto, about which the pilot book was quite informative. A previous capital of the country (I did not discover if the use of all the same letters in both names had any significance) and a short distance from

Kobe, the city had been declared by Roosevelt in World War II to be an historical site that was not to be bombed; thus it was spared the annihilation visited upon most of the country. As it was December 18th, the weather was freezing, but on the train-ride up to the city, I realised that this was an advantage; firstly, it had removed all the foliage, so that almost everything could be seen, and secondly, perhaps more significantly, no tourists of any sort were to be seen. I wandered around the silent streets, hired a taxi to the most significant sights, and took photographs, free of people, as much as I liked.

And these sights were worth seeing. I had certainly seen pictures of the shrines and temples, but the reality of seeing these Shinto symbols inspired awe. They were massive and ornate, the latter being more sensually overwhelming than the former. I took in Nijo Castle, but by that time was so cold that I had also to harbour in a local eatery – though I did not know of sushi and sashimi, I was certainly quite prepared to try it – in order to feel my toes and fingers. Again, I could not but note the extraordinary politeness of the people. I found this strange to master; an 'uncle' friend of my parents had been a Japanese POW, and his wife indicated in no uncertain terms that it was an awful experience about which he would, and never did, talk.

The voyage back to UK was unremarkable and routine, which made me ruminate upon the vagaries of the strange life that I was leading, strange even within the confines of the merchant marine. Almost without thinking about the issue, I had joined a company which offered as varied a nautical life as could be attained. Most of the other companies of high repute (Blue Star, Bibby, Cunard, Royal Mail, Palm Line et al.) enjoyed limited runs to a limited number of ports (that generalisation did not apply to tankers of course, but many of their ports were miles from anywhere, were very dull in themselves, and were visited for hours, not days). *Chitral* was a good ship on which to work, but three trips had created a sense of routine that I did not particularly wish upon myself.

But other matters obtruded. After years of planning, and looking for a travelling companion, Margaret had made the trip to Europe, England in particular of course. I met her in London; I had the possibility of this leave lasting as long as seven weeks. I devoted a considerable amount of planning to her visit, she being, in my recollection, attractive, intelligent, sexy and an excellent letter-writer. She came home with me and we had the week together, though Mother did not find her quite as marvellous a girl as I had described. The problem was that nor did I.

From a sparkling bright girl, she had notably and unfortunately become somewhat physically dumpy, intellectually commonplace and rather boring. It occurred to me that her letters, mostly of high quality but always in print script, had been ghost written or received substantial assistance from someone else, perhaps a parent, and that the underlying purpose of the European trip was to bring back, or remain with, a husband. This was obviously not her 'fault' but was mine; I had met her when my judgment was impaired by 'immaturity', and though I was now no wiser than I had been when on *Oriana*, opportunities to mingle with the opposite sex had subtly changed my view of the real world. One night she said to me, "You don't like me anymore, do you?" By that point I had realised that she didn't even like sex, which was not a message received some twenty months before, and although I did not reply, I knew she had hit the nail on the head. Two days later I delivered her back to her travelling companion residing in 'Kangaroo Valley'. I think the relief on both sides to have been palpable, though such words were not exchanged.

One problem that I faced was one that I should have anticipated. This was the MGA. I had quickly discovered that while I was now earning more than ever before (the wage was by no means generous, but because the seagoing life was rent- and board-free, the income available for frivolity was pretty good) the need to spend money on it increased almost exponentially week by week. The starting problem was regularly a bother but was something that no mechanic that I ever met could solve, and the brakes were so unreliable that I hesitated to go anywhere far afield or ever attain a speed that even that car could manage. Consequently, it was constantly in a garage undergoing repair. Fortunately, Judith was still around (though going to cosmetician school and therefore often unavailable); she was enjoyable company and seemed to understand the need for 'cheap dates'. As always, of course, everybody else was out doing an honest day's work while I had leisure and sought pleasure.

Things did sometimes turn up, however. A couple of my parents' friends, living a few miles away, knew of my predicament and invited us over for a dinner with a nice young lady whom they knew to be footloose and fancy-free. The husband was, I believe, in insurance, and had a hearty manner that bespoke a satisfaction with life and the ability to put strangers at ease. His wife, and Mother's friend, was a delicate soul whom, I suspect, was in her youth a beauty of some note. She also fancied herself a good cook – which she most certainly was not – but they were always good company. We anticipated a light-hearted evening. I was told that this young lady whom I was to meet had recently given up a relationship and was more than eligible.

It was actually an evening that I enjoyed, and I was pleased to meet Alex, a girl of some good looks, but less as attractive a personality. I sat next to her and realised that if I was egotistical, she herself believed that she was God's gift to the world. Not only was the ex-boyfriend her constant topic of conversation, but he was a successful London broker, owned London properties, and drove a Bentley. Although she didn't say so, I also gathered that he was quite the stud. It was all that I could do just to keep polite, for hearing about this magnificent being made me want to meet him, not her. But our hosts, seemingly quite oblivious to this soliloquy, made up for this piffle, and the evening on the whole passed successfully. On leaving, she gave me a card with her address and phone number on it; I threw it away before we got home.

A few days later I was appointed to *Salsette,* a cargo ship similar in most respects to *Comorin*. Where it was not similar was in its use; it had been chartered to British India (B.I.), a P&O subsidiary, to maintain the East Africa run, one, again, unfamiliar to P&O personnel. (The P&O Group, as distinct from P&O-Orient Line, was one of the world's biggest, and B.I. was itself a company with, at times, over 150 ships, almost all cargo vessels. Its routes were world-wide, except for the Americas; by itself, a major force in shipping. All that *Salsette* had to do to change its appearance was to paint two broad white stripes around the black funnel.)

Salsette in dry dock

I joined the vessel in South Shields, a drab location that had by then seen its best days. The work was, however, minimal, the ship undergoing a major overhaul, mainly in dry-dock. There was, of course, little enough to do ashore, so my main entertainment was a Saturday afternoon spent in Sunderland watching a Division 1 match between Everton and Sunderland. This I quite enjoyed, though the result I do not remember; I was a not-too-ardent fan of the London teams of West Ham, Arsenal (which team originally played just down the road from us in Woolwich) and Spurs. But just getting around and seeing people was stimulation enough for me, a ship in dry-dock being about as soul-less an environment as one could imagine. Of course, I could familiarise myself with the ship, it actually being a twelve-passenger freighter, as was *Comorin*.

The ship being thoroughly refurbished, we were soon back in the Royal Docks. I was to be the 4th officer and a few days later the 3rd mate, Dick Andrews, arrived, a personality with whom I was happy to sail. It transpired that he was a knowledgeable jazz fan, and one evening he suggested that we should go up to central London to hear the great Sonny Rollins. I, of course, knew nothing of this great man and blithely went with him up to Ronnie Scott's Jazz Club, which, again, meant nothing to me. Upon arrival, I was surprised to see how small a venue this was, but we managed to get in, though without a table, simply by going through the door; I had expected there to be 'a performance' and to have to pay admission, but this was much easier. I found a stool by the bar upon which to perch, ordered a beer, and sat and watched the very young audience. Before long Rollins came in to an enthusiastic reception, his tenor sax before him. Not a man to waste any time, he forthwith began; I knew at once that I was well out of my comfort zone. But I was not alone; the other members of the quartet ceased accompaniment after twenty minutes. I ordered another beer, for I was beginning to get saddle-sore. Undaunted, he went on for another hour ... all the time without the trio! When he finished – the place was as silent as the grave while he was playing – I gingerly removed my sore rear end from the stool, barely able to stand, the deadening effect of more beer notwithstanding. The barman, an obvious enthusiast, asked whether I would be back for Ornette Coleman; as gracefully as I could I grunted negatively. Even an armchair would not have induced me to return. Andrews and I returned, he very cheerful, to the ship.

Salette's propeller being replaced

To recover a bit of prestige, a couple of days later I noticed that there was a concert at the Royal Festival Hall, with Giulini conducting two Mozart wind serenades. This was music with which I had to admit to a lack of familiarity, but as Mozart is never unapproachable, I suggested that we travel up there. And we did, though it has to be said that this music was actually somewhat more profound than I had expected. Nevertheless, it was a good evening; Peter Shaffer chose his music well.

The preparation for the voyage was somewhat different from the norm, this because nobody aboard had ever been to East Africa. And, again, there arose the strange names; everyone would know of Zanzibar, even if few had been, but none knew of Mtwa! (It transpired that the cargo for that port was marked thus, but the place is Mtwara, not that that was much more enlightening, for on the chart this looked like little more than a roadstead.) However, off we duly sailed into the unknown.

Firstly, however, the passengers boarded. And these were a bit unusual, as there were only two of them, and they were, though strangers to each other, like sisters, even twins. One was a Dutch lady, in her mid-twenties, and the other a similarly aged girl from London. Both were comely enough, not beautiful, but each was sufficiently statuesque for us; we young bucks were initially delighted. But all overtures, then and later, fell on stony ground. Both were polite, but firm. Their privilege, if it could be so called, was that they were seated at the Captain's table. I actually felt a bit sorry for them in this respect, Captain Cooke being no conversationalist and, in truth, was a rather dull man. He was always polite to his officers, but it seemed that he favoured the solitude of command. Unfortunately, my lingering recollection of the poor man was that, being on the eight to twelve, he always came up to the bridge before he turned in for the night, and if we were in sufficiently warm climes, he preferred to come up clad only in his sagging Y-fronts. Even in the pitch dark this was not a pretty sight.

The mate was a different cup of tea. New to P&O, most of his prior experience having been on tankers, he had few of the social graces that the company seemed to favour. Being a small man, he had, we thought, a significant Napoleonic complex; at all times he made sure to assert his rank, especially to the junior officers. He actually acted differently with the 2nd mate, Michael Carter, a bearish shambles of a man with a giant sense of humour and proportional maritime experience, one upon whom the assertion of rank would just make the asserter look foolish. The other person of significance was the R/O, Chris Hall, a young man of abundant humour and good sense. He, Andrews and I made a good trio, all being of similar age and with similar views on life.

The first port was Aqaba, Jordan. True, this place had little to do with Africa, but we had some crated machinery to discharge. The geography, and politics, of the region were interesting in themselves. From our anchorage, looking from west to east, one saw Egypt, a United Nations camp, Israel, more United Nations, Jordan and Saudi Arabia, all apparently spoiling for a fight over this desperately unpleasant corner of the globe. And all too soon, they were all to learn another lesson in fighting … and how not to do it.

We could not go ashore in Aqaba, but we could in Port Sudan if we so wished. This particular port had a reputation among seamen in general as being one of the world's least pleasant. And this was how it appeared to me as I took a brief walk around the wharf. The heat was almost intolerable and made the worse by the swirling sand. Much of the transportation was by camel, animals with undoubted attributes, but the old saw that the creature is a horse designed by a committee is apt enough to remain funny. The town itself was as flat as could be, and was, to me at least, made doubly dull by the sandy look of the place. I noted some pleasant buildings, but thought they probably dated from when Sir Herbert Kitchener, with young Winston Churchill in tow, had made his incursion into this sorry country. We couldn't wait to speed on towards Zanzibar.

In fact, that fabled name was an historic memory, for almost precisely two years before our arrival the islands had merged with Tanganyika to become Tanzania, a logical consequence of geography. However, Zanzibar was only an anchorage, and therefore without transportation ashore, a fact which somebody on board who had visited the place before said was a blessing in disguise. He described it as a Hole.

The first real stop was Dar es Salaam, Tanzania's capital. It was a natural harbour, but the port was antique in its cargo facilities and transportation. The first real African destination, its dilapidated effect was unfortunate, and the necessary unloading accomplished, we departed without regrets. We then moved north up the coast to Tanga, all the while having Droopy Drawers Cooke on the bridge; it was a very low-lying coast, and deep-sea mariners loath an unseen coastline that lay just over the horizon.

But the effect of Tanga was altogether more favourable. A large inlet with no mooring facilities for securing to a quay or pier, we were obliged to anchor almost within the shade of the jungle. Service to and from the ship was by barge, our ship itself providing for shore-side transportation its lifeboats, a pleasant hourly duty for the cadets. What is more, our task to oversee cargo handling was rendered easy by the fact that we were anchored in the large bay; any attempt to broach or steal cargo (though we had no alcohol nor much that was worth plundering) was easily seen, and all those who worked on the ship had to leave by passing the gangway watch. So life was pretty easy for the officers as well. And further, when we arrived the B.I. agent came aboard and declared that while we were in port, we were honorary members of the Yacht Club, a pleasant building close to the ship. "But," he said, "you won't be able to pay; you will be presented with an account when you leave … make sure that you write out what you have; there have been occasions when extra digits are added to chits, and it's too late to do anything after the chief steward has paid the bills."

Salsette

On the second day, Andrews and I went ashore to the town. Once seen, however, there was no need to go again. We decided to go to the Club, and before we could find a taxi, a Mercedes coupe arrived beside us and we were offered a lift. The driver, a sprightly gentleman-farmer type, explained that there was still a great deal of German influence in the country (Tanganyika having been a German colony until, after the war, Britain felt that an extra bit of red on the map of Africa would look rather splendid) but that the British Army was still a presence, the region still being subject to some anti-white prejudice. There was still a bit of Mau-Mau unpleasantness, he added.

The Club was like something out of a novel set in the Empire of the past. Wide and airy, it was well protected (we were, after all, still very close to a jungle), with comfortable wicker chairs and a wide bar to match, it included the expected fans, lots of servants, billiards and ping pong; frankly, better than being at home! Our driver friend bought us drinks and extolled the virtues of the colonial life; we had to agree, it looked pretty good. He was a farmer, but of course, that did not mean that he had to actually work, merely run the farm, labour being very cheap. He left us shortly, presumably to go and supervise someone, and we tried ordering, ensuring that we wrote 'Two beers', not '2' which can easily be transformed into '22'. We vowed to return at the first opportunity.

Next day we honoured our vow, bringing Chris with us (R/Os had to monitor calls from London once a day, but to call his job onerous would be hyperbole) so that we could sample the lunch. Happily, it was a good lunch, with unknown but tasty white fish.

However, other business interfered. There were ten or so people in the bar (all colonials like pre-prandials) and we sat down next to a table that looked of interest, being a family with two girls, maybe fourteen and eighteen. Naturally we engaged in conversation, and we found our companions to be a Sergeant-Major in the British Army and his family. It transpired that he was here to train members the Tanzanian Army, and of course, we were three young fellows who looked respectable enough and quite suitable to engage in conversation with two young ladies. To put it mildly, it was a pleasing interlude. We even asked them if they would like to join us at some time on the ship for a meal, an invitation which only the elder young lady (Sally) took up.

Next day (one must not hurry things too much) we invited Sally back, and one supposes that the wearing of a uniform cemented the impression of our reliability, for she seemed to have a really good time. For some reason, I was selected by her to be the fortunate one to entertain her in my cabin by myself, but she was a virtuous girl and nothing untoward occurred. Nor indeed would I have wanted it to; I knew enough of sergeant-majors and their equivalents to know that they were the fiercest of all the non-commissioned ranks and never to be crossed with impunity.

On the whole, the stay in Tanga was idyllic. The weather was wonderful, hot but with balmy breezes. The pace of life (which is to say, discharging and loading) was languid and not disturbed by any night shifts. We had to keep a watch on the bridge – the anchors could have dragged – but we had four cadets on board to fulfil that need. It was with some reluctance therefore that we departed this piece of Nirvana, though we anticipated being back for some supplementary cargo on our final run up to the Red Sea. Unfortunately, upon leaving we found that quite a lot of numbers had been added to our bar bills; we had been insufficiently diligent in *writing* the numerical entries.

However, there was absolutely nothing wrong with the next port, this being Mombasa. This again was on a low-lying coastal strip, but this was of no moment; as soon as we moored, we saw that the city was decked out for the visit of H.M.S. *Eagle*, Britain's largest aircraft carrier. Naturally the several thousand young men on board were a considerable boost to the local economy, not to say especially so to certain professions. Our berth was close to the port area, so we enjoyed some of the benefits of all these extra visitors, including the fact that all the restaurants were open the entire day. We three caballeros decided to go to a nightclub, where of course, certain ladies could be entertained with bottles of champagne at twenty pounds a pop; they seemed to be doing pretty well. Unfortunately, Andrews seemed a bit taken by the charms of one of these overweight 'ladies'. This not being to the taste of either myself or Chris, we left the jollity and returned to the quiet of the ship, there to have a scotch together.

The issue that Chris and I set out to discuss was, of course, the fact of Andrews' behaviour. Chris was about my age, but a bit of a babe in the wood, despite having been at sea for a few months. I myself found Dick's earlier activities rather inappropriate, but all he had really done was pay for something that others, like the two of us, would accept 'for free'; was his having so acted therefore in any sense 'right' or 'wrong'? Chris took the view that the whole escapade was completely repugnant in and of itself. I found little guidance from 'Ethics'; "… if we speak of conflicting moral attitudes as 'contradictory' we run the risk of unconsciously assimilating moral disputes to empirical ones and of inventing in the logic of moral discourse elements analogous to those which are bound up with the notion of contradiction in empirical discourse …" to which one can say little other than 'hallelujah!' (So it goes for several pages; I understand the words, but not what they mean). In fact, the issue did not disturb our friendship, but to Chris and me it made us a bit uneasy in our own certitudes.

Next day, a gentleman appeared on board looking for someone to accompany him on a trip to the Tsavo National Park for a day's tour. He was a photographer and sought out from ships those who would like to see animals in their natural environment and cover his expenses, and it took only ten minutes to find six of us who would be most pleased to take such an excursion. Two of those were our passengers, whose final destination was to be Mombasa, but who were happy to delay their departure for a day to go on a guided tour. The trip was set for the next day, with an early departure, and a picnic lunch to be supplied. Our guide was the sort of person that inhabits 'Happy Valley' and 'White Mischief', a big, slow-speaking man who looked as though, if need be, he could wrestle a gorilla, and besides the girls, Chris and two junior engineers decided to come along.

We boarded the inevitable VW mini-van before the sun arose and roared off to the west, although it was actually more appropriately 'sedately drove', for Kenya had major infrastructure problems. The roads were in appalling shape, full of potholes, far too narrow for the country's main arterial road, and clogged with elderly trucks. Unfortunately, as our guide explained, the railways were even worse, a handicap for a port that was the gateway not only to Kenya, but the best way to deliver goods from the east to Uganda, Burundi, Rwanda, and both Congos. The transportation problem was one that plagued the development of the whole of East and Central Africa, for if the westward arteries were poor, the arterial 'roads' from the Congolese coast were little more than compact mud trails. So although on the map the distance from Mombasa to Tsavo is modest, in effect it was a very onerous way to travel. Even as I write, some sixty years later, the Mombasa to Nairobi (and beyond) rail link is overburdened, antique, understaffed and over-politicised, and still a topic for discussion in 'The Economist'. The reason for the lethargic pace of unloading cargo in East Africa's ports, as I understood it, was simply that there was no point in unloading ships with rapidity, the poor infrastructure including a lamentable shortage of secure warehouse space.

But our driver knew what he was about, and we arrived at a Lodge for wetting our whistles and planning our route (fauna doesn't just wait about for the tourists; one has to know whether and where they were drinking, feeding or resting up, the latter apparently being lions' favourite occupation). We then set off into the bush, which, to me, was surprisingly bush-free (why should I be surprised? We were there in the midst of the dry season!). This meant that all was brown, dusty and dry. In fact, the first animals that we saw were baboons, but they were so difficult to see, despite being only yards away, that our man had to point them out to us. Fortunately, the animals seemed not in the least perturbed by our presence, but at least this meant that I obtained some pictures that, on my own, I could not have taken. Other animals that we saw, at least to my knowledge, were antelopes, a totally comatose lioness, and an elephant. The latter we simply came across as we drove slowly through the bush. He, of course, saw us first, and when we circumspectly stopped some distance from him, he didn't look too happy (inasmuch as I knew how an elephant expressed happiness) and we watched and photographed. Our guide said that he wanted to keep to a distance from which he could see the creature's tail, as it would indicate when or if he wanted to charge. Apparently, the behaviour of a bull elephant is highly unpredictable when he is in musth, which can be seen, if one is close enough (or, more correctly, too close) by virtue of a visible thick discharge from his head, behind the eyes, and which indicates that he virulently dislikes on that occasion everyone and anything. I saw no reason to test his mood, particularly as the Volkswagen, as with most of its ilk, sounded as though it were having a minor stroke. Photos taken, we repaired to the lodge for lunch.

This welcome repast we took near to, but a safe distance from, Mzima Springs. It had to be acknowledged that the Chief Steward had outdone himself, though I suspect that this was because our two ladies were disembarking, and he reasonably wanted a good report if any were sent by them to P&O's Head Office. I should also add that these two were good if quiet company for the day, but I still did not know their names!

Mzima Springs are well known in this region. Although this is by no means a well-watered area, geological formations have created the Springs in this unlikely place. The animals living there, mainly hippos and crocodiles, never go far afield, and their lifestyles, including their excreted vegetable diet, maintain a natural balance that the park wardens naturally wish to maintain. I recall being high enough to see what we needed, comfortable enough to consume an adequate amount of Tusker Beer, and safe enough not to concern myself with the hippos, which I knew to be quite as unpredictable as most wild animals.

I much enjoyed this outing, as I had never been to a similar place before and could not easily see me visiting another such in the future. Back aboard, I noted that *Eagle* had sailed, apparently to Singapore to create some mayhem, so the next day (discharging cargo had virtually ground to a halt) two of us took a trip to Nyali Beach, which we understood to be Kenya's Bondi or Waikiki beach. And it was … but it was totally deserted! This, I thought, must soon become a tourist trap. It did.

The port of Mtwara was something of an anomaly, a port whose purpose had passed it by. The British had attempted to give life to the southern part of Tanganyika initially by encouraging the growth of a groundnut industry (which was an idea whose story was short and brutish in Africa as a whole; the industry developed its markets slowly and ineffectively), and later by touting it as the terminus of a central route into northern central Africa mainly through developing an East-West railway. The schemes never really took off, and when *Salsette* went there, the port was a mere shadow of what was planned. We unloaded what we had by way of manufactured goods and headed north again to Tanga. Despite some wishes to complain about our earlier 'bar charges', we generally agreed that it would be churlish to do so (and which might result in a few job losses by those who obviously had little by way of alternatives) loaded some coffee and agricultural products and sailed north to Suez.

It was a mark of the ubiquity of the Commonwealth that on this voyage all of the ports visited (except Aqaba) had, to a greater or lesser degree, enjoyed an association with the organisation. The last on this voyage, however, showed that 'enjoyed' could not always be an appropriate word. Famagusta was the principal city on the East coast of Cyprus, and a resort for the international jet-set to frequent. We berthed in the harbour but were immediately aware of the tense political situation which was everywhere evident. In the 1950s the activities of EOKA, a militant Greek-dominated independence movement, had been one of the main international news items in the British press. Although the situation was complex and always in flux, Greece had encouraged Greek-Cypriots to eject the British and, as a by-product, get rid of the Turks (less than 10% of the population). To put it mildly, this was unwise; Cyprus was geographically in the armpit of Turkey, and Turkey possessed the second-largest army in NATO after the USA. By the time we were there, the United Nations had sent Canadian and Finnish troops to the city, and they were evident in their patrols around the walls and streets of this ancient city. I took the opportunity to walk around, saw the absolutely perfect beach (occupied, but I suspected by few tourists), noted armed UN troops everywhere, and took pictures of some of the dramatic ruins. The island, having a history going back to before 1,000 BC, is a veritable museum of Mediterranean civilisations, the Phoenicians, Assyrians, Egyptians, Romans, Greek, Byzantines, Genoese, French and British, to name but a sample, all having governed or dominated this ancient land. I actually spent far more time looking at the city (though I could not go outside the walls) than I did on the ship. And the careful observer could reasonably guess that things would soon get worse rather than better; after World War I, the Greeks having chosen the right side in the nick of time, decided to invade western Turkey, rousing the ire of the recently defeated Turks, who with the Allies then gave the weak Greek army a military and diplomatic drubbing. This humiliation radicalised successive governments in Athens, until the military took over and had, with their usual ineptitude, left their country in precisely the economic and political state that they had sought to avoid. We left Cyprus that evening; I would have enjoyed a delay of at least two days in so fascinating a place.

Before arrival in London we visited the entirely uninteresting ports of Sunderland and Hull. Before arriving there, however, I was told that I was to leave *Salsette*, pending promotion to 3rd mate, and go on leave. Leave in London, however, did not include any hanky-panky with Louise. She had written to advise me that she was shortly to be married (to the fellow whom I had earlier met). This struck me as 'not unexpected', as I had obliquely gathered from her that her target had always been marriage. My view at that time was that most of such individuals (for example, Margaret) were much too keen to tie the knot, indeed any knot. Obviously, I had that idea in mind (eventually) for myself, but to me it was a question a bit like going to Heaven; one wants to get there ... but not quite yet. (And I believe that the 'expected' occurred; some years later I received a two-page letter in which she implied, but did not state, that she regretted her decision to marry so precipitately. There was no return address.)

I was soon appointed 3rd mate on *Cannanore*, a vessel similar to *Comorin* and *Salsette*, and drove to London in the MGA (it had reliable periods, but as the uncertainties occurred without warning, the very uncertainty of the uncertainties was singularly nerve-wracking). I had, however, received notice from Susan that she was enrolled in a photography course in Ilford, a scruffy London suburb, but close to the Royal Docks, and I thought that I might give her a ride up to Somerleyton/Oulton Broad, visit her home, and again collect some automobile wisdom from Uncle Jack.

I was quite surprised when I arrived in Waveney and entered Susan's house. Far from a small dwelling, I found it to be a converted guest house or small hotel surrounded by several acres of lovely green sward, the 'house' to me being more of a minor palace than a family home. Susan warned me, however, that her father (as I have said, quite a formidable man) had just days before recovered from a bout of malaria, a periodic affliction that left him weak and a bit temperamental. She told me that during the War he had been a Japanese POW, and in Malaya, where malaria was endemic, one could barely avoid catching the disease in the absence of quinine, and of course, his captors had not bothered with such niceties (on each ship on which I had sailed to the Far East, bowls of anti-malarial pills were front and centre on the dining tables; even in 1966, one had to be careful). She told me that when the malarial symptoms recurred it could be difficult to control him – this I could believe, both she and her mother being quite small women – but that comment about these episodes, and indeed any reference to the war, was to be studiously avoided.

Inside, the house was frankly quite perfect, with mainly Asian furniture, and I was delighted to see a superb stereogram. His taste appeared very middle-of-the-road (Tchaikovsky, Beethoven, Rachmaninov etc.), and, being taken outside, Susan showed me his cars (apart from the family VW), which comprised a 1932 Invicta and a 1936 Jaguar, both beautiful roadsters in quite perfect condition. She even showed me the polished chrome engine (the cleaning of which was one of her jobs!). Naturally, she said, they were in perfect working order; I could only drool. I left the house after a wonderful afternoon tea, a mite envious.

Back in Somerleyton, I had a discussion with Jack about the car, and my sense of balance was somewhat restored. He declared that he felt that I had done the right thing, despite the probable consequences. As a young man (Mother said that he had been quite the young buck) he had lusted after a sports car. Although he had always worked on the Lordly estate and had job security, he had never had 'quite enough money' to indulge in a sports-car; His Lordship did not pay his 'retainers' very well, but accommodation was tied to the estate and a pension, though feeble, was attached to employment; it was an almost feudal existence. As time progressed, however, his savings had increased, but for long not to the extent that enabled him to afford such a car. But when he could manage it, he felt that he would look ridiculous in an MG, besides which, he married the local school teacher, the bucolic but very companionable Rita, whom Father preferred over all his other relatives. He said that he always regretted missing the boat; you only live once, and he felt that I, at least, should not in the long run regret having had such a perky car. He was, needless to say, quite correct.

After this philosophical lunch, he asked me if I would like to go shooting on the estate. My response, "Why not?" arose in part from my never having fired a shotgun, and I thought that it would be a good atavistic way to experience a cold November afternoon, followed, of course, by a suitable imbibition. He therefore loaned me his over-and-under 12-bore gun, and off we tramped to the fields and meadows. And there we stood for a few criminally cold minutes until a couple of pigeons took to the air. The first I missed, though he did not, but the second I brought down quite easily. However, and it was a big 'however', I immediately thought that this was an uncivilised thing to do; I had brought the bird down, but not killed it, and Jack had to end its life by bashing its head against a tree. I thereon lost all enthusiasm for a 'sport' of this sort, the bird in no way deserving death in such a way at the hands of a callow youth in the name of leisure or passing the time. I have never since found it necessary to fire a gun.

Back in London I re-joined *Cannanore* but cannot say that I greatly relished the schedule; East and West Pakistan and India. On November 8th, we departed London, by which time I had decided that this was not likely to be a happy ship. Captain Firth, despite the presence of his wife for the trip, was a baleful presence whom I never saw smile. Indeed, he seemed to take pleasure in berating the 2nd mate (the navigator), a rather weak character, about the manner in which the charts, the chartroom, the log, and all navigational appurtenances were maintained (Basil had been the same, but his 2nd mate hadn't cared a fig for such behaviour; either a brave man or a fool!). On this vessel, the mate was Mr Foote (late of *Khyber*) but he had changed into a taciturn, rather sour figure, one supposes because, too late, he had realised that the seagoing life was more suited to the young and footloose, and not to happily married fathers.

I was content with being 3rd mate, though that position included being the ship's doctor and the flag officer, both of which could, but may not, be sinecures. All letters are represented by differently coloured flags and each had a meaning attached ('C' is 'yes', 'O' is 'man overboard', 'L' is 'you should stop, I have something important to communicate' etc.) but widespread use of signal flags had largely died with Nelson, and the idea was now antique. Nevertheless, we still had to know all twenty-six meanings. And if there were some important event, a ship might be required to 'dress overall', which meant to have flags suspended from all the longitudinal wires and stays from stem to stern, a fairly frequent requirement for passenger ships, but rarely needed on freighters (perhaps required for a British coronation, but they are somewhat infrequent, the 16th century notwithstanding; there were few other suitable occasions).

The 3rd mate habitually kept the twelve to four, by no means my favoured watch. However, on this ship it was not too bad an assignment, for few bothered those on the bridge after midnight, and most of the unpleasant activities took place while one was asleep; I was also fortunate to have ascribed to me the junior cadet, Brian Neilson. This young man was one of the most literate and erudite persons who crossed my path while I was at sea. He suffered from an unfortunate appearance, being dark and swarthy and somewhat hunched, to the extent that I thought that he suffered from mild kyphosis, but he had a rare breadth of mind that kept us in good conversation night after night on the long trip to Karachi. I quickly came to the conclusion that he was not long for a nautical career; he undoubtedly should have been at University. (I believe that this was in fact his only trip to sea, though what became of him I do not know.)

A more significant personnel issue arose with the Captain. His wife, a pleasant lady who was well liked by the officers, suffered a mysterious ailment shortly before arrival in West Pakistan, and had to be flown home with her husband from Karachi. This was a matter of some relief for all of us. Foote took over, as it was expected that Captain Firth would soon be back. In fact, his wife's indisposition was more severe than first thought – he returned to the ship only at the conclusion of the voyage – but Foote was a good replacement, taciturn, but a reasonable man with whom to work.

Karachi was, as I had earlier thought, not a place where one would dwell with any pleasure. Not especially hot in November, it nevertheless suffered from the impediments of maladministration and poverty. The equipment operating in the docks comprised elderly cranes of a type that the Royal Docks had long since sent off to third-world ports and was made the worse at night by the most Gotterdammerung of scenes, great flashes of lightning emanating from the gantries and shore connections, often of sufficient intensity to read a book. A supervisor told me that the demonic scene arose from the age of the equipment, the extreme unreliability of the electricity supply and, as much as anything else, the ignorance of the crane-operators (as often as not, he told me, the variable electric current would cause large numbers of fuses to blow – as in 'lightning bolts' – the fuses then simply being replaced by any nails of sufficient size that happened to be available, the supply of correct fuses having long since been exhausted). Frankly, I couldn't wait to leave for East Pakistan.

As before noted, the Ganges-Brahmaputra Delta is the world's largest. How many people the system supports is difficult to calculate, but because of it being one of the world's most fertile regions, it directly supports a population in the hundreds of millions. It floods frequently, is subject to cyclones, rising sea levels, tectonic plate movements, and unpredictable changes in its course. There are a number of significant cities in the vicinity, but in 1966 the primary problem – though whether it was actually seen within the country as a problem is doubtful – was population growth. At the time of our arrival, the population was over 70 million, but fecundity was encouraged by society's need for children to support the aged and infirm and to tend the crops, mechanisation being too expensive. The primary regional export was jute, used mostly in the manufacture of packaging materials, clothing, roofing, electric cables, cordage and ropes.

Our destination was Chalna, a port that existed more in the imagination than reality; the pilot station was seemingly right out in the Bay of Bengal, and when we 'arrived' we simply anchored amidst the mangroves and awaited the barges and labour that was to discharge and then load our cargo. But as this was not to happen for a good number of hours, we kept an anchor watch (it was a muddy, unstable bottom).

Such a watch was exceedingly boring. I was perhaps fortunate in having Neilson on watch with me, as I was nearly his equal in chess; I had, anticipating tedium, conveniently brought a set with me to the bridge. After a couple of games, I think one each, at about 2 am we heard a yell from the foredeck. Upon turning the aldis lamp on and shining it on the bow, we could see three or four figures moving around among the mooring ropes, the yell having come from the deck watchman doing his rounds. I quickly told Neilson to rouse the other cadets, and get them to the bow, and then I ran down to the foredeck, grabbing a brass wheel-spanner on the way. On the way forward, only some 70 feet in all, I could see some men scrambling to throw one of our mooring ropes overboard (these were fairly substantial items, 50 to 200 feet in length), and then make rather desperate attempts to get over the bow, presumably to swim ashore. Two of the cadets arrived, I of course being the first one there. One man was partially over the taffrail; I brought the wheel-spanner, a formidable weapon, sharply down upon his forearm. He yelped and was gone. Just beside me the cadets reached a man who was trying to reach a rope ladder suspended over the side; he fell into the water, a distance of perhaps thirty feet. In moments a motor started, and we saw a boat speeding upriver.

We collected ourselves and surveyed the scene. Of the possibly five men, we only saw four in the boat and wondered if one of them had survived the fall. We knew that one was injured (probably with a broken arm) and threw a lifebelt overboard, but there was no response that we could see (there being virtually no light, the only lamp being the forward anchor light, which was designed only to be seen from a distance of at least three miles). We had lost three mooring ropes, they with possibly one of them drowned.

I woke Foote to tell him of the night's activities. He was not a man to shower expletives upon me, "What the hell do you think you were doing?" being as far as he went; I had very little to present as a defence.

The matter rested there. We, fortunately, had two new mooring ropes in the forecastle storage, and two old ones that were (barely) serviceable, so in fact the loss was not extreme. It was, however, something of an ironic theft; the main export of East Pakistan, being the jute already referred to, was usually delivered to Dundee, where it was made into various goods, particularly mooring ropes (it was cheap, strong, flexible and light to handle). But in the 1960s jute was giving way to polypropylene, cheaper, stronger, more flexible, much lighter, and easier to manufacture than jute or coir products.

In any event, we were only 500 or so miles from Chittagong, our penultimate port in South Asia, which probably had available the cheapest supply of mooring ropes in the world. We arrived on December 20th, a completely inauspicious day; this was a devoutly Moslem country, and we rightly thought that there would be absolutely no recognition of Christmas. We were correct.

The days passed slowly. The weather was fiendishly hot, and the ship was in no manner air-conditioned. We set up a sort of bar and barbecue immediately aft of the bridge, but as the local cargo-handling facilities were almost entirely limited to manual labour, of which there was a super-abundance, there was not a moment's peace. And other matters came up. I was called down to the gangway on one occasion because two men had come aboard with a covered hammock, seeking assistance. I went to the spot, and upon asking what was up was shown that the hammock contained a very sick man whose friends, the bearers, had smuggled him aboard for some medical help. Despite my absurd role as the ship's doctor, I was quite unable to do anything, for he looked pretty far gone and there was nothing that I knew to give him. But we gave the men some food and said that he had to see a doctor. That, in itself, was more than ironic. Britain at that time was losing doctors fast (to the Americas) and replacing them with Commonwealth practitioners whose expertise those nations could not afford to lose.

The local agent came aboard the next day and amid the chaos of loading asked if a few of us would like to go outside the city to see the sights. I swapped my watch with the second mate and a car that took us some miles into the countryside, in fact to a rather delightful lake on which we rowed around in a small boat for an hour or so (a bit of a busman's holiday, but none the worse for that in the midst of relative peace and calm). But the general view gained from this day, indeed from all the days in this benighted country, was of poverty and desperation. I don't think that it has ever much improved.

On January 14th, we arrived in Cochin, India, but only for a short time. It was certainly nicer than Pakistan, but by then, we had all had enough of the subcontinent.

It was a delight to sail back to the calm and coldness of Europe, essentially with only one minor incident to disturb the routine. That was when the Serang came to me to seek some assistance for one of the members of the crew. This poor man was quite evidently sick, but with no apparent need for anything that we had in the (reasonably well-equipped) dispensary (it contained a bed, so I suppose that to some it could be termed a hospital) I sought Foote's assistance. He said that Black Draft usually did the trick (a loathsome concoction contained in a fearsome-looking bottle, one dose of which had a remarkable ability to instantly cure ailments). It didn't work, so he said that an injection of similar stuff into the man's rump would probably cure the problem. This now became my problem! We decided between ourselves that the worst result would be to jab the needle in (during 2nd mates' training, we had practiced injecting an orange, apparently pretty close to the gluteus maximus) and have it break, so we elected to use the strongest needle that we could, actually big enough to frighten a horse! I prepared the dose (it was an ampoule to which distilled water had to be added) but was disconcerted to find that my patient had a rump that appeared to comprise only bone. I jabbed it in, but it didn't actually go 'in' on the first attempt, and on the second I was only able to get about 10% of the medication in under the skin. Still, it had the desired effect; instantaneously he got better and leapt out of the surgery.

We were about half way up the Red Sea at that point, so the R/O called our agent and requested that a doctor come aboard when we arrived in Suez. And, indeed, a man did arrive, but upon talking to him it appeared that his expertise was limited to having served during the War as a medical orderly with the 8th Army … he wasn't that much better qualified than I was! However, he effected another miracle; our patient never again complained of any disability.

(Lest the learned reader be put off by this sorry medical tale, I should add that if there were a real emergency, there was a 'radio surgeon' (I believe located in Rome) who would talk one through an operation if there were no alternative, and, of course, there was always the chance of a large passenger vessel being within a day or two's sailing; most were quite well equipped for childbirth, broken limbs and that sort of thing. Even so, things could easily get hazardous if one were chronically ill; few vessels could safely land a helicopter on a cluttered or even a normal deck to air-drop a surgeon.)

At the end of February, we arrived in London, and I was happy to realise that I now had sufficient sea-time in to sit for my 1st mates' ticket. I decided to again use the Warsash facilities and take the exams in Southampton, partly because I knew the qualities of the instructors there, but mainly because David was still at that University. Firstly, however, I had to get in a bit of 'living' and to sell my car, as it was apparent that it was simply too exotic a vehicle for me to maintain. As my parents had two cars, this was not a problem, and in fact their Austin A40 was more suitable for my 'social needs' than was the MGA.

I stayed at Warsash from mid-April, and Elly having moved away, part-time fun was out, so sat for 1st mates as soon as I could. I was very pleased to get the ticket on May 1st.

Canberra in Sydney

7 Canberra and Cathay

I was gratified to receive a telephone call from Head Office, shortly after reporting that I now had my Ticket, that I was to be appointed to *Canberra* as 3rd mate. On May 22nd I reported to the mate in Southampton and made myself at home in a rather nice cabin overlooking the passenger deck immediately forward of the bridge. I made the acquaintance of the deck officers, as assorted a bunch as one could expect to collect.

Captain Riddelsdell was a strange man in appearance and manner. He looked bearish, was short and stooped, and because of an injury received during the War, spoke with a gruff cloudiness; he was called 'Woof-Woof' by the officers, which was actually a very good description of his vocal manner. He appeared severe, but was not an unpleasant man, somewhat belying his far-from-handsome appearance. He was not particularly approachable, but that may have been because his was not an easy job, representing as he did the cream of P&O's fleet. The fleet Commodore was on another ship.

The Staff-Captain was Mr Lefevre. Since last sailing with him, I was told that he had taken some sick leave because he had had hurled at him a pot of boiling water, this by his wife because of a shipboard liaison that he had enjoyed and of which she thoroughly disapproved (an occurrence that should have happened to many senior officers far more than often than it apparently did). Whether this rumour was true or not was never made clear to me, but judging by his mood during the voyage, it rang true enough.

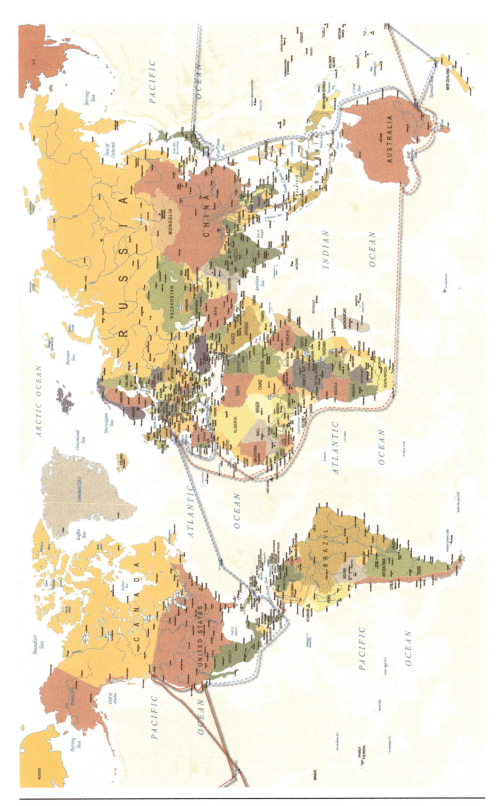

The mate, Peter Love, was a charming man, who subsequently became the company's Marine Superintendent. I never heard a bad word spoken about him, and probably would not have believed it if I had. Next down in seniority was Malcolm Rushan, the thoroughly professional Navigator, as on the albescent *Oriana*, whom I increasingly felt was under-employed; a natural commander, calm and competent, he could organise people and things, and would probably take easily to a corporate executive job ashore.

The 1st mate, John Christey, was an amiable though high-strung man (with whom, as 3rd mate, I would be keeping the twelve to four), but who, despite his competence, was permanently on edge about everything with which he was concerned; he was the finest ulcer candidate that I had ever met, ashore or on a ship. He was happily married, without a roving eye, and, I believe, had a young and revered daughter. I could hardly have asked for a better companion with whom I could expect to spend nearly 70 hours a week in close proximity. His cabin as next to mine, two decks below the bridge.

The 2nd mate was an altogether different type. Pocock was aptly named, but better would have been 'Peacock'. As handsome as the Captain was plain, this boy/man strutted his stuff in the full awareness of his grandeur, and he regarded any attractive woman as meat for his grinder. It irked me that he seemed to have the pick of any girl that he liked, regardless of the fact that to me he was completely transparent.

By this time, I was happy not to be at the bottom of the tree, the two 4th mates (Woollard and Tadman) being good fellows with whom it would likely be a pleasure to sail. I knew that the trip that we were to undertake, much the same as *Oriana's* round-the-world voyage, would inevitably throw up a few challenges, and this somewhat variegated group was likely to be able to manage without trouble anything thrown at it.

After we sailed from Southampton, I was apprised of some of the characteristics of the ship. Because there was more aluminium in the structure than was the norm, it was supposedly the tallest passenger ship in the world, but some of its features were less notable. Firstly, it had some difficulty in maintaining the twenty-seven knots that *Oriana* had maintained without effort, and secondly, because the engines were in the stern, she operated, unless carefully trimmed, by the stern and at a draught greater than specified. She also had cameras at the stern for aft visibility from the bridge; they never worked after the maiden voyage. Additionally, there was a sophisticated anchor cable isotope mechanism whereby the bridge could without watching the cable exit the hawse-pipe know how much cable had been let out. A neat idea, but I was told that it had never worked, even on the maiden voyage. Lastly, if the wind was blowing from bow to stern, smoke would ever land on the passenger decks;

however, if it was blowing from astern at a speed above the ship's, the deck could be covered with soot if the fuel mixture were unbalanced.

We departed Southampton bound for Gibraltar, where I again declined to go ashore, having just left English beer anyway. One little contretemps disturbed our departure, however; a missing passenger (though where one could get lost in this port was a mystery) and we left late on his account, steaming towards Naples, two days away.

The passenger complement did not lead me to believe that this would be an exciting voyage, though I had not inspected the possibilities directly because my rank now precluded supervision of the lifebelt drill. This disadvantage, being much the same as on *Oriana*, I could accommodate without difficulty; things would improve in Australia.

In Naples, we were greeted on the quay by our passenger who had missed the ship in Gibraltar; he had enjoyed quite the experience in rejoining us. He had quickly been to our agent's office in Gibraltar and been found a flight out – but not to Italy. Because of the virtual blockade by Spain of the British colony, there were no aircraft connections to anywhere other than to UK (no other nations wished to alienate Spain, so European destinations other than in UK were simply not available) he had then had to fly back to London, then fly to Rome (there were no direct London to Naples flights) and from there get to Naples as best he could. I am glad to say that he reached the ship's berth on time to clamber aboard, but he only just made it. He had little choice, because he was a civil servant stationed in Aden; to get there without *Canberra* would have proved a very daunting task.

Sailing south through the Straits of Messina, we began to realise that international (Middle East) news was beginning to assume unusual importance. It appeared that Egypt and its allies – Syria, Jordan, Iraq and Lebanon and eight other Arab nations – had suddenly declared the Straits of Tiran (the narrow entrance to the Gulf of Aqaba, at the head of which lay Aqaba and (Israel's) Eilat) to be closed to Israeli shipping. Israel had earlier declared that the closure of this waterway would be a casus bello, a warning supposedly unnecessary because in 1956 Egypt had guaranteed that the passage would remain open after the cessation of those earlier hostilities.

The news that we received (the R/O's were very busy) was that on June 5th, the Israelis had taken pre-emptive action. Firstly, they had destroyed most of the Arab air forces while they were at their airfields (and had used the tactical advantage of time-delayed tarmac-penetrating bombs to render the runways operationally irreparable) and at the same time attacked the Egyptian armies in the Sinai by not driving down the 'paved' roads (which the Egyptians had carefully blocked with their tanks, presumably because they thought that the Israelis would invade by driving down the roads!) but by-passing those defences by circling through the surrounding desert, surprising the Arab armour (most of which was Russian-made; the tanks reputedly contained crew heaters for use in Russia's freezing cold, but in the searing heat of the desert could not be turned off).

It did not take London long to realise that the position of *Canberra* would soon be critical; we were therefore ordered to substantially reduce speed until it became clear what was to happen in the Canal Zone. But this became quickly apparent; the Egyptians had been taken completely by surprise, their leadership was abysmal, their troops ill-trained, and Nasser's misleading statements caused Syria and Jordan to attack Israel and lose for Jordan the West Bank, and Syria to lose the strategic initiative by ceding its Golan Heights. The war was over in six days, the Israelis suffering under 1,000 casualties (the Arabs lost some 20,000), and some 400 tanks to the Arabs' hundreds of tanks and over 450 aircraft. (For a contemporaneous, if febrile, account of the conflict, see 'The Tanks of Tammuz' by Shabtai Teveth, published in 1968; compare this to a more seasoned commentary in 'Enemies and Neighbours; Arabs and Jews in Palestine in Israel, 1917–2017', by Ian Black, published in 2017.)

As it was entirely likely that there would be no Canal transits for a while (blockade ships were immediately sunk at both ends, and it was not reopened until 1975, the 'yellow fleet' of fourteen ships, so named because of their increasingly sandy colour, being interned in the waterway for the duration, a fate so narrowly missed by *Canberra*) London ordered that we turn around and divert to Australia via The Cape of Good Hope, a route that required some 3,000 nautical miles of extra sailing.

The turnaround required us to dock in Gibraltar, both for refuelling and for mundane requirements such as the provision of charts for a route almost unknown to P&O. Gibraltar, being a major naval base, had all that was needed.

The major irony of this whole episode was ironic indeed. Our passenger who had missed the ship upon our earlier visit to The Rock now had to disembark to fly back to London, there to fly onwards to Aden; a great story for the grandchildren, I'm sure, but at the time, one can be equally sure, a very poor subject for mirth.

The voyage down the West coast of Africa was pleasant enough, being mostly conducted out of the sight of land. There was the traditional 'Crossing the Line' ceremony, an event which I witnessed from the bridge during an otherwise lazy afternoon. What I also witnessed, however, was of substantially more interest. Looking aft from the bridge, one's view immediately beneath was of the first class swimming pool. There I saw, for the first time, two girls, obviously friends (they had to be, the first-class passengers' age probably averaging 65 or more). One was quite young and appeared to be in her mid-teens. The other, however, was a statuesque raven-haired exotic with great presence and an interesting, and very alive, face, by no means beautiful, but imbued with vivacity and personality. I decided that she and I had to meet.

That evening, we did. Why I had not seen her before was because she had been until then the subject of the superficial ministrations of Pocock. She, Virginia, was well-named, being full of self-confidence and ready intelligence, always immaculately dressed. She was an Australian model, returning to Sydney to continue her career after the mandatory (for Australians) European trip. As somebody in that business would probably be, she knew how to handle herself; although I had her attention when I brought her to my cabin for a (very friendly) drink, at which time she fitted beautifully into a tight and nicely revealing sari, she made it clear that snuggling was all that I was could expect. I got the message; also, that she could, in extremis, handle me without difficulty.

I had been to Cape Town on *Mantua*, but the arrival of *Canberra* was an altogether more significant matter. The ship was dressed overall and we received a substantial number of dignitaries, for large ships of this importance just didn't come down to this part of the world (which is not to say that the city was ignorant of ships, the British company trading to South Africa being Union Castle, the owner of very fine vessels, but all of which carried substantial cargo due to the vagaries of the passenger trade). Cape Town itself being a most attractive city, even without ascending Table Mountain, the passengers poured ashore. What they actually found, however, was a torn society.

South Africa was going through one of its tumultuous periods. The country was blessed by magnificent scenery, great weather and abundant natural resources. Its religions were Dutch Reformed, rugby and cricket. Its curses were a deeply divided population, the divisions being the whites (both Boer and 'British'), coloureds (Indians, of which Gandhi had been one, mixed races, miscegenation being banned, 'honorary whites', which is to say Japanese, Koreans and later the Chinese) and the Blacks, who were regarded as little more than paid slaves, of low intelligence and little potential. One common factor between the races was a love of cricket, a game made for long sunny days, perfect green pitches, and Pimms for the spectators. In the 1960s the unlikely had happened inasmuch as a man of mixed race, Indian and Portuguese, had risen to the top in South African cricket, but who, because of his racial mix, was not allowed to play at the first-class level. He, Basil D'Oliviera, was condemned to the lower leagues of South African cricket (which meant coir pitches and segregated crowds, with black spectators corralled behind barbed wire fencing) until his skills and reputation came to the attention of John Arlott, the Walter Cronkite of British commentators. He, with a deep brown voice and a warm Hampshire accent, was a revered BBC (the only game in town) commentator, and he had sufficient influence to persuade D'Oliviera to come to England to play for a minor club, from which he soon graduated to one of England's leading county sides.

In 1967, his talents had become undeniable, and being an all-rounder and qualified to play for England (as a good bowler, and a good, if not better, batsman, he could easily fill a necessary role in any first-class team) he was an obvious team member. England was to tour South Africa in 1968, and there was much consternation in England when the team was announced; it was immediately noted that it omitted D'Oliviera. The selectors declared that this was because of his variable form, and not politics, but when one of those selected withdrew and D'Oliviera simply could then not be excluded (the South Africans even offered him a handsome bribe to be 'unavailable'), South Africa's Prime Minister, John Vorster, declared that if he were included, the English team would not be permitted to play in South Africa. Only whites (and D'Oliviera was a handsome fellow who was not visibly of mixed race) were allowed to play whites; it was reported that at this announcement the South African Parliament rose to cheer.

Because it was such an 'outdoor' and sports-mad country, it is probably not going too far to say that this exclusion from the world's sporting communities – not just cricket – was a body-blow to apartheid. It still had resilience, but its death-knell had sounded.

This developing scenario had not, of course, played itself out when *Canberra* was there, and it was unquestionably a port that passengers were very glad to visit; the originally scheduled ports included the desperate Port Said, Aden (or Djibouti) and Colombo.

We now set sail for Fremantle. But this was a unique voyage for me (and most of the officers), for it was the first time that I had experienced the need to employ a great circle route. By way of explanation, look at a globe. The shortest route from Cape Town to Fremantle was not along a parallel of latitude, but by way of a southerly curved line towards Antarctica. But that route contained some unpleasantly foggy waters and occasional icebergs. Thus, there was a 'limiting latitude', below which one did not sail; all navigators learned of this issue, but until 1967 few had gone through the calculation.

It would not be true to say that the trip across the bottom of the world was full of interest. And we were also somewhat cursed by a westerly wind, which meant occasional smoke and crud on the decks. But the tedium had its good points inasmuch as everybody perforce became much better acquainted, for after a day or so it became too cold on deck for comfortable recreation. It was also the first time that I had seen an albatross, one of which glided with us on our port side for a couple of days, and for an hour or two alighted on the extremity of the bridge, at which time his magnificence was obvious. This great creature just stood there, presumably awaiting an improvement in the ship's warm updraft before he took off to assume his customary position just off the bridge wing; I do not recall seeing him have to flap his wings.

About half way across the Southern Ocean, when Christey and I were discussing some completely unimportant titbit, we became vaguely aware that the ship had begun an unusual vibration. Normally this could be caused by changing the engine revolutions or by the decrease in the depth of the ocean beneath us, the latter of which was hardly likely in our location, where there was at least 2,000 feet of watery nothingness. Looking forward, we saw a group of passengers peering over the bow and gesticulating to us on the bridge. I was sent forward to see what was happening, and upon looking over the railing saw that a whale had become trapped over our bulbous bow. It was letting out copious amounts of blood and was probably either a bowhead or right whale. After being hit by 45,000 tons of steel travelling at twenty-six knots, it was plainly dead. I remained on the bow, and Christey reduced speed, altered course a few times, and eventually, after many manoeuvres, the poor cetacean rolled off to its grave.

Such excitement was rare. I continued with my pursuit of the glorious Virginia, but as it became evident that she regarded me as some kind of dork (and, indeed, as did I in such circumstances) I spent more time reading than normal given the 'possibilities' on such a ship. (I always brought with me some of my own books, as the ships' 'libraries' with which I became acquainted were obviously selected by the illiterate and ignorant.)

We duly arrived in Fremantle, where, having by then been at sea for quite a few weeks, the only relief being the brief Cape Town stop, many went ashore to stretch the legs. I was not entirely surprised to find that the port proved as dull as expected. However, there was a surprise for me in the shape of a letter from Sandra, from whom I had not heard for months, and to whom I had not given a schedule of ports. I could only surmise that she had located me from the Sydney office, the second biggest of P&O's homes.

Three days later, we arrived in that city. I soon located Sandra, and our stay being set for a few days, forthwith brought her aboard for some comfort. Firstly, however, I bought a paper; there on the front page was a picture of Virginia posing on Bondi Beach! I could plainly see what I had missed; I needed some compensation.

I am pleased to be able to say that I received a lot more than my fair share of compensation. We had a good dinner on board, and upon repairing to my cabin found to my untrammelled delight that this was very much a changed girl. She had, I suspect, been somewhat restrained by society's values in Ceylon, but the considerable freedom permitted, nay mandated, in Australia had changed her to a very affectionate young lady. These were the months that followed the scandalous trials in England of 'Lady Chatterley's Lover' and 'Fanny Hill', wherein much more explicit depictions of love, sex and lust than hitherto permissible in polite society were now commonplace, but as I could not express the experience in a purple passage that would justify having referred to D.H. Lawrence, I will not attempt to do so. In brief, I had a life-enhancing experience.

A few hours later, I bumped into Christey on his way to breakfast. "I couldn't sleep most of last night," he declared. "What the hell were you doing?" That felt good! I had no answer.

The usual festooned quay saw us depart Sydney with the usual style (named after their country's capital, the ship seemed to mean something special to Australians and was always lavishly welcomed in its ports, unlike *Oriana*, merely a celebratory name for Queen Elizabeth I). I would rather have stayed in the port for a few more lascivious days, but it was not to be, for we were bound for Nuku'alofa, the capital of Tonga, a port somewhat off the beaten track, but selected for *Canberra* because the ship's draught was a bit too much for Suva. Tonga is not exactly a well-known country, but it had two claims to fame. The first was that at the coronation of Elizabeth II one of the more colourful celebrities was Queen Salote, a dramatic and distinguished woman who in 1953 took her one trip to Europe to attend the coronation, and gained great admiration from Londoners when she rode in an open carriage to and from Westminster Abbey in the pouring rain, deigning to utilise the hood that was provided because a queen should not copy what one's onlookers were doing. The second claim to fame was that the country loved rugby, the sport that they play in Heaven, and because Fijians were habitually very large men and surprisingly agile, that tiny nation could produce a team that could play on equal terms with the rugby giants, Australia and New Zealand. I would have liked to indulge in a tour here, as I had earlier in Suva, but this not being a cruise and my now being too senior, I just had a walk around town; rather charming, but I would have liked a better introduction to such an unusual place.

One tends to think of the Pacific Ocean as vast and uninhabited, but it is in fact a most interesting part of the world to traverse, there being all sorts of very low-lying islands and atolls that can be a real danger to navigation, and only an occasional volcanic outcropping (the Hawaiian Islands, for instance) disturbs the tranquillity of the scene. (Not that 'pacific' was necessarily a good word to describe this ocean, for both to the north and south of the equator one can encounter ferocious storms. Fortunately, we did not). And, of course, to Honolulu we were bound. But there, a longer walk around town than I had earlier enjoyed did not charm me any more than had my previous visit.

Although the run down the West coast of Canada and the US was accomplished much as expected (though this time without visiting Seattle) in Los Angeles we ran into a spot of bother that demonstrated another minor issue with *Canberra*. In the normal course of events, Los Angeles was easy enough to enter and exit. But on this particular occasion we arrived in the middle of a tug strike, and although it was a somewhat spread-out port, the piers at which we were to be berthed were relatively close together, and thus were difficult to approach. But while *Oriana* had four transverse thrusters (propellers) and thus could almost move sideways, *Canberra* had only a single bow transverse propeller. Though this was much more powerful than any two of those on *Oriana*, it was of little assistance in turning around the corner of the pier, and some damage was occasioned to the ship's starboard quarter. Although found upon berthing to be merely a cosmetic injury, nothing unsightly was permitted to mar the appearance of this big white beauty. Men were sent down to paint away the scratch upon our being securely moored, but the problem was noted (had there been some underwater spreading out of the end of the pier – as there was in some ports – the starboard propeller could well have been damaged, an expensive and time-consuming problem). As time passed and the big ships frequented more unusual places (for example, Alaska and the polar regions), damage to a propeller could become a significant issue, the replacement of one being by no means simple (all ships that I came across carried at least one spare propeller), usually requiring the use of a dry-dock. However, in this instance, no problems arose, and after we left, the strike was evidently settled.

Through the Canal, on to the Caribbean, I was fortunate to become acquainted with two New Zealand girls who were on their ritual trip to Europe; P&O must have been thankful that young people in the Antipodes seemed to be better paid than their counterparts in UK, for I do not recall ever meeting the English young undertaking such trips alone, but antipodeans seemed to find it a normal rite of passage. I had bumped into these inveterate travellers often enough to appreciate their qualities; one Diane Cossey I found to be wholly agreeable, especially while beside her on the Port Everglades beach.

Upon return to UK in August, we were at the aft end of the summer cruise season and I was pleased to see that we were running a cruise to some interesting places. We had the usual stop at Gibraltar (recall that when the Barbary apes go, the citadel falls from Britain's grasp; to me they seemed to be reproducing remarkably well), then Athens (which seemed to have prospered since my last visit) and then an Istanbul anchorage.

Istanbul, I had long wished to see. Proceeding up the Dardanelles was a passage of the utmost interest. It may be an exaggeration to say, but perhaps not by much, that the pusillanimity of the British Army and Navy (particularly the latter) allowed World War 1 to continue when a vigorous attack in 1915 could have saved Russia and knocked Turkey, Bulgaria and perhaps Austria-Hungary out of the War. The Admirals, not wishing to lose (obsolete) ships decided not to press on even as Turkish determination wavered.

Many of the world's great crises arise because of unseen opportunities or mundane but momentarily important events, and the failure of the Gallipoli campaign, at the time largely blamed on Churchill, was one such unnecessary disaster; on August 8 1915, Admiral von Tirpitz (from 1911 Commander of the German Navy) noted, "Heavy fighting has been going on since yesterday at the Dardanelles … The situation is obviously very critical. Should the Dardanelles fall, the World War has been decided against us." (See Decisive Battles of the Western World, Volume 2, by J.F.C. Fuller at P. 264). (But see 'Sultans of Spring', 'The Economist', July 15th, 2017 for 'what might have happened'.)

History being seen at its actual site becomes much more alive. And this is as it was with Istanbul itself. The city of Constantinople, Byzantium and Istanbul (as you may choose) resonates with the rise and fall of Christendom in the history of the Near East, and it is no coincidence that the Stavrianos book referred to earlier began its tale in 1453, when Byzantium fell to the Ottomans because of the indifference – until it was too late – of the Christian West. I really wanted to go ashore, and this time took the opportunity to pay for a tour. (It is to be remembered that at that time there was no bridge joining Europe and Asia, so one could see either one side of the Bosphorus or the other, and the consensus seemed to be that the European side was much the more interesting).

The tour, actually rather an exhausting one, encompassed fascinating places. The Hagia Sophia Museum and the Blue Mosque were breath-taking, though having been more accustomed to English Gothic magnificence and Italian pictorial splendour, the Spartan Islamic equivalent was startling, especially in light of the fact that there must have been immense baroque and Orthodox grandeur in all of these places prior to the Byzantine Empire falling. Any belief that the Ottomans believed in simplicity for its own sake, however, was negated by visiting the Topkapi Palace.

The fall of Constantinople in 1453 was accompanied by widespread killing of its citizens and destruction of the Empire's old and substantial buildings. At the time the sack of a city and the ruthless massacre of occupants was an accepted part of conquest, but in this instance the Sultan, wishing to make the city his capital and aware of the dwindling number of people living in the area, caused the destruction to cease and imported citizens from Anatolia to re-create a great city. He also engaged in wholesale and Islamic-style construction of palaces, places of worship, barracks and 'factories'. Central to the reconstruction was Topkapi Palace, a combination of living quarters and buildings designed to show off the magnificence of the Ottoman Empire, which after this victory expanded westwards into the Balkan peninsular. The lives of the Sultan and his entourage was characterised by opulence; every surface was a decorative opportunity! The display of jewels, in particular emeralds and rubies, was quite spectacular. The opulence is in the stones, but the 'too much' level is soon reached; I have not seen many emeralds (though the British Crown Jewels and those in Sri Lanka are impressive enough) but here the gems themselves were just too large. These were not to be worn or carried, but simply displayed!

As this was the late summer, and a glorious evening, instead of turning back southwards into the Sea of Marmara, Captain Riddelsdell decided that it would be a pleasing diversion to go north into the Black Sea, something that the pilot was quite happy to accomplish once he knew that he would be going home with a bottle of Scotland's finest product. It was an interesting little run, though we were in that sea itself for only an hour or so. It did help give some substance to my understanding of this historical and much troubled part of the world. It also helped me to see that a Nelson or a Napoleon would likely have forced the Dardarnelles and Bosphorus Straits, probably without difficulty, if either had been in charge in 1915. Such are the vagaries of history.

On our way across the Mediterranean we enjoyed the same perfect weather, and in the course of a pleasant evening on the dance floor I came upon two nice young ladies whom I had not before noted. We did nothing special, but when we reached Lisbon, I thought that we, with a junior R/O, could take an afternoon ashore and see some sights, including the Tagus Bridge, a newish and impressive construct, visit some of the city, and then relax with a picnic on the adjacent beach. This was enlightening (the statue of Prince Henry the Navigator near the mouth of the Tagus is not large, but as prominent as it should be given that his role in exploration demonstrates the value of being a state on the Atlantic coast – the mainly Mediterranean Spain required ships very different from the Atlantic-facing Portugal – in the creation of the vast Portuguese Empire, as opposed to the rapacious Spanish conquest of much of South America and little else).

Back on board we collectively enjoyed pre-dinner drinks, a quick after-dinner dance, and then off I went to bed, being on watch at midnight. At about 11 pm, I was suddenly awoken by a glass of water being thrown at me! It was a quick exchange that I had with these two girls, but it seems that my unenthusiastic reception of their suggestion for some cabin frolics had not gone down well; they thought I deserved a lesson. I got the message; I had thought that the chasing was what *we* did, not what comely young passengers did!

This time Christey's tune was different, he having heard every word of the altercation. Actually, he did little other than smirk. It was all that was needed.

And so we returned to Southampton, this time for another, and longer, voyage around the world. I was glad to see the Staff Captain changed, but other than that we were basically the same bunch of officers. While I was happy to see much the same parts of the world, the long run down to South Africa and then across to Australia was a bit tedious, although I had to admit upon reflection that this was a very selfish view; I was well fed, had variety every day, keeping watches on a run like this was no hardship whatsoever, and all of the people with whom I worked were personally nice to know.

Nearing South Africa, however, the first-class children's hostess, Leigh, asked me if I liked Patricia. "Which one?" I replied – there were two, one young and lithe, the other, well ... frumpy.

"Don't be silly," she said, "I mean the tourist chilly-ho." I grunted.

I recall a philosophical discussion taking place one breakfast when we were sitting with the Assistant Surgeon. He, Dr Ireland, as a two-stripe officer, was entitled to his own table, but given the fact that he hated socialising with any passengers, he was able to find an excuse at virtually every meal to join the junior officers, FAPs, nursing sisters and children's hostesses at the generic junior officers' table. He, a young New Zealander, termed 'Baby Doc', was a very charming fellow, and this was his first ship (and probably his last, for a ship's doctor's job was unexciting, most issues with which they were faced related to imagined sea-sickness. But it was an awfully good way to see the world for a trip or two and then establish a practice wherever one's fancy alighted). After our departing Cape Town, he was musing on the foibles of men; "I had a seaman come to me yesterday," he said, "who complained 'Doc, I've got it again!' by which he meant The Clap, and I began to worry about this, because that wasn't the first time it had happened. But now that I think about it," he continued, "I see an astonishingly sexual environment around us, and I think that it's because of the continuous mild vibration going on all the time on the ship, but we're not aware of it. Look at this," he said and put a glass of water down on the table before us, and we watched as a slight wobble on the water's surface became apparent. "Not much," he said, "but it's going on all the time while at sea, and sometimes even when we are in port because of the generators, which never stop." I won't say that we were all surprised into silence, but I long remembered the discussion; not that one can do much with the information, but the more I thought about it, the more I thought it a not unlikely explanation of what I had seen going on. Several of our table-mates looked on attentively, particularly Patricia (the neatly packaged Chilly-Ho), Valerie, Linda and Patricia, all FAPs, Leigh, first-class Chilly-Ho, Isabel, a nursing sister, and Tony Dyson, a 4th R/O.

In ten days or so, we were back in Sydney, but, for me, the incentive of a vibrating ship for moments of pleasure was now unnecessary. I hired a car, and Sandra and I drove around to see a few of the local sights; again, I was struck by the quality of life that Aussies enjoyed. But the stay was short, for we were off again for a cruise, this one around the Pacific (it was not really a cruise, for it was to execute a figure 8 around that ocean, but it was a sample of the needed inventiveness in finding satisfactory uses for these big ships, and such a route did indeed find a satisfactory Australian response).

After Nuku'Alofa we moored in Honolulu, this time for some twenty hours. I was able to collect a gang together of Tony, small Patricia, Valerie, and Linda, and we hired a Chevy for the day, to us a very spacious and high-powered car, to the locals a very ordinary machine indeed. And around Oahu we drove ... except that when we found a good beach on Kaneohe Bay, we decided that that was enough exploration and encamped on the beach with our victuals. It was the perfect spot for whiling away the hot afternoon, and as for Tony and me, we could only regard ourselves as being in some sort of paradise, naturally having carefully selected the most attractive of the female staff (nobody ever postulated that life was fair; we certainly did not do so) and were content.

Of course, we did not have the whole afternoon available (there is very little actual time off on any passenger ship's route, and I could only get the afternoon off by a bit of watch-switching) and returned to the ship for a quick post-mortem and the usual foie gras, steak, savoury and ice cream repast. The end of an extremely pleasant day.

But it wasn't. After a little relaxation in my cabin with Beethoven (of whom Christey was not a fan), I got a call from Patricia to ask me down to her cabin for a nightcap (early for her, but not for me, as I was on watch at midnight, at which time we were to depart for Japan, Vancouver and California). Naturally, I thought that a good idea.

It took me some time to find her cabin, because non-deck-officers' accommodation was about ten decks below mine. I opened her door and was greeted by very low lights and Patricia dressed in a virtually invisible nightdress ... well, not exactly invisible, but almost completely transparent. I was immediately embraced and thrust into a very comfortable position on her bunk. She was a slight girl, but I knew from the day on the beach that she had on her not a spare ounce of flesh on a shapely body. I had an idea what was required, but in beginning to 'get ready' I was told quite clearly that being a Catholic, she would permit no sex, but was very enthusiastic about cuddling and fondling. As might be expected, I did not much object to this treatment; I think that I even forgot about my scotch and ginger ale.

After a pleasurable half hour or so and getting myself a bit over-charged, I realised that before long I had to be up on the bridge to get ready for the ship's departure. In endeavouring to get ready, she made it quite plain that I was not going to easily get out of her cabin and stood up to prevent my leaving. As I stood, she took off the flimsy apparel that still remained on her; one could call her a picture of perfection, but I didn't. I realised that she was quite out of control, and that although I was obviously stronger than her, to actually force her away from the door could make things even worse. I sat down to collect my thoughts ... at which point she fainted right before my eyes!

This was obviously significant trouble. In wondering what to do, I thought of calling Leigh, but then thought of Isabel, down-to-earth professional help (she could be called a bit of a dour Scot) whom I knew to be friendly with Patricia. Firstly, of course, I had to deal with a comatose naked lady and decided to put her into bed (it surprised me how difficult it is to pick up and deposit a completely relaxed body, especially when I wished to ensure that I did nothing untoward) and in a few moments, I had put her under her sheet. I phoned Isabel (Izzy, as we called her) and she was up with me in but a few minutes. Her inspection indicated that Patricia was in no distress, but that Izzy 'had expected this' (I wish that somebody had told me!) and to leave the situation with her. I was happy to do so and finished off getting into uniform and sped up to the bridge.

Captain Riddelsdell was unconcerned, but the staff captain gave me a hard time about being late. I could do little but be contrite; what was to come of this I did not know.

Next morning, I found that Patricia had essentially been granted sick leave, and in talking to Peter Love, the mate, found that the whole incident was over, as far as I was concerned, and that no opprobrium was attached to me; small comfort, actually, as I felt that I had walked into a situation of which others could easily have warned me. However, being a willing participant, I put the matter down to inexperience and the lust of youth, and in the final analysis recognised that I had avoided a bullet; this I could treat as a lesson. I did not feel that Patricia was herself culpable, she being a rather strange being, almost 'trapped' in her looks and her psychology. I later heard that such a relationship had occurred on her previous ship, but inasmuch as it is easy to be wise after the event, I gave no particular credence to that tale.

There was to be a final denouement, laughable if it had not had an element of tawdry drama. A few days later Pocock approached me and asked if I would mind if he 'had a go' with Patricia; in replying that I had no possessory rights and it was certainly not my role to give 'permission', I left him to it. I soon heard, I think from Leigh, that Patricia's response had been nicely direct derision. Given his Don Giovanni personality, I doubt that that even bothered him (he was reputed to have the strange habit, before he got 'down to it', of requiring a shower with his intended target; I suspect this story to have been apocryphal – but only 'suspect').

This incident somewhat curtailed my social activities for the next section of the voyage, as I thought it quite probable that there were all sorts of rumours going around and that it was best just to let that sleeping dog lie. The Vancouver-San Francisco-Los Angeles-Honolulu leg was in any event fairly busy with promotional activities (all sorts of travel consultants/agents coming aboard, fashion events staged on deck, local dignitaries aboard for photo-shoots … that sort of thing) so I kept my watch and did little else. The routine, however, sometimes changed unexpectedly; one morning, on my rounds, I found a dead man in the first-class lounge. As nobody was around at 3am, the medical team dealt with matters quickly and silently; nobody other than those directly involved even knew of the event, the deceased being laid to rest ashore in Los Angeles.

The section of the voyage from Honolulu to Yokohama was somewhat ominous. As we headed West the barometer began to drop, and we began to receive news of a tropical storm that appeared likely to develop into a typhoon. As before recited, severe low-pressure areas in the deep oceans can cause extremely dangerous weather, the effect of the 'low' being exacerbated by Coriolis Force. Although a complex phenomenon, the effect of which mariners are most aware is that low-pressure areas in the Northern Hemisphere, unpredictable in their path, turn into huge clockwise cyclonic wind-systems. A vast system was generally headed for Eastern Japan, as was *Canberra*. We were to precede it to Yokohama, but probably not by much.

Arrival in Yokohama was in mid-afternoon. The weather was nasty but did not mean much to a ship as large as ours; the problem was the typhoon's unpredictability. The Captain decided that in the circumstances the passengers should be allowed ashore, and other than doubling up the mooring ropes, little needed to be done unless the weather deteriorated. I repaired to my bunk to get a decent sleep.

I was awoken at 11:45 am and upon arriving on the bridge was surprised to see that we had left our secure berth and were anchored in Tokyo Bay. All was calm and normal … in fact, strangely so, the sea being flat calm and with no wind, a very eerie calm. Rushan, the navigator, was already up there with the captain, and he briefed Christey and me with the fact that we had encountered the edge of the typhoon and had left the berth for the safety of the comparatively wide Bay, and were then in the eye of the storm, riding it out with both anchors down. It seemed that I had missed any excitement.

But I hadn't. In about an hour the wind began to rise, and we put the engine-room on stand-by. I could not immediately see why we did this, but I soon found out. The wind increased alarmingly quickly to such an extent that it was difficult to hear orders being given. And I soon realised why the engines and bow thruster were ready; the Captain had to use them for what seemed like hours – but wasn't – to keep the anchors from dragging. If any passengers had been about on deck in that screaming wind, it would for them undoubtedly have been quite frightening, but both Captain and Navigator knew what they were about (though I doubt that either had been in such a situation before) and by the time my watch was over, although I did not leave the bridge, the question was one of how quickly we could get back to the berth, the wind by then being relatively normal; necessarily, for we still had quite a number of passengers ashore.

But the cyclone was finished with us. The pilot came back to the bridge from his cabin, and by daylight we were again properly berthed. It had been an experience from which I learned much, a large part of which was that keeping a cool head was one of the most important attributes of being a good seaman. Few that I had ever heard of had been through the eye of a cyclone (or hurricane/typhoon, whichever term applies), and been able to learn from the experience; all of the officers matured that night.

Our passengers, of course, were mostly unaware of the night's events, largely because being in Tokyo Bay meant that no rough sea was experienced; even the ferocious howl of the wind was inaudible from inside the ship. Thus, two days later, all was shipshape. We sailed for Kobe; there I did not again try any erotic manipulation, even a sauna, which some worthy told me was something so pleasurable that I had to try the Japanese version before I met my Maker. I disagreed – without even trying it. I never had another chance to see whether I had wasted yet another of life's sensual opportunities.

Nagasaki was our last port on this part of the run. Of this notorious city I did not know what to expect, be it devastation, new buildings or pastoral tranquillity (shortly after the bombing it was thought by some that in the vicinity of the blast, no vegetation would flourish for nearly 100 years. However, nature prevailed). I took the opportunity to visit Nagasaki Peace Park, where a special ceremony is held every year on August 9th. One of the ironies of this memorial is that Nagasaki was not even the intended target of 'Fat Man'; too much cloud prevented its use on Kokura, and in many respects (not least the rumpled terrain) limited the Bomb's effectiveness. However, though its power was not measured by the tens of thousands of casualties, its effect was almost immediate, the emperor declaring to the nation (which had never before heard his broadcast voice) on August 15th, 1945 that "the war situation has developed not necessarily to Japan's advantage. Moreover, the enemy has begun to employ a new and most cruel bomb." (He was not to know that the USA had no more ready bombs).

Discussion in the wardroom that evening was, of course, centered on the morality, for want of a better word, of what had occurred so few years before, some of the senior officers, including Captain Riddelsdell (who was not present in the wardroom; he rarely was) having seen action in the Pacific. Though the British contribution to the defeat of Japan was dwarfed by the American, the British and Australian Navies had jointly made efforts to bring as many warships to the theatre as was possible and had, of course, suffered substantial initial losses on the way to victory. The general consensus was that there could really be no discussion about it; the war had to be ended by the bomb if the weapon was available, and talk of surrender by starvation was addled thinking. I certainly subscribed to this view (I was brought up reading the Hammerton volumes, and their photographs in particular made no bones about the propensity of the Japanese to fight to the absolute end while inflicting as many casualties as possible); I still believe the logic to be unassailable. I frankly found it irrational when, years later, I discovered while at university that some still 'debate' the use of the weapon, a debate that was by no means an intellectual excursion.

Japan was soon left astern as we headed south to Australia. But this was not destined to be a peaceful cruise through the tropics. The typhoon may have evaporated, but there were sequelae; the weather system responsible for our night in Tokyo was still around and made for some fierce winds, not helped, one supposes, by the geostrophic force having, at least in theory, to reverse its clockwise propensities. (It might be a good idea for some hardy soul to accurately watch the bath water drain out of her bath while crossing the equator… though, on second thoughts, there is probably somewhere out there an unread thesis on the subject; there seems to be at least one on virtually every conceivable matter.)

Passenger ship schedules are strict, necessarily even more so than freighters'. Our need was to arrive on time in Sydney, and our transit across the Equator, at twenty-seven knots into a rough head-sea, was quite uncomfortable. Two days before arrival, I entered the chartroom just after mid-day to find a serious discussion going on between Riddelsdell and Rushan about our schedule and whether the severe pounding that the ship was taking (virtually no passengers went to lunch) was warranted; deliberately defying the set schedule was not something to be lightly contemplated.

I was at that moment standing close to the front window on the bridge, however, when the matter was decided for us. I saw approaching us at high speed an enormous wall of water, the biggest wave that I had ever seen. As it came, up rose the bow to something that felt like 45 degrees. Then there was the trough, and down the bow crashed; I honestly thought that I was going to see the ocean floor, so steep was the descent. Few were able to keep to their feet, but then came the other side of the trough, a veritable wall of green water that crashed against the windows (which were 102 feet above the waterline) and seemed to want to force the ship further down. The bow staggered up, and we were back to mere rough weather, though 'mere' is the wrong word. It was evident that some damage had occurred to us, but that we were fortunate to have been heading right into the sea.

Immediately speed was reduced to less than twenty knots, and all slowly returned to rough-weather normality. The lookouts reported that there were some shattered portholes, that deck equipment was damaged, and that the public rooms (not that many of the 'public' were up and about) were chaotic, chairs, furniture, and glasses being scattered hither and thither. There were some passengers who were injured (some foolhardy individuals always appear at moments of crisis while the rational seek security) but they were few; some even thought it a bit of an adventure.

It was interesting to think of the event in retrospect. The term 'rogue wave' was not yet coined, but this was a phenomenon similar to an experience of Sir Francis Chichester in his round-the-world voyage; a wave took his small vessel in its grip and turned him end over end, depositing him safely and unharmed, an event over which he had no control whatsoever. I thought afterwards – and, of course, we all discussed it – of my feelings. My personal response was one of awe, for I distinctly recall the sight before me of what I felt was the ocean floor, absurd though that was. It was not fear, I suppose because cause and consequences were so rapidly each upon the other that such a thought had no time to develop, but it was an event that none of us had any wish to repeat.

Next day we limped into Sydney, relatively shipshape and in appearance none the worse for wear. Rarely had we so looked forward to arrival in port and to its tranquillity.

I myself was fortunate enough to have some lovely arms to ease my sorrows, and ease them she did. On this occasion, I recall no comments from friend Christey.

One tends to think of the nautical events referred to above as being in the realm of 'Moby Dick', *Mary Celeste* or simple fiction. But this is by no means the case, for the sea is not a medium upon which to be complacent, even for the skilled and experienced mariner. In December 1944, as the Pacific War was drawing towards its conclusion, MacArthur's forces had targeted Okinawa, an island which needed to be captured because it lay between Allied airfields and Japan itself. However, this schedule was disrupted by nature. On December 18th, there arose a typhoon that was inadequately forecast by Halsey's meteorologists. The fleet, caught out at sea in an area not far from the incident experienced on *Canberra*, having inadequately bunkered, lost, by sinking, three destroyers and over 100 aircraft, thereby setting back the planned events by some days. The error should not have been unexpected, destroyers being narrow of beam and having very little righting moment if not fully bunkered; they simply roll over with the heavy seas, their deck-edges being so close to the grip of the seas ('simply' is a totally inadequate word; to experience the sensation must be quite horrible to those who actually feel the capsizing of a ship of any size). Halsey was found at fault, but being a fighting and very aggressive Admiral, received little censure for what were avoidable losses. Of course, by that time the US could sustain such losses, but of what comfort could that have been to the wives and families of those so needlessly lost?

After what had until then been an unusually scintillating trip (for me, 'interesting' may be a better word), the voyage back to Southampton was remarkably ordinary. I even re-established a relationship with Patricia that was as it should have been; friendly and talkative (she even bought me a record of two Haydn 'cello concertos for my birthday; hers was six days after mine, but I do not recall whether I bought her anything) and we co-existed as if nothing had happened. Perhaps, in her mind, it had not.

Arrival in England was just before Christmas, and we enjoyed what I believe to have been a novel idea at that time; a Christmas cruise. Naturally, all of those who worked on the ship would have far rather been at home, but the atmosphere on board was jovial enough, and while Lisbon, the Canaries and Gibraltar were good enough, of more interest, at least theoretically, was Bathurst (now Banjul), capital of The Gambia. One has to say 'theoretically' because at the best of times the city is barely visible, but we could never see it because, firstly it is barely above sea-level and we were at anchor in the harbour, and, secondly, the whole time we were there all was covered in thick mist. It was hot, and to the British 'hot' and 'Christmas' are words that should not co-habit.

****

The next voyage to Australia commenced on January 6th, 1968, and was as pleasant a sojourn at sea as one could wish, the Southern hemisphere being bathed in summer. By now the long days at sea between Southampton and Cape Town and that city and Fremantle were simply to be enjoyed. There were virtually no passenger girls, and all were aware of the 'dangers' of intra-ship dalliance. Therefore, one did one's work and became very familiar with one's sextant (the company did not provide them to us).

I thought that on this occasion, because I would likely see Sydney many more times, I would vary my routine a bit and give Christine a call and get together; Sandra was great, but variety is the spice of life. Therefore, I wrote to her and suggested an afternoon of frivolity, and when I phoned, she thought that a good idea, but asked whether she could bring a couple of friends. Naturally, I thought that a good idea.

They came down to the ship for an early lunch, and I was delighted to see that one of the friends was a lass called Winsome ... and she really was! The other friend was a fellow, a law student at the University of New South Wales; I didn't quite know how to treat this lucky guy because I didn't know to which girl he 'belonged' (and I never actually found out) but he was a good person to talk to. Christine had the peculiar fringe, and dressed rather clumsily, but as there was an officers' dance that evening on board, I thought that Mother would prefer me to invite her to the evening rather than the comely Winsome. We spent the afternoon on Bondi Beach watching all the beautiful people and left the beach in the late afternoon. I had to do a bit of explanatory work with Patricia, just to ensure that no scene would occur, but she took things in good heart; after all, there was still the lustful Peacock if all else failed.

On Canberra's bridge with Winsome and Christine

I descended the gangway to await the taxi, and it duly arrived. What arrived, however, was totally unexpected. Out of the car stepped one of the most beautiful girls that I had ever seen! I had thought the fringe an unfortunate choice of hair-style, but it was apparent that she had that afternoon spent some hours in the care of a master hairdresser; she was now a lovely sort of slightly gingery blonde with what could be described as a 'pixie' hair-style, she had a lovely face, and eyes that themselves could turn heads. Further, she was wearing a flowing but simple long black dress, quite demure with bare shoulders, and wore it with great elegance. I have described her as ungainly; now she was as gainly a girl as I have ever seen.

I brought her aboard and could sense the stares that I was getting, for most of the officers had selected as partners either passengers recently on the ship, or female (or male, in the case of the FAPs and others) officers. In a city like Sydney I certainly was not alone in having a guest from ashore, but I might as well have been (how could a homunculus like Frost find such perfection? – actually that was me asking myself the question). We had a great evening, and she gladly came to my cabin when the dance was over, but so taken was I that I acted in a completely gentlemanly way ... simply because I felt that that was expected of me. I took her home in a taxi, delighted with so successful an evening, but that was the conclusion of the relationship. I felt that I was very lucky ... but luck should only be pushed so far (in other words, I felt that the law student had the inside track, and this was not a girl with whom to make an ass of myself, a role at which I was a consummate master).

With some regret, we had to depart Sydney, and on the way across the Tasman Sea to Auckland I thought that I should see something of that city; Diane had insisted that I should visit her parents when I was in port, and I duly sent notice of my impending arrival. I was happy to receive a reply; I would be picked up on arrival by one of the Cossey family. And her father obliged.

Diane was a very charming girl with a very attractive face and great personal charm. Her distinguishing feature was her hair, which was pulled back from her face into something akin to a skull-cap (she was, of course, still in Europe at the time) which, I suppose, made the most of her features. I was therefore quite taken aback when I arrived at their house for lunch and met her mother and younger sister; they looked exactly the same as Diane, hair included, except for the apparent age differentials. I knew that an elementary, but not definitive, vision of how people would look in maturity can often be gleaned from their parents, but this was uncanny. (I need hardly add that the impression was wholly favourable respecting Diane, but I had earlier inferentially understood that there was an eligible young buck against whom I was being measured, and if this were so, I would have liked to measure up the competition. I had the feeling that I didn't quite make the grade.) But after a nice lunch, they took me on a drive around the city, which appeared to comprise little other than suburbs with a small downtown area of modest skyscrapers. A delightful place, actually, but even from the perspective of New Zealand, a place distant from practically everywhere else.

The voyage across the Pacific was sufficiently pacific. I saw a little more of Honolulu, again without seeing many more of its potential charms, but did not get to visit the *Arizona* memorial, which I would like to have seen. But other than that important symbol, I saw little that I could do in just a day; to see the place properly would obviously require a lot more time.

Life on board was not relaxed, but by now I was so familiar with the ship that I knew that it was time for a change; of ship, certainly; of lifestyle, probably. One matter that did come up twice, however, was this old chestnut of marriage. In Sandra's arms in Sydney the issue was elliptically alluded to by her, but the conversation was unproductive as I could not see a footloose fellow of twenty-five, with no prospects, settling down until absolutely ready – if that could ever occur. The second time the topic arose was during a tourist-class children's bridge-visit when, as junior officer of the watch, I had to describe to the visitors how the bridge mechanisms worked. Being tourist-class, the Chilly-Ho was Patricia, and she brought to the bridge a wholly noisy group of five to eight-year olds. These children's bridge visits were always enjoyable, the small ones being very inquisitive, in awe of the 'dressed-up' officers on watch, and especially entertained by the 'steering wheel' (not very impressive a fixture on *Canberra*, but that didn't matter; we could put George on duty and then anyone could pretend that they were steering the ship; of course, they all wanted to blow the whistle, but that was one joy too far). Even I (Christey was actually conning the ship) realised that the one thing that children love to do is to laugh (provided that one was not too scatological in one's humour, though that theme always resulted in uncontrolled mirth ... but I knew of an officer who was reprimanded for a joke about Kelvin's Balls – look it up!). One mother, who was carrying a toddler, said to Patricia on leaving "He would make a good father, wouldn't he?" to which she quietly replied, but loudly enough for me to hear, "And he wouldn't make a bad husband either." It was beyond me why young women were so keen; we were all so immature!

My main part-time pleasure (sic!) being my tape-recorder, of which I had purchased a top-of-the-line Ampex, I always looked forward to visiting San Francisco, where, on Market Street, there was what I considered the world's finest open-reel tape shop (it had literally thousands of selections that I had never seen elsewhere, all the way from Bach to Xenakis). This technology was actually the best type of music reproduction to have on a ship, as it was disturbed neither by the ship's rolling nor by vibration, and absent magnetic problems, there was no degradation of sound such as occurred with vinyl. I had also, by the chief R/O's request, been asked to take over the afternoon broadcast of a classical music programme that was piped, if listeners wished, through the ship's radio system, lamentable though the sound reproduction was. It was one of those tasks that nobody seemed to want to undertake but which I enjoyed; the ship's record selection was quite good, if unduly conservative (evidently a selection created by a committee).

During one of our usual breakfast discussions, an interesting concordance came to light. I was talking to a 3rd R/O about his life and from where he derived, and he said that he had gained his qualifications in a college in Ilford. "Oh," said I, "I know somebody who studies there, a very nice girl that I met on *Chitral*." He looked interested (he was a bit of a geek, but a very nice fellow). "Her name is Susan," I concluded.

I saw him blanche a bit as I described her (I even had a picture of her in my cabin, so any uncertainty could easily be overcome) and he gasped, "So you're the guy!" He declared that he had had the hots for Susan, but she was apparently holding firm with some officer in P&O and he and others could get nowhere. To say that I felt awkward would understate the case, but I knew that at some time in the future I had to have a little talk with the delectable Susan. He actually went on a bit about himself, because he was concerned about his life in another and very significant way.

On a big ship there was a large body of radio officers, sometimes four, sometimes seven. There was on *Canberra* the usual number, but the 2nd R/O was a bit different; we saw him very frequently on the bridge, doing chart-work, taking sights, talking about the Collision Regulations etc. – and, of course – quite often in repairing the radar. I asked him why he was doing the two jobs, and he said that there was absolutely no future for marine radio officers (they were probably the most technically sophisticated of all the ship's officers). "There will soon be no need for sights, repair of radars (just installation of circuit boards), knowing Morse code and semaphore, how to repair solid-state radios, everything we presently do … all will be electronic and just need a technician," he declared. "But I like it at sea, so I am studying for my 2nd mates, and will go on from there and become a deck officer." This was the only occasion upon which I heard such prescience respecting where the nautical world was headed. (I do not believe that the word 'digital' had at that time any meaning other than when related to fingers). He was, of course, absolutely right; sextants are even now 'on the bridge' and the use of astronomical sights still practiced ('just in case'), but GPS is so much easier and break-downs, if they occur, would be of worldwide, and likely catastrophic, scope.

For some two years, I had been occupied in my limited 'spare' time in working on a correspondence course through the International Personnel Management Association (IPMA) a London college. Started while on *Salsette,* I had a vague idea that this certificate might, eventually, provide me with other marketable skills. When I told the 2nd mate about my plan, he scoffed. "I know lots of people who undertake correspondence courses; I have never met anyone who completed one!" Words that incentivised me). By May 1968, I had covered all of the courses except for Corporate Finance, one that despite the difficulty of learning in this field with no mentor I thought that I could ace given last-minute cramming; one could fudge 'Industrial Psychology', but one had to actually know something for finance to be even partially understood.

As expected, when we arrived in Southampton, I was notified that I was leaving *Canberra* and that I was entitled to a couple of months' leave. I departed the vessel with some regret as it had provided me with some great experiences of all sorts, and for such a large agglomeration of people, it was actually a 'happy' ship.

My first task was to speak properly to Susan, and my second, I decided, was to sit the IPMA exam as soon as possible. The first I could effect immediately.

I did not look forward to this discussion with Susan in the least. While she was a lovely person, it had often occurred to me that I had led her on, despite the fact that I knew that she was not really my type; she came from a family where Father dominated everything to such an extent that both wife and daughter, though intelligent, did not feel that they had decision-making roles. I, through my parents, had been brought up to see the marital relationship as one of equality; though one did not 'revere' one's partner (too mawkish a term), one respected their opinion. If choosing between a milquetoast and a firebrand, I would veer towards the latter … that much I now knew.

I drove to Ilford and spent a pleasant afternoon with Susan. She was her gracious self, and I was glad to meet her room-mates, all most pleasing. However, when the crunch came, I balked. I excused myself because of the other girls, a feeble and weak let-off.

I again travelled to London and sat for the IPMA exam; I thought that I had done reasonably well ('The Economist', if carefully read, could provide anecdotal material for almost any business scenario that one chose to weave). I was disappointed to receive notification a few days later that my exam results were good, except for Corporate Finance, where I was plainly out of my depth. But my 'passes' would last for a year; I could take the paper again. With this I had to be satisfied.

It is perhaps opportune to digress into thoughts about the 'golden age' into which I had fortuitously and unknowingly been born, for my life at sea had occupied the interregnum between the Pill and HIV. Suddenly the former rendered all sorts of dalliances possible, and the latter, yet to appear, had been preceded by VD and a few other menaces, most of which could be avoided without much effort. It was then something of a game; before long it became a gamble with possibly dire consequences.

My social life now being a desert, I decided that I would again look up Judith. She was still attractive, well-toned and gregarious (frankly, I could do a great deal worse). As for intellect … well, I won't get into that. We had good times, without doubt, though I was aware that there was another fellow hanging about waiting for me to stumble; this was a small village with young people notably absent. However, while I was away at sea, Mother had become acquainted with a girl who lived only a mile or so away and assisted in the local grocery while on vacation from university. Mother's firm recommendation was that (this) "Judith has lovely ankles" which I thought, even on a mother's considered opinion, a basis insufficient for a lustful relationship. She was a pleasing young lady, and her wrists were pretty good too, but this was not a relationship that I saw going anywhere; I asked her out once, an invitation that fell on stony ground, but I saw no purpose in giving her a second chance, and I saw no special merit to her ankles.

However, my leisure was over; I was to join *Cathay* as Junior 2nd in the Royal Docks in London. A nice promotion and quite timely too.

Cathay was as similar to *Chitral* as two peas in a pod. Orientation was simple, and the route was to be the shortened Far East run, which is to say that things were changing. In light of containerisation, P&O had decided to institute a new sort of ship for the transportation of containers to Hong Kong and beyond and perhaps to other destinations entirely. These new ships, yet to come into service, were bigger and faster (and designed entirely differently from, say, *Salsette* and *Comorin* because of their cargo being nothing other than standard-sized containers). In the meantime, a number of ships, *Bendigo*, *Surat* and *Sunda* among them (a veritable geography lesson!) had been renamed *Pando Cape* et al and taken over the routes to be served by these new fast vessels. *Cathay* and *Chitral* were therefore almost redundant, designed for outdated cargo-carrying techniques, but, in the interim, useful for passenger service and cargoes such as rubber, tobacco etc. that did not take so well to containerisation.

The 'making' of a ship is, of course, very dependent on those with whom one sails. I knew none of the officers but quickly became acquainted. Captain Harris was a gentleman in every respect, having none of the airs of a martinet about him. I took him to be somewhat forlorn, for on one occasion, when discussing families, he said that he was proud of his daughter attending Cambridge, but sorry that he didn't even know what she was reading; he could look forward only to retirement. The mate was a small man, but very pleasant to all and sundry; the sort, all too rare on many ships, with whom one could sit with a beer and talk about anything. The 2nd mate was very quiet; I barely recall him. (I was Junior 2nd; the twelve to four.) The 3rd mate, Steve Pinney, I knew, but vaguely; on *Mantua* the senior of the two cadets (the sassy one) had been Chief Cadet Captain at Warsash, and beneath him were three Senior Cadet Captains, each in charge of a 'watch'; Steve had a watch different from the one in which I was housed. Viewed from afar, I had taken a bit of a disliking to him. He was, to me, sallow in appearance, sharp in speech and without humour. I saw little of him, however, and after he departed from the School of Navigation, he joined Shaw Savill, one of the best of the cargo companies but one almost entirely limited to the Australian trade. After a while he decided that he wanted more variety and joined P&O, thus becoming junior to me though he had graduated before me. To round out the group we had three good cadets: Rose, Thorogood and Clowes.

It was only a day or two before I found out that this was an excellent bunch with whom to work, and far from being a bit of an old misery, Steve was one of the brightest people whom I knew and possessed of a highly developed sense of the absurd and humorous. I greatly enjoyed it when I took over from him at midnight; he delighted in telling tall tales until well after he should have been asleep. My watch seemed all the shorter for his absurdities. On August 23rd, we sailed, bound for Cape Town.

The Captain's Cocktail party was much less substantial an affair than it had been on the big ships and was followed by a select party for the 'special' passengers, who were on few voyages such as ours. I was asked to go, I suppose, simply because I was available, and I suspect that the mate was unenthusiastic about the task. It was held in the Captain's cabin, and the first person to whom I was introduced was, to my great surprise, a charming young lady called Mary. We had a chat and I found that she was destined for Delhi, where she was to be Assistant to the First Secretary at the High Commission (we were not to go to Bombay; she was to fly up from Colombo). Things were looking up.

One of the components of the Junior 2nd job description was to have his own table, and as there was only one sitting on this type of ship, I was a bit concerned about those with whom I was to be closely associated for the next month or so. In fact, I found myself to be very fortunate; I had a small coterie of HSBC employees, two young trainee-managers, a manager and his young wife, and another person whom I do not recall. (At the time HSBC was a Hong Kong-based bank with its main management (mostly British) in London. It was the main Bank in Hong Kong, but it was rivalled by the Chartered Bank; both issued their own notes and coins). I realised that I had struck it lucky, the manager being maybe 45 years in age, but with a personality much leavened by his German wife, almost a girl, who possessed a very un-Germanic sense of humour. One of the 'bank boys' was a rather studious young man, the other the exact opposite … I called him Flash Harry, about as unlikely a banker as I could conceive.

Next day I noticed from the 'Special List' that Mary was indeed listed. She was the daughter of one of the significant directors of Ellerman Lines, one of the biggest British shipping companies; it traded, as far as I remembered from the ship recognition books, practically everywhere in the world. I assume that comity among shipping companies dictated that when someone important, or related to someone important, from a British shipping company travelled by ship, they were given some special attention. An idea occurred to me.

Officers watching Chitral New Year's Lion Dance

That evening I approached Mary (there were for some reason few rivals for her attention) and suggested that one thing that I really needed to do before attaining a higher rank was to learn to type, and that perhaps she would help me, as I owned a typewriter on which I had to that time proved quite inept. Surprisingly she thought that a good notion, so I approached the mate to clear the idea with him, and he seemed quite happy to agree that the best place to learn was in my cabin.

At dinner, I told the table of this plan, and Flash, with his usual generosity of spirit, said something to the effect of, "You're barking up the wrong tree!" I didn't think I was, in part because of the nanosecond that it had taken Mary to accept my idea. However, in order to give some bottom to the scheme, I had a word in the ear of the head waiter that it might be a good idea to relocate Mary to my table in place of the nonentity to whom I did not recall having yet spoken.

Next day the change was effected, and I began to very much look forward to the voyage ahead. (Recall that we were ten knots slower than *Canberra*; time was with me.)

The pre-dinner (and sometimes post-dinner) routine quickly established itself, and it went extremely well. Mary and I got together for a brief and anodyne drink – she was no drinker – and did a bit of keyboard practice. I learned very quickly that, again, the Catholic sensibility was a road-block to complete success in my primary area of interest but having never come across anyone who enjoyed canoodling so much, that was no hindrance to much enjoyment. The typing lesson occupied almost ten minutes each session, if I could stretch it that far, but did not progress very well ... not that that mattered a tittle. Additionally, it was not entirely unrewarding to see the Flash Harry frustration, for he could be a bit pompous, and in my opinion, though entertaining enough at meals, would probably not make a great bank manager; although he didn't know it, he benefitted from being taken down a notch or two.

There were, of course, other things to learn. For some reason, I had been given the job of giving the ship's morning broadcast, and in sailing on and on, day after day, and seeing land only in arriving at and leaving Cape Town, I had to exercise ingenuity in saying anything interesting. The Pilot Book, however, usually offered something enlightening. On the way to South Africa, for example, we had passed by the Namibian Skeleton Coast (though it was too far away to be visible) which the Portuguese had declared to be 'The Gates of Hell' a name now forever associated with the wreck of *Dunedin Star* in 1942 on the storm-tossed, foggy desert shore. Again, when traversing the northern part of the Mozambique Channel, we passed over the spot where the coelacanth had been discovered by fishermen in 1938. I had not heard of this particular fish before, it having been thought to have been extinct for millions of years, but pictures revealed an ugly, almost half-formed denizen of the deep ocean; had those fishermen not accidentally brought it to the surface, we might still be ignorant about its survival.

Whether anyone listened to my broadcasts I did not know, but it was an enjoyable little excursion into finding out about things of which I would otherwise have been unaware; with a passenger load of only 250, there was little enough to occupy active minds.

Early in September we arrived at our anchorage in Colombo and discharged our few passengers bound for India and Ceylon, and departed later in the afternoon, rounding the south-western point of the island – redolent of the *Khyber* chapter – after a few hours. In the meantime, at lunch, Flash had important news to impart; "Did you know that two girls have boarded?" he asked. I declared that I did not know this important fact, but he dug deeper. "I can get them up on the bridge during your watch tonight," he said, to which undertaking I responded with scepticism, "I'll bet a bottle of wine that you can't. And remember that a time well after midnight will be necessary as the captain will want to see the southern tip of Ceylon before turning in."

The evening passed quietly and at midnight I took over from Stevie, as he had now become, and he had plenty to say about Colombo, which was new territory to him. I then spent some time discussing things with Martin Clowes, my cadet, and prepared for a boring watch, the Bay of Bengal rarely being busy. It was a perfect tropical night, with light breezes, a crystalline sky and the captain content with the next leg of the voyage.

At 1 am we were disturbed. It was Flash, and he was accompanied by two girls. As it was pitch-black, we could see all the navigational instruments but little else, and our visitors could see nothing, there not even being an illuminating moon. We introduced ourselves to Judith and Susan, Susan being peeled off by Martin to the starboard side of the bridge. I was left with Judith on the port side. They were the Shepherd sisters from Canada, and on board for a trip to and from Hong Kong and back to Colombo, where their father was working for the Canadian Government in the field of Hotel Management training under the aegis of the Colombo Plan.

It is difficult to meet a new person in complete, or near complete, darkness. But in this instance, this was no problem at all; I knew something of Vancouver, she had a good knowledge of ships and the sea, having sailed from Vancouver to the Far East with APL, and I found that her conversational skills exceeded mine; she even worked in HR. Further, she was obviously the right age, being two weeks younger than me, and possessed a good sense of humour – she even liked my jocularity, not something I could always take for granted. It was also readily apparent, even in a few minutes, that she was no milquetoast. (And her name was easy enough to remember!)

We parted after an hour or so of most pleasing conversation; I looked forward to seeing her next day. Martin enjoyed his watch as well, so he told me.

I hot-footed it down to the dining saloon the next morning and had another important conversation with the head waiter. This most accommodating man knew his stuff, for by dinner that evening we managed with the two ladies to have a perfect table, even with Flash Harry there; he never proved a problem actually, humour, if well-judged, never coming amiss, though I was beginning to see him as rather immature. His companion was, to me, far more like conventional banking material.

On the afternoon watch, another glorious day, Martin called me over to the starboard wing of the bridge and pointed out a rare sight; before us, on the foredeck, were two sun-bathing girls. One was a rather young and demure English girl who very much kept to herself (Barbara was her name, but that was about all that I knew of her) and then there was Judith (remember, I had not actually seen her other than as a shadowy figure in the starlight) beside her. I immediately knew that here was something special. Built like a Rolex watch, she was curvaceous in all the right places, and, I thought, would not have appeared on the foredeck at such a time without knowing exactly what she was about (it was the first time that I saw any passenger ever going on the foredeck at all beneath the bridge, certainly one that I had ever looked at!). Clowes looked at me. "You want to marry that girl, don't you," he said. I did not know what to say. The watch over, I retreated to my cabin and enjoyed a necessary pre-prandial scotch. There was soon to be the Captain's Cocktail Party for the new passengers, and I made sure that I got there as soon as the door opened (I believe, there being so few new passengers, that it was held in the captain's cabin). The two girls entered after a fashionably suitable interval, and immediately made their impression, Judith in a long pink/fuchsia-flowered cotton dress, Susan in a very similar blue dress. Only then did I realise that they were pretty tall girls, and I noted that Judith had a point to make with the mate (I suspect about some dirt or oil on the foredeck) and, seeking him out, cornered him against a bulkhead and forcefully told him that 'something had to be done about it'. The poor man (remember, he was quite small and unassuming) quickly acquiesced; he was plainly out-gunned and out-maneuvered. I was probably introduced to Mr and Mrs Shepherd by one of their daughters but do not recall it; the scotch was having more than the usual effect. We then repaired to the dining saloon and the needed bottle of wine (we even agreed on the best wine, a white Barsac, as cold as possible; actually, it was nauseatingly sweet, but from that time on my alcohol allowance became well exercised. Today I doubt that Barsac is even crafted). *Cathay* had a small but pleasant dance floor in the forward lounge and a group that we called 'The Prickly Heat Trio'. As always, I searched assiduously for glamorous partners and actually found that Judith was willing to have a try-out; knowing my limitations (waltz and quick-step, though at school we had been taught even the rumba and tango – both well beyond me), I stuck to those boring themes that I could just about manage. As expected, she was an excellent dancer (inasmuch as she easily avoided my heavy-footedness), and we actually enjoyed a pleasing hour or so; at least, I did.

But there was one big problem: Stevie.

Not what you would call an impressive figure of a man, and certainly not, to me, handsome, he made up for these lacks with great personal charm and an acute sense of humour; some even seemed to think him 'cute', whatever that word meant. His great disadvantages were that the 3rd mate kept the evening watch and thus missed the prime social (dancing!) hours, that he did not have his own table, a tactical advantage that I employed as much as I could when I knew that he and I had the same objective, and that he knew nothing of the ports to be visited, sometimes a significant advantage but that on occasion (like my Athens and Naples escapades) one could really botch up.

We soon arrived in Penang, again an anchorage rather than a berth, and Stevie, unbeknownst to me, invited Judith ashore for a carefully planned afternoon. He arranged for a motor-bike and had decided to take her to a secluded beach on the other side of the island. As the afternoon wore on and they had not returned, I began to get concerned but not nearly as concerned as her father. As officer of the watch I was looking after the gangway and preparing for our departure, only a half-hour or so away, but he was pacing up and down in a state of mild excitement. (He was by no means an excitable man, but, obviously, he could get exercised if he lost a daughter in the wilds of the Malay jungle; he was getting quite heated!)

Fortunately, the two arrived in the nick of time in what I believe was supposed to be the day's last launch. She seemed unconcerned, but Stevie explained that they had been swimming on the far side of the island, the bike broke down, and realising that the ship was about to sail, sped back (the ship would not have sailed without them, but of that they could not be sure). However, I told Stevie that one just doesn't swim in the Straits because of sea-snakes and jelly-fish; he was accustomed only to safe old Australia, where one had only to worry about sharks and crocodiles.

Nonetheless, I had actually become a bit better acquainted with the family at a lunch. As I had been invited to join them, I asked my steward to ensure that my best white uniform was pressed and ready for use, and I sallied forth with the intention of carrying out the research that I had by now found essential; see from the mother how the daughter would turn out. And I had enjoyed the lunch … for the most part. Mr Shepherd was physically very like (Waveney) Susan's father but had far more friendly a manner and from what I saw, treated his wife in much the same way as my parents regarded each other. All went well, and then I ordered dessert – bilberries and cream, as neutral a selection as was available. But as I reached over the table, my sleeve caught my bowl and tipped the whole thing down my front (bilberries are a smaller version of blueberries, but, as one might guess, had far more potent a colouring; even a few would markedly stain the teeth. This was, therefore, remarkably inappropriate a choice of dessert, but I learned the lesson!). As for the mise-en-scene, I felt encouraged, for all the women, mother and daughters, had no compunction about expressing their views, especially, as I expected, Judith. This I liked.

We edged our way down the coast to Singapore. Although I had traversed the passage between two islands that constituted Keppel Harbour a number of times, I had never been officer of the watch when we were berthing. When our pilot came aboard, he, a notably short man with very poor English, seemed to favour the fast passage to the berth, which was frankly difficult to approach. As we sped between the two rows of ships, I could see both captain and mate getting very nervous. When the pilot indicated that we were nearly there, the two looked at each other, and the captain promptly ordered full astern and for the 2nd mate, on the bow, to drop both hooks. This sort of emergency response I had never before seen, but it was remarkably effective, the concern that the stern might swing around to port and strike a moored ship proving unwarranted. All ended well … but I would not want a repeat performance.

I was happy, especially after that event, to go ashore and have lunch with Bob Hammond. Needless to say, the topic of our stressful arrival did not come up, for I suspect that he would have bewailed the nationalistic fervour that had promoted local pilots with scant big-ship experience to positions that should have been filled by deep-sea Masters. Nevertheless, it was an enjoyable lunch; where we went I neither knew nor cared, but my appreciation of Chinese cuisine was much enhanced.

Returning to the ship, now calm and peaceful, most of the crew and passengers taking walks or tours, I had a restful afternoon and indeed evening as well; I do not recall having any dinner companions.

But at breakfast I discovered that I had missed out on an entertaining evening. Apparently without any particular motivation, a number of my table guests had located a moon-lit terrace with a suitable bar, and taking the opportunity offered, had leaped into the pool, none, however, having any swimming gear. Judith and her sister had simply stayed in their underwear. This was grist for ribald conversation!

Surprisingly, Flash had some more interesting news for me. Unusually, a few new passengers had boarded in Singapore, presumably either for the voyage to Hong Kong or for a Far Eastern Cruise (it now seems absurdly Eurocentric to describe this part of the world as 'the Far East', 'Asia'/'Asian' being far more appropriate. But, to a degree perhaps today difficult to understand, ethnocentrism prevailed; "the Wogs begin at Calais" was still thought more of a truism by the British than most of them would like to admit). Flash declared that there was another 'girl' on board of more than passing interest (on second thoughts, his ability to pick up 'tips' probably cast him for a future Bank Governor more than all of the plain bankers who were to be ground down by their system), a fact of which I had received no inkling.

But as I soon found out yet again, the Captain's Cocktail party was a good entrée into the newly aboard. I was again invited – perhaps because I was one of the few who actually enjoyed these opportunities to drink the ship's scotch at another's expense and I also kept the most convenient watch and was introduced to Colonel Sheppard, the Commander of the British Army Garrison in Singapore, and, presumably, to his lovely wife, details of whom I do not recall. But I do recall many details of Julia Sheppard, his lovely daughter.

It was quickly evident to me that I had a real dilemma here. Firstly, I had happened upon a really first-class girl who exhibited an intelligence and sensibility that I instinctively felt was very close to mine, though I had a rival of some substance. But, secondly, this Julia was not to be lightly dismissed; she was certainly attractive, but was less 'composed', in a lissom sort of way, than the Judith that I had met only a few days before. The problem was acute, as although I felt that Stevie probably didn't have the legs for maintaining a relationship, at least at this point, this Julia was plainly a quite sensual girl, one whom it would be foolish to overlook in light of the uncertainties of life (one of those being that Judith was apparently 'pinned' – whatever that may mean – to the trainee surgeon still in Canada). I decided that all I could do was play a waiting game ... but that certainly did not involve going back to the head waiter for a further favour (actually, this was probably irrelevant; Colonel was a very senior rank, almost certainly to be seated at the captain's table. No favours were needed).

On the way to Hong Kong, socialising proceeded. However, feeling that I was somewhat left out in the Stevie stakes, I tried to have my way with Julia. Although unsuccessful (she had a boyfriend, though how to maintain a relationship when the army was plainly to soon depart Singapore was beyond me) I did my best, as I thought her enthusiasm showed that she was far from unavailable. Time was not, of course, wasted; I recall that in a John Updike short story he described how the most sensual part of a woman was the small of her back; on that basis, Julia was an exceptionally gifted girl. We also took an afternoon in Hong Kong to go to Repulse Bay, where I further recalled the (apocryphal?) statement by Florenz Ziegfeld: "Always judge a woman by her legs." Strangely, everything that I knew about 'shepherding' demonstrated that all of the women that I then knew in that category were superbly endowed. (There is a sort of louche symmetry to these unimportant things, it should be noted. Ziegfeld had a loose association with the Folies Bergere of Paris; it was from that inspiration that he formed the infamous Ziegfeld Follies, a Broadway sensation in the 1900s. One can only note that 'bergere' is the French for Shepherdess ... Ziegfeld knew his world; his comment was simply a truism. At times, fate seems to play its cards with subtle mischievousness.)

But the afternoon in Hong Kong was followed by one of the most delightful evenings that I had yet experienced, certainly while I had been at sea. The HSBC manager and his wife invited Judith, the 'bank boys' and me to their apartment for a parting evening. There was no question that we had constituted a very convivial group, even Flash being a strangely cherished companion. As is the fashion in Hong Kong, the apartment was small but exquisitely furnished, though in the rather heavyweight Chinese style, and there were two servants, an amah and a cook. There was therefore no question of helping our hostess, whose company by that time I was only too happy to enjoy. Our meal was, of course, Cantonese (Canton, only just up the river, at that time might as well have been on the moon for all purposes other than its cuisine) but was preceded by an excellent selection of Scotches (of which at the time I had only 'blended' experience) and as good a selection of wines. Our host was at his convivial best, and even had some amusing stories about the Bank ('amusing', I suspect, only after handsome portions of Mr J. Walker's best).

To conclude the evening, our host played for us a selection of his favourite records. One in particular stayed with me. Out of the blue, he said, "How would you like some Nina Simone?"

I said, "Fine," although I had never heard of her, and he put on 'Lilac Wine' and 'Break Down and Let It All Out', two of the most moving songs that I had ever experienced outside Strauss' 'Four Last Songs'. It could have been the scotch, it could have been the company, it could have been the occasion, who knows? But I have never forgotten the evening. We parted after midnight.

Next day I decided that it was time to purchase some Chinese table crockery, because it had become apparent to me that most of the world completely misconceived the Chinese way of life and culture but that we would soon enough face reality. Napoleon may or may not have said, "China is a sleeping giant; let her lie and sleep, for when she awakens, she will astonish the world," but his prescience indicates that he *should* have said it. My set of twenty or so bowls allowed me to wow them back in England; how to properly use it was beyond me.

Our long journey back home commenced all too soon, for we could happily have stayed in Hong Kong for much longer. But the Indian Ocean beckoned.

It was during one of our evenings under the stars and with pre-dinner wine (Stevie and I, maybe a cadet or two, Judith and Susan, and any young ladies who wished to join us, of which there all too few) that we discussed life and the future as vigorously and with the futility that the young so love. It was decided that we would plan to have a reunion in the future, basically in Europe when we two were entitled to some leave. The plan was quite simple, inasmuch as the sisters would join *Cathay* on its next trip to Colombo on its return from Hong Kong, and they would thus return to Canada after seeing something of England and perhaps of Europe. What we would then do was quite open, especially to me, but I was beginning to formulate my own ideas anyway. In Judith I had also found a forceful presence to offer some guidance.

It was after one of those frequent nights of perfection experienced in The Bay of Bengal in the North-East monsoon that I took stock of my position. I was twenty-five, living a first-class life of enough money (there was little on which to spend what was in fact a fairly modest stipend), excellent working conditions, a great deal of interesting travel, convivial company (and sometimes profoundly better than that) and could look forward to fairly rapid promotion. The latter, however, was significant; opportunities for getting ahead came up fairly rapidly because of mid and senior-officer wastage. It appeared obvious that the life of a Bon Vivant could become rather flat, especially when I could see that 'home' to many mariners that was at bottom somebody else's home; one heard too often of domestic routine wherein the returning husbands didn't even know where their offspring went to school. Fortunately, I had by pure chance met up with the most charmingly didactic companion.

Despite the depredations of Stevie, who was actually quite adept with wooing the objects of his desire, Judith and I engaged in many conversations about the future, especially mine! With wisdom seemingly beyond her years, though she was, as it were, 'in the business', she set about charting a course for me that included university (which I myself had now concluded had to be in my future) and the end of this mostly rewarding seven years at sea. It appeared that access to a university in Canada was a much more user-friendly process than it was in UK, as I knew from David that time was really not of much import to UCCA (University Central Council of Admissions), which tended to find candidates a position at a university suitable for it, rather than a position for which one might choose to apply. I decided that I was going to set the new course of my life as soon as I could, but not to bother with that awful Corporate Finance hurdle.

On the way across the Indian Ocean (the Shepherds disembarked in Colombo) and around Africa, I planned, as best I could, my route through the rest of my life. I read as many British papers as I could find (though they were almost entirely unavailable in South Africa, most English-language news media being unavailable because of their anti-apartheid bias and the South African alternatives being journalistic tripe), with a view to seeing what alternative careers I could dig up in London, to where many people that I knew commuted daily from deepest Sussex.

Thus, as soon as I could (which was very soon, as the turn-around occupied only a few days) I made an appointment with the assistant marine superintendent for a discussion about any ideas that he might have. He, of course, was an ex-deck officer, so it might even be that something would come up within P&O itself.

Before my discussion with him I carefully perused the 'Times' and the 'Daily Telegraph' jobs and saw that there were a number of job opportunities that actually encompassed the sort of expertise for which an IPMA diploma might render me suitable. Thus armed, our discussion was general, but with one specific job at IBM as the focus of my future planned weltanschauung. Mr Jones, however, really senior to me by only one year, was dismissive and, I thought, unhelpful.

Obviously, the future was up to me. (To be fair, I could hardly expect him to be particularly welcoming to what he would probably have seen as another defection from already-depleted sea-going ranks.)

Back aboard *Cathay* for another voyage we welcomed the next lot of passengers; they struck me as especially unremarkable. In fact, I have no recollection of any of my table companions and I did not even go ashore in Cape Town (this was a sign of professional ennui; when one stays aboard rather than go ashore in really interesting ports, the spark of the enjoyment of travel has plainly sputtered).

In Colombo the Shepherds came aboard, and Stevie and I were very happy to see that the ladies' plans were going well. In the meanwhile, he too had decided that he would leave the ship at the end of the voyage, and that if we were to have a bit of a group hug in Europe, we collectively decided that we would try for a ski holiday, our return to London being scheduled for early in March (I was more than happy to replicate my Leysin experiences, which, despite some inexplicable disappointments, I could recall only with pleasure). He indicated that he knew a girl who might be interested in coming with us (a bit of a surprise to me, as I had hitherto thought him very much actively prowling), and I was rather interested to see somebody, anybody, who would be interested in his rather laconic ways. As far as the two of us were concerned, the passage from Colombo to Hong Kong and back again could not pass quickly enough.

In Colombo again, Judith and Susan boarded. However, I was quite disconcerted to see that Judith brought with her a big, handsome all-American guy, a Peace Corps volunteer who was a graduate farmer from Washington State. He I just didn't like the look of; he resembled a hero from an American movie. Fortunately, it transpired that he was not going with us, though Arnold, upon being spoken to, presented himself well, and when Judith explained that he was just a nice guy, but not too sharp, I felt the 'danger' to be allayed. As the Shepherd parents were shortly to be leaving for UK on *Oriana*, and from there going by ship to Montreal, things were working out excellently.

But there always had to be some flies in the ointment. This time they were Mummsy and Gayle, two Americans taking a rather exotic route back to some desperate place in the USA. Mummsy was a blowsy 'lady' (not the right word!) who bore the cross of her crass twenty-something daughter (who, I judged, would look just like her mother in only a few weeks) an ill-educated drop-out obviously in need of a 'boy'.

Departure Colombo was a moment of joyful expectation. I had arranged to have Judith and Susan on my table and cannot recall who made up the number – all that I had to do was avoid approaches from Mummsy and Gayle, who were accommodated with some unfortunates … though we saw plenty of them in the bar (rum and coke, I suspect). My pleasure was assisted, however, by some perfect weather as we proceeded to Durban, which we thoroughly enjoyed every evening before Stevie was obliged to go down for dinner, and we encouraged the cadets to likewise enjoy themselves with us, in part because we could then invite another passenger, a singularly beautiful young girl returning from Malaysia with her parents. We thought her a teenager, and very quiet and unassuming; I personally thought that the rigours of English school or university would be quite hard for her (she reeked vulnerability) but it was not within our power to do much other than perhaps boost her self-confidence.

Four days later we berthed in Durban, few on board other than me having ever seen the place before (it was relevant to say that that city was quite anglicised though with many Zulu inhabitants; Port Elizabeth seemed to me a dull, religious sort of place, and Cape Town a city where, if entering a store, one felt the need to use Afrikaans before trying English). The two girls went on a tour to a nearby Zulu village – where Judith insisted in standing on an ostrich egg to prove its soundness. This young lady, I found, had all the moral courage and sheer chutzpah that I would rather have liked to possess myself (I should have been aware of that characteristic on that first evening months three months before when she cornered the mate and got her way only by way of sheer force of character … though she was also the taller of the two!).

Just as importantly, Stevie brought aboard the young lady whom he thought might like to go skiing with us, she at that time living in Transvaal, and soon to leave for England. I was not surprised to find Susan (let us call her Susan L.) to be as she was; very well put-together, quite refined in a North-London way, and very passably attractive. I thought it an excellent idea for her to go away with us reprobates for a week or two.

Arrival in Cape Town was perfect. The late morning was hot, cloudless and bright. I took a walk ashore down Adderley Street for a bit of civilisation and decent coffee, did my watch-keeping, and then assembled our group for the evening. For this, we sought out an Italian restaurant (with Chinese cooks and waiters we had much the same old English menus as all P&O ships enjoyed, and which was pleasantly leavened by frequent Chinese specialties; but no Italian). Good eating, but then the highlight of the evening was ascending Table Mountain by cable car. By this time a northerly wind had created a most glorious 'cloth' hanging over the mountain edge and, looking South, one could easily imagine, and perhaps believe that one could see, that the next land of any sort was the Antarctic ice-sheet, some 7,000 kilometres away. We were, I think it no exaggeration to say, over-awed; it was, in a word, magical and never to be forgotten.

Evening cloud over Cape Town

I also recall that I encountered another strange aberration of the South African sensibility while sipping my morning fresh coffee (with fresh cream!). One of my favourite magazines was The Gramophone, a well-written quality British publication with lots of pictures of musicians, record sleeves and orchestras. I sought one out in a couple of bookstores, but found none, not even outdated samples. However, I did find a locally produced 'equivalent', and quickly realised why the real thing was missing; there were many supremely gifted black musicians in the real world, and recognition of any such qualities was verbode. So, therefore, was the magazine. (This ethical stupidity had been the focus of a drama in 1962, when Stravinsky had come to South Africa to conduct his music and been told that he would conduct some concerts with white audiences and only one with a black audience. Declaring that he conducted only for 'people' he, as the most famous composer of the day, forcefully made the point that he would not be constrained by such odious strictures, his demands eventually being impossible to refuse. Yet the wall still took years to be breached, it being in that same year that Mandela was arrested and imprisoned for conspiracy to overthrow the state.)

In order to give passengers some breaks from the eternal seascape, our voyage to UK included the Canary Islands and Le Havre. I would have liked to see something of the former, for it was one of those unique volcanic islands arising from the West African seascape, but tendering on *Cathay* was a somewhat primitive business. Of more significance, I sent my resignation letter off to P&O … with, naturally, some trepidation.

I saw no reason to step ashore in Le Havre. The rainy pier at Tilbury was welcome enough (it should, however, be added that at the best of times Tilbury was a miserable place, but it was changing profoundly because of the container revolution. Today's Tilbury would be totally unrecognisable from the workaday berths of the 1960s).

A visit to the Marine Superintendent in London, effectively an Exit Interview, though such a thing had yet to be thought of, was not entirely unsatisfactory, inasmuch as Captain Dunkley did not try to persuade me of the error of my ways (the more I saw of such individuals, the more I realised that the grandeur of being the Commodore of the Fleet, or even a Captain, was often countered by the realisation that they were there only because of not having earlier thought of going ashore when best able to adapt to a new calling). Anyway, I thanked him – though I was not sure for what – and began to work on our anticipated holiday.

Meanwhile, the remnant of the Shepherd family had arrived in London on *Oriana*, Susan L had also mysteriously arrived in North London, and even more mysteriously, Arnold seemed to arrive out of nowhere. (I didn't remember him being invited at all, but, as I say, he did not play the part that I thought that Moviedom would have assigned to him). All six of us were going on the skiing holiday, and we researched suitable locations. We collectively settled on Mayrhofen, a small ski resort in the province of Tyrol.

We had ten days of ski and fun. The picturesque chalet was as rural as one would expect in such a small place, and the food very good, if strange (I took especially to raznjici, which I never again in my life sampled). The skiing was excellent, though primitive; however, on the first or second day, Arnold skied into a tree and broke his leg; thereafter, he really was hors de combat. However, I myself had a rather different and far better seminal moment. Stevie and I shared a king-sized bed. One night we had a knock on the door, and Susan L came in. "Steve," she said, "I think someone is trying to come in the front door; would you please change beds with me, as my room is very close to the front door?

Somebody is prowling." I was fully and absolutely awake as this attractive and very well-designed girl climbed in beside me, wearing only a rather flimsy nightgown! For what seemed like hours, I tossed and turned, uncertain about the obvious; she, meanwhile, apparently (I think) fell asleep. I was eventually awoken by Judith entering the room with tea for Stevie and me; she seemed not in the least fazed by the presence of Susan in lieu of Stevie. I felt like a bit of a loser, I should add; I never found out what Susan felt.

But Judith had her own moments, one that was not entirely uncharacteristic of her occurring during one of our post-gluehwein dinners. Stevie had a sometimes-acerbic sense of humour, and one of his less appropriate bon mots fell on her sense of propriety quite heavily; she pondered for a second ... and threw a full glass of tomato juice in his face. We all sat in stunned silence; Stevie eventually laughed, and all was forgiven.

After Austria, we all went our own ways, the Shepherds and Susan back to Vancouver on the Polish *Stefan Batory*, Susan L to London, and Stevie, as far as I knew, back to P&O, though I did not hear from him for five decades.

The following week I received a call from P&O, through the marine superintendent's office. The question posed was whether I would take the job of assistant nautical inspector, based in London's Leadenhall Street. It took no time to accept unreservedly, even though one supposes that normally one knows what sort of job one is accepting. I considered only that if there were one place where there was an abundance of opportunity, both for things that I could do and for determining what suitable avenues lay ahead in other arenas, the City of London would be the finest of choices. But no more going to sea!

The P&O-Orient Line Ships in which I served had varying tales of sale or destruction;

- a. *Khyber* apparently has two versions. Either it was scrapped in 1962, or it was sold to ship breakers in Kaohsiung, Taiwan, in 1970 (under a different name).

- b. *Mantua* – sold for scrap to the Pakistan Gulf Trading Agency in 1976.

- c. *Malwa* – sold to Taiwan interests for scrap in 1975.

- d. *Arcadia* – sold for scrap to Taiwanese interests in 1979.

- e. *Himalaya* – sold for scrap to Taiwan interests in 1974.

f. *Oriana* – a rather sad ending, sold in 1986 as a floating attraction and hotel firstly to Japanese interests and then to Chinese interests, it declined into a rusting hulk until severely damaged in a storm in 2004, after which it was then ignominiously scrapped.

g. *Comorin* – sold in 1972 to Alonso Garcia and then scrapped in that year.

h. *Chitral* – transferred to E&A (a P&O subsidiary) in 1972, broken up (Taiwan) in 1975.

i. *Salsette* – sold for scrap in Kaohsiung in 1979.

j. *Cannanore* – sold for scrap in Taiwan in 1972.

k. *Canberra* – broken up on Gadani Beach, Pakistan 1997 (see 'A very Strange Way to go to War' by Andrew Vine, Aurum Press 2012).

l. *Cathay* – transferred to E&A in 1970, then passed on to People's Republic of China, but its actual fate seems not to have been determined and it may still be in operation.

(Much more information on all of these vessels is readily available on the Internet.)

West Star Glacier Bay

8 Leadenhall Street, Canada, West Star & CPR

As I had not been asked to apply for the job of assistant nautical inspector, it was my assumption that somebody in authority (perhaps Dunkley!) knew that I could do the job, simply because I had never heard of such a position and had no idea what it entailed. Working in the City of London to many would mean dark suit and bowler, but I had seen enough of the London workworld to know that such an image was by then outdated. To Father, my getting a job in the city, especially at the Head Office of such a prestigious company, was like a dream come true; to me it gave unparalleled opportunity to explore new fields, not at all necessarily associated with ships and the sea.

More significantly, my relationship with Judith blossomed. I had invited her home for a few days' respite from the rigours of London, though by this time her family had departed, and she, I am glad to say, quite took to the hardship of Sussex country life. I had decided that she was what I desired for my significant other, but the more distant future I had to regard with less certainty; not only was she 'pinned' to the orthopaedic surgeon, but there was a worrisome gynaecologist residing in Vancouver who was ardent but with some odd reservations about marriage (for example, spouses had to take separate vacations). To cement our relationship, I thought it a good idea for us to take a little trip, and what could be better than a trip to Shakespeare country and to Stratford-upon-Avon, she having her (appropriate) degree in English?

We drove off into the unknown and before long found ourselves in Stratford, a rather charming Cotswold-type town somewhat marred, in my view, by the rather brutish Royal Shakespeare Theatre. We stayed in a typically twee guest house, wherein Judith had a communication problem ("What will your husband have for breakfast?" our prim hostess asked. "What hus—?" asked Judith. "Oh, Michael, haha…" said she, "Cornflakes and poached egg," neither of which I would ever order). Our hostess pursed her lips a bit but took the American accent for the usual transatlantic mishmash (who would know a Canadian accent!). I enjoyed my full English.

We enjoyed a little tour of the area – as picture-perfect an Olde England as it is supposed to be (which is to say, nothing at all like the rural England where people actually live). We went to the theatre and found that 'Pericles, Prince of Tyre' was being performed that evening, so that, of course, we saw. This is hardly a play at the epicentre of the Shakespeare canon, even when leavened, as it was, by Judi Dench in the role of Marina. Frankly, it was pretty heavy going; it is small wonder that scholars are doubtful whether much of it was written by Shakespeare at all. Still, we were glad that we had had the experience (of course the fame of Miss Dench was at that point limited, neither of us knowing much of her at all).

Next morning, we drove back to Sussex, but on the way passed Fairford. This being April 9th, 1969, we actually witnessed the first British flight of Concorde, a moment of aeronautical fame. A sight not to forget.

Once returned to domesticity we enjoyed some 'acquaintance' time, Mother in particular needing persuasion that this was the right partner (Father thinking her wonderful!). However, it started off very well when Judith decided that it would be nice to have a Canadian-style shrimp cocktail. As we had no ketchup or similar concoction, we visited the village shop (where one of the other Judiths worked, of course!) and bought a chili sauce, which looked exactly like ketchup. We mixed that up with some horseradish and dolloped that on some excellent prawns. The problem was that Canadian chili sauce bears resemblance to British chili sauce only in its colour. Father (who didn't even like curry!) looked as though he were about to have apoplexy upon tasting it; it was indubitably the hottest sauce that he had ever tasted. The point of the exercise was, however, quite different from what would have been my embarrassment if I had prepared the dish; Judith was able to take it in her stride and duly laugh it off. It was a good bonding moment with possible in-laws, she making what could have been a troubled introduction into something about which we had a snicker for years to come.

A few days later, Judith was off to Montreal, where, I knew, were waiting the arms of the nearly-qualified surgeon. She seemed to me, however, to have some ambivalent views about this fellow; her doubts basically being that he was more impressed with himself than with her. And as I knew that she liked me, I thought that ultimately her impeccable taste would prevail. But I could only wait and see the game played out. Meanwhile, motherhood had its own game. Mother asked me "But will *she* have *you*?" followed by, "She's a bit strong-willed, isn't she!" (which I thought a bit ripe coming from her!).

On the basis of there being no immediate reason to change my plans, I set about developing a future life for myself. The first thing that I did was apply for a university place. One needed at least two 'A' Levels to obtain a position, but I felt that my tickets were sufficient for me not to be turned down out-of-hand. That did not happen, but the actual impediment was more serious. After writing to the UCCA, I was advised, as indeed David had told me, that by applying in March I had precluded getting any place for at least a year and a half; applications were taken only as early as October for the following October! As I would therefore be nearly twenty-seven when I *might* get a place, and therefore be a spent intellectual force, I felt myself snookered. Other plans had to develop, though now at least from a secure job situation.

The commute to London was not a journey that I much appreciated. The daily train originated in Hastings, and I caught it at a very small country station that resulted in seventy-minute journey to Cannon Street. Although I usually managed to get a seat, the train atmosphere was distinctly humanoid, especially on rainy days, and from having an insufficiency of news, I actually had a surfeit of time to consume the Daily Telegraph.

But the job was not too bad at all. I was taking over from another fellow of my seniority (John Smith, I'll call him) as he had found a job near his home, and I quickly came to realise that there wasn't really a full-time position here, it comprising scheduling for various ships, giving 'expert' advice to the legal boys in the event of accidents or claims, preparing 'sailing orders' for ships as they were about to sail off into the blue yonder, and ordering bunker fuel for the big ships as requested by their Chief Engineers. I was under the direction of Captain Sperling, a charming old salt with many years of seagoing experience who usually fell asleep in the afternoon following a pub lunch (oh yes, and P&O provided lunch vouchers in sufficient amount to get a pork pie and a pint every day; excellent idea, I thought), he in turn being under the direction of Mr Mackenzie, a director who had probably seen at least seventy-five summers, but a nice old fellow anyway. Captain Dunkley was also above us, an éminence grise with, I thought, an unmerited reputation for gruffness.

John and I almost immediately found ourselves with a new and significant task. As I had earlier understood, there was increasing difficulty in finding adequate use for the big white ships. The Boeing 707, already mentioned, and the faster general pace of life were in any event contemporary shipping problems, but the closure of the Suez Canal had magnified time and bunkering issues, destinations and new and unexpected costs. The most intractable problems existed for the use of *Cathay* and *Chitral* – there was simply insufficient call for them given the new classes of container ships, and the Government and other employers (an obvious one would be HSBC) quickly losing enthusiasm for paying their employees for longer trips by sea that BOAC could provide at less cost. John and I were charged with finding new uses for those ships in particular, but other liners in general, and bring our thoughts to the attention of Mr Mackenzie and his harried assistant, Roger Brown, a very pleasant young man who was permanently on edge because he was operating at the very limit of his capabilities. The problem was that so was P&O; the company operated the finest fleet of elegant and comfortable deep-water ships whose 'due date' was recognisably upon us.

We worked on two possibilities in particular. The first was to base the two vessels in Fiume (now Rijeka, then part of communist Yugoslavia) or Trieste from where their limited speed would be no hindrance to cruising to the Dalmatian Coast, Greece, Turkey and the Black Sea. There were two problems; they carried only 250 passengers and were as much cargo ships as cruise vessels, which cargo-carrying capacity was not needed, and, more importantly, could earn no revenue.

The second possibility was to develop new scenarios entirely; the Baltic was under-served (but who would want to go to Leningrad, the only interesting city on that sea? Who had heard of Riga or Talinn?) and there was talk of Alaska becoming a destination of choice (but, firstly, who would want to go to such a cold and destination-deprived place, and, secondly, the Jones Act precluded foreign ships carrying Americans from US port to US port; could this impediment be overcome?).

Perhaps the greater problem was the ships themselves. Excepting *Canberra* and *Oriana*, the bulk of the fleet were not really cruise ships at all. They all had substantial cargo capacity with derricks and other comfortless ships' gear, and their decks, while having swimming pools and suitably-placed bars, were very limited in 'entertaining' facilities; after all, conventional first-class passengers to Australia spent more time resting, reading, eating and drinking than did the newly targeted cruise passenger, which could be described as the young, hip and well-off. We directed suggestions to Mr Mackenzie, who was, I have to say, quite open to discussion, but as with many in the shipping industry, somewhat aghast at the profound and rapid changes generally taking place over the whole nautical world (as an example, Noel Mostert (see 'Supership') had sailed on *Ardshiel* in 1966, a new behemoth at the time, a type of vessel that soon rendered the Suez Canal almost irrelevant). P&O had also noted that K Line, a Japanese company with vast numbers of ships, operated from two skyscraper floors in Tokyo, while the P&O Group, with fewer ships, maintained offices all over London, each component company having a complete office, separate facilities and employees.

However, in addition, life in London was not quite what it was cracked up to be. I liked the office environment, inasmuch as there were friendly and capable people with whom to work, but it was unvaried, the train journey was too tedious, and times at home began only late in the evening. I also cared little for 'living for the weekend'; in short, it was more fun to be at sea!

But change was on the way. Firstly, I arranged for a room to occupy during the week (in grotty Eltham, near Bob Hope's birthplace, but less than 30 minutes from the office by train) and Judith had arranged to obtain information from two B.C. Universities (UBC and Simon Fraser) that painted a very different picture from that of UCCA respecting admission policies; in short, my qualifications seemed satisfactory, but if upon investigation proved inadequate (who, over in BC, had heard of a Foreign-Going 1st mates ticket?) deficiencies could easily be made up at local colleges. As soon as I could come over, I could immediately apply, and SFU operated all year-round (in other words, everything didn't close down for the summer). The die, for me, was cast.

My parents were, of course, less than wholly enthusiastic about this scheme, but, as I had chosen my parents with the greatest of care, accepted the inevitable (and that was how it was beginning to look; after all, I had already been away from home for 7 years) with good grace – this was how the Empire was created, after all!

Meanwhile, I had to have an interview at Canada House (my interviewer, of course, had no idea what a nautical inspector did) which, I think, lasted about three minutes, but I made sure that I went to as many operas as possible (I never need to see 'La Traviata' again) and to all the plays that caught my fancy (though the G.B. Shaw and Noel Coward canon I would thereafter never miss) as I thought Vancouver to be a cultural desert. I was actually wrong in this regard, but the 'colonies' were the 'colonies'!

In beginning to prepare for a major transition in life, I was, of course, fortunate in my nationality, my choice of destination, and the fact that I was relatively accustomed to foreign parts, though I had already decided that Vancouver was a city easy to embrace. The cost of getting to Vancouver was ninety-nine pounds, ship and train included, and all I had to do was ensure that, in the event of the failure of the relationship, I would be able to stay or return. I had so often left for foreign parts, however, that to actually leave in November was no big deal; I caught the train to Liverpool, where I joined *Empress of England* for the five-day crossing. The stabilisers were faulty, and as the weather was unfavourable, usually the dining saloon was half-empty. I was in steerage (or tourist) class with three other young fellows, but this was not a social trip; all were 'drawing our bows at a venture' and probably equally nervous about what awaited us.

Montreal was inviting enough … until one stepped off the ship. It has to be remembered that my career hitherto had consisted of going to hot, or at least warm, places. This place was colder than anything that I had yet experienced, even in Britain, where the Gulf Stream kept things relatively warm in all but the coldest weather. As a result, I took to going underground, where I found the Metro to be far superior to the Underground; clean as a whistle, running quietly on rubberised wheels, and with shops and warmth that belied the severe weather outside. This interlude I enjoyed; at last I was on the last leg (of life/the journey?). The train itself was not by any means luxurious, but better appointed than any British train of my experience, and less crowded than expected.

This was a three-day trip, but I was surprised how slowly we travelled, and to a degree, how big is Canada; we seemed to take forever to go around northern Lake Superior (which looked as cold as sin) and then eventually arrive in Saskatoon, where I thought that I would step off the train and buy a paper. I took one step off the train and stepped right back – this place was absolutely freezing! It made Montreal seem tropical.

Of the train itself, I had no complaints, the food being more than adequate, the domed car absorbing, and the sleeping quarters quite acceptable. The transit through the Rockies was disappointing because it was at nighttime, but I felt quite under the weather anyway (psychological pressures by then having overtaken me).

We arrived at about 10:00 am on November 25th, and of course, there she was waiting for me, dressed, I am sure very deliberately, in a smart red suit, looking her best. We went to her apartment. There now occur, of course, a few terminological changes; 'apartment' for 'flat', 'pants' for 'trousers' (though much of Britain thinks differently), 'trunk' for 'boot' and the like. A smart apartment greeted me, we lunched on shrimp vol-au-vent, and, beautifully planned, Judith returned to work … an excellent idea.

The domestic arrangements were perfect, with a sitting room tastefully decorated in a light brown, and a bright and airy bedroom that could have brought some parental problems … had they been around. In fact, the Shepherds were by that time in Jamaica, where Mr Shepherd was in a job very similar to that which he had enjoyed in Colombo. I had no unpacking to do, my luggage being brought by CP to me later that afternoon, so I relaxed, at least to the extent possible, until Judith returned from work. We quickly went out, however, because her boss, something of a bon vivant, had suggested that the best place for such an occasion was Hys' Prime Rib, where he was a friend of the head waiter. I, frankly, was not much interested in roast beef, as in English cuisine roast beef was brownish, toughish and thinnish, but it would have been churlish to point this out.

And thank goodness that I didn't! This was one of the finest meals that I had ever had. We had both recovered our form, at least to the extent possible, the head waiter looked after us as he would with his own children, I was introduced to the Manhattan cocktail, and the prime rib, a beef-cut of which I had never heard, was surpassingly good at medium rare, again something with which I had not before been acquainted. If I recall correctly, this wonderful experience cost $17.50.

Life settled down. I needed a job, and Judith, in HR at Eatons, Canada's premium department store, found me employment as a parking lot attendant in the downtown core, from where I made enquiries about getting some education. Again, not too difficult, as I could attend a Community College commencing in January, completion of which, after two terms (semesters), would comprise the first year's university (four years being required in Canada).

Christmas came and went, but it had become relatively routine for me to be in strange places at this time of year, and we took the opportunity to slowly become familiar with each other's domestic foibles. Very shortly afterwards, I was able to start on the first year's courses. I chose what I liked and what was mandated, but most courses were ridiculously easy; History, for example, "Does anybody know where Serbia is?" and economics well below what I learned from David's set books from his university days.

Life settled down quite nicely, and I found that not only were we getting on well, but that love had reared its stately head. So, what better than to propose on Valentine's Day – what could go wrong? Well, what could go wrong is that I was turned down, though apparently, I just chose a bad time (which showed that my antennae needed repair!). Thinking that the next day would be a better day, I prepared escargots, fillet steak with béarnaise sauce, and served a good sauternes (sic!). This time no mistake … immediate acceptance!

The ring was not so easy, as Judith was inclined not to want one (though I believed it an insurance policy!). But a Ceylonese classmate told me how to have it inscribed in Sinhala, a geographical coincidence that went down exceedingly well.

Meanwhile, Eatons had turned up another job that suited me very well; a Saturday parts-man in appliances. I knew nothing of refrigerator parts, but a supervisor was always to advise, and things were even better than that sounds, for I was 'assisted' by three nubile young girls, all daughters of other employees of the company (I actually never found out what they did at their desks, besides filing, but they certainly assisted in making my Saturday workday – which paid for our groceries – pleasant enough).

We had decided that the wedding was a no-brainer. As the Shepherds were resident in Jamaica, and that was the obvious place to enjoy both a holiday and the nuptials, Mr Shepherd began to arrange things. Being an instructor at the hotel school, the venue was obvious, the school being located a mile or so north of Kingston, and their rented house had plenty of accommodation. And I found that my parents could also come over, Father always having wanted to go to such exotic places.

But my cup ranneth even further over the top. Upon hearing that in September we were to travel to the Caribbean for ten days, two of the young ladies working with me, Linda and Joyce, declared that they would like to go too! The fact that Judith would be there (I believe her Eatons' 'rank' was above their mothers', but she was in any event regarded as being a perfect temporary guardian for these two young things) meant that any parental reservations were allayed. They received the necessary consent.

Thus, at the end of August we arrived in Kingston – the traffic was every bit as savage as I had remembered – and were greeted by the Shepherds and Susan, who was still living with them, and a couple of days later, my parents arrived. The house was typically Jamaican, open and airy, but well protected from the afternoon rain-storms. There were surprises (one went outside in the morning to pick the breakfast oranges, very little talk was audible during an evening on the veranda, so noisy were the frogs, and we were never unnecessarily disturbed, Brutus, the family Doberman, being amiable but looking ferocious) but servants looked after the cooking, cleaning and gardening. Indeed, this was a pretty good way to live.

The mechanics of getting married were not necessarily so simple. Mr Shepherd had engaged the services of the new Bishop of Trinidad to officiate, but the pre-Marriage Certificate had to be obtained (not so simple in such an anti-bureaucratic country) and then notarised. Finding a Notary was not simple; when we did find one, he had already sampled a few tots of rum. As it was unbelievably hot at the time, Judith decided then that she no longer wanted to get married and to go home forthwith.

Fortunately, next day she changed her mind. Wedding day proved exceedingly hot, and the ceremony at Constant Spring Church went well (as did the excellent Prime Rib, obtained with much difficulty, although with not Sauternes but Chianti). However, as we had and have no idea whether there was a residential requirement for the wedding to be valid, even now we cannot be sure that we are legally tied!

Judith and her parents before the Wedding

The Honeymoon was of the sort of which dreams are made. We drove to the northern part of the island, visited Montego Bay and rented a chalet near Ocho Rios, dunked ourselves in Dunns River Falls, and enjoyed some of the world's finest beaches. And let me not forget to say that I was the subject of many pained male glances; one, perhaps two young girls on a honeymoon … but four!

It was a shame to return to Vancouver, but study had to go on. The next semester saw the same sort of courses, though suddenly Economics became much more difficult, our lecturer being the estranged wife of Saunders of 'Samuelson Saunders' Principles of Economics'. I got full marks, but suddenly it was much more difficult than the first half of the course (one poor soul in the class was having his fourth attempt at it; I advised him that he might be best to try another discipline, advice that I suspect he ignored). As before, I retained the Saturday parts-man job and had a few other 'nothing' jobs, but it paid for the groceries; for many reasons, Eatons was the perfect employer.

The net result of this tuition system was that by April 1971 I had completed two years' worth of university and had been accepted at the UBC, where I knew standards to be high. (I had long since absorbed 'Anarchism' by George Woodcock, a professor there). In choosing my courses there I selected those that I thought I could ace and was also accepted in the third-year Honours Class, part of that scheme being so that I could get into the Faculty of Law, the second-most difficult Faculty (after medicine) by which to be accepted. But summer employment was a problem, the part-time jobs that Judith had found for me being poorly paid. I therefore enquired from a friend of hers if he, in the Employment business, could locate anything for me. He did; work as a timekeeper for Canadian National Railway. The job was located in the middle of the forested wilderness, but one earned money that one simply could not spend!

While the location of the job was far from 'civilisation', there were reasons for the remoteness. I was transported by train to a siding near the hamlet of Blue River, a town that I never actually saw. The job entailed ensuring that a rail gang was properly paid, I having to liaise with the foreman, who each year collected together 15 Portuguese labourers, who lived in rail cars on a siding, and each day departed for a section of rail that needed some maintenance. As there was nothing else to do, they would work long days, I would be left in the rail 'camp' with the cook, and I would keep a record of their time spent on the job, plenty of it, of course, being overtime. Naturally I was completely separate from the gang, did not speak the same language, and myself had absolutely nothing to do other than read books. The idea, I suppose, was that I was effectively incorruptible; necessary perhaps, but the foreman was a good man, and the gang earned, in effect, good money because they worked such long hours. In addition, the cook, indeterminate as male or female, produced excellent food in lavish quantities, my problem, if I had one, being that after my steak I generally liked a clean plate for my fruit pie; the guys seemed to think that a bit too prissy. For me, a very boring and inactive job ... but I was ready for that. But it didn't last long.

One day (May 20th, to be precise) I received a phone call from Judith. Her secretary, plainly a diligent type, had seen an advertisement in a paper for a merchant marine officer with a foreign-going ticket. "Get on the next train," she said. "Come to Vancouver, and we'll catch the next ferry to Victoria." I did as requested and two days later found myself in an interview with Mr Case, a director of West Line, a division of West Tours, an old tourism company operating from Seattle. The interview was short and sweet, one view of my Discharge Book demonstrating that I had a ticket that he really needed.

"Okay," he said, "I need a chief officer for *West Star*, cruising to Alaska. We have been taken over by Holland America and need a foreign-going ticket. Are you interested?"

My positive response was, "Yes, but when do you need me?" to which he replied, "You start as chief officer tonight, okay." Fine with me though that was, I had no uniform with me, but that didn't matter; a quick call to Judith and she came over from Vancouver by the next ferry with my uniform. On the ferry with her, though of course unbeknownst to her, was another applicant, who appeared before Mr Case two hours after me. That fellow, Malcolm Pearson, had a ticket virtually identical and contemporaneous with mine; he was forthwith made 2nd mate. Such are the vagaries of life as it really is.

I should point out that it now appeared that this was evidently not too much of a 'venture'; Holland America was cut from the same cloth as P&O, a very well-established and reputed company, with fine ships and very high standards, though more attuned to North American trade than was P&O. It also hardly needs to be said that that company had outsmarted P&O, for they now operated the premier tour company in Alaska, though there were other companies that had undertaken this cruise scenario before, but none of which had the scope of West Tours, which operated tour busses, hotels, exotic destinations and all manner of frontier excitements.

When *West Star* arrived in port, I saw an unusual looking ship of 4,437 gross tons, virtually a motor-boat in comparison with my experience of ships. I introduced myself to the Captain, a cheerful Scotsman named Harry Blackwell. We had a good talk, his primary issue at that time being whether I had my Masters', as he was the only Master that had to this date been located by the Company, and a deep-sea ticket was required to man the vessel when it was not devoted to Alaska cruising. I pointed out that I was about three months short of sea-time to take that ticket but did not point out that I had no intention of staying at sea. He was delighted to hear that I was available until early September, permanently, as it were, as I would need no relief for some four months. There were a couple of other things that really appealed to me; firstly, our (sic) Union had negotiated a day-for-day leave scheme (which is to say that for every day worked on six-hour watches, we received one day of paid leave) and, secondly, officers were paid overtime. In other words, I would be paid for eight months while only having to actually work for four, and that I would be adequately paid. I then introduced myself to the mate and the 2nd mate who were to leave the ship that day. These old salts, Steve and Archie, whose combined ages doubtless exceeded 150 years, had only coastal tickets, which to that point had sufficed because only at the end of the summer cruise season would the ship be travelling to the Philippines for other employment (Holland America wanted to maximise income from their ships, for in the past anything operating in the North-East Pacific was essentially laid up in Seattle or Vancouver for the winters). But I use the word 'only' coastal tickets with some deference, for these old guys had operated in some of the world's trickiest waters more on acquired knowledge than by adequate equipment. For example, in navigating the Granville Channel, a narrow unlit passage between two islands off B.C.'s coast, navigation had been effected by blowing the whistle and, if one echo returned before the other, adjusting the course so that the ship would revert to the channel's centre with equal whistle-response time. No deep-sea mariner that I had ever known would have thought the exercise of navigating by whistle-blasts viable, even possible. The two did inform me, however, that the job was not too difficult, Canadian pilots being on the bridge most of the way north to Prince Rupert, and US pilots in charge for the rest of each cruise. Thus, although they had intimate acquaintance with one of the world's most intricate coasts, they barely needed to use that knowledge. They also indicated that the cruises were a trifle boring; each lasted eight days (each end of the cruise occupying a day for discharging and loading) and the ports were always the same – and that if you like the glamour and vigour of Hong Kong, forget it!

I was then introduced to the bosun and the SIU (Seafarer's International Union) representative, the latter a man called 'Tiny' (presumably because he wasn't, all of him being unable to sit on just one chair). This was my first experience in dealing with Canadian mariners, and I realised that, as mate, I had landed in a fire-pit. As will be appreciated, although the P&O white ships had plenty of English sailors, they were all the equivalent of petty officers and long-time employees of the company; the bulk of the crews were, however, from South Asia or in some cases from Hong Kong. All, however, accepted P&O discipline; no fighting, no drinking and no drugs. I had never witnessed a serious crew disciplinary problem in my years with P&O.

Now Captain Blackwell advised me (he had spent most of his seagoing career with, I believe, Donaldson Line/Blue Star, a good solid worldwide exposure to the sea and Scottish seamen) that the crewing problem was not insignificant. Because *West Star* operated in Alaska during the summer, but went to East Asia during the winter, where local crews were hired at far less cost, it was impossible for West Line to engage quality SIU men; they just didn't want to be working for only six months a year, and indeed, quite reasonably so. Thus, he said, what we generally got were men who were unable to find steady employment in the solid B.C. shipping companies. He further told me that the Canadian authorities required Fire Plans for all ships, regular lifeboat drills, and a Planned Maintenance schedule. Why these were absent, he said, was because the original owners of the ship had gone belly up, the vessel had laid on the stocks and rusted for two years, and that it was my job to fill all of these missing requirements.

Patently, this small 'summer job' was to be no sinecure. I began by looking for fire-plan materials, and found enough to know that such a plan, of which I had seen many, was a bit of a slog, but rested upon fairly obvious principles. For the life-boats we could have an early practice, and for the Planned Maintenance Schedule, this was basically an administrative job prepared by Head Office. For that reason, I spoke to the Marine Superintendent, Mr Wiggins, a sad and tired-looking man whom, I fancied, had not actually been to sea. He was, however, an easy man to deal with, pleasant but taciturn, and probably a bit put off by this young mate who seemed to know how an efficient company, which West Line's shipping component was not, should be operated. He was, however, easier to deal with than was the bosun.

This individual, a large florid man who seemed to have only tug-boat experience, was not so easy to handle. I indicated that I wished to introduce the painting maintenance routine right away, as the ship exhibited quite a lot of rust spots, and a cruise vessel should always look smart. Therefore, whenever overtime was required (coming into port, for instance) the two hours' minimum could best be utilised by paint touch-up and sheave greasing. These suggestions went down like a lead balloon; he could see no reason why two hours' overtime pay should not be the reward for a 20-minute berthing. Tiny, an ominous presence, seemed to agree with him.

But on the whole, I was happy with my lot. Viewed from afar, *West Star* was quite a pretty ship. It did not look as though it had lay unloved for two years, and I was happy with my shipmates, Blackwell being of a somewhat unsettled disposition, but he looked and sounded like a Captain, and Malcolm being a quiet, but very pleasant fellow. Further, we had a married couple as Entertainers, she, an attractive Country and Western singer, and he, a brash young man, a British carny-type. Although I loath country music (cowboys braying at the moon I just found stupid) this was a popular duo; her name was Dodie West, a name that was close to Dottie West, a very popular Country singer. Many passengers were very happy to be entertained by someone so well-known; that they had the wrong person seemed not to matter.

We sailed at 7pm after the pilots had boarded and transited the Gulf of Georgia (now more appropriately named the Salish Sea). I kept the twelve to six but was not too worried about the coastal complexities (which were quite strange to a deep-sea mariner) as we had pilots in control the whole time. I knew I could not have done the job myself, though Steve and Archie could have done it with their eyes closed. By any measure these were the most complex waters in which I had sailed, and, to me, had totally inadequate shore lights by which to discern one's position. Any idea that I had harboured about the superiority of the deep-sea ticket over the coastal equivalent was quickly laid to rest, even though there were a host of other disciplines that were studied by the former that were unnecessary for coastal mariners. And when we crossed the mythical line into the USA, the same expertise prevailed (except that some pilots favoured 'left and right' in lieu of 'port and starboard').

Steaming up the Alaska Panhandle was therefore interesting and not a little intimidating. The ship's culture was quite different from my experience; the officers were mere technicians designed to get the ship from one port to the next. There was no Captain's cocktail party in which officers were required to participate, there was no idea of officers' tables, and far from a wine allowance, we were prohibited from drinking, though the Captain, on occasion, did have the more important passengers in his cabin (a by no means exotic accommodation) for small parties.

The route, however, was invariable. We sailed from Vancouver to Ketchikan, then to Juneau (the state capital), then to Skagway, over to Glacier Bay (not a port, but the mouth of a glacial inlet), to Sitka and then to Prince Rupert, a Canadian port. Apart from Sitka, which, because of its past and very visible Russian heritage, was really quite interesting, the ports were of very little note. All of them featured numerous vendors of 'gold' trinkets, displays of gold panning, and a large number of under-lit and smelly bars. The passengers loved it all, most of them coming from the US mid-west, where the largest body of water that most had seen was their bath, and 'Culture' was C and W. There was no doubt that Chuck West, the founder of West Tours, knew his market; each trip was full. And I did not dislike it; there was a lot of organisational work to do, but I was being paid more than I had ever received before, and it was limited to four months' work and eight months' pay; thank goodness for The Canadian Merchant Service Guild!

We were allowed to take wives on one trip per year, and despite the minute cabin that was allotted to me, we had a good time seeing the very fine scenery, bergy-bits calving from the glaciers, and walks on the decrepit board-walks. Malcolm was a good fellow to know, as his background was so similar to mine, and Judith found him quite a charming fellow (Archie would have been a more knowledgeable 2nd mate, but what we would ever have talked about? Malcolm's sex life at a Holiday Camp where he had been a Red-Jacket gave rise to hilarious tales, especially over the scotch that I smuggled aboard).

Not all was roses, however. There was much crew drunkenness, and I learned upon which members I could rely. There was no George, and the passage being so difficult, good helmsmen were of value; one such was Bob Ward, a gangling Canadian of great experience who had for years worked for CPR (which company operated the West Coast CP fleet), and we utilised his services for difficult passages. On one occasion, we had berthed and two were missing from the tie-up crew. I asked the bosun where they were; he said that they were 'sick'; I knew what he meant and asked him to bring them up on deck. He looked at me, started visibly shaking and looked about ready for an apoplectic fit. This, I knew, was trouble, but I recalled the advice of the Royal Marine Instructor ("Never take on a drunk or drug-addled opponent.") and simply stood there waiting to see what he might do. He blinked; five days later, he was the ex-bosun.

When Judith and I were both aboard I saw a good deal more of the passengers, and, of course, of the entertainment staff. Premier among them was the Cruise Director, one Jeraldine Saunders, a flamboyant lady of abundant personality and much, though faded, allure, who at one time had obviously been a real looker (she had been born in 1923) but had retained great elegance and vivacity. Her job was to keep the passengers content, which she did with ease, and she and Judith found that they enjoyed each other's company. Among Jeraldine's accomplishments was fortune-telling (and what she told, and wrote, for Judith has never been revealed to me!), but of far more note was that she was learning something about the Great American Cruise Passenger, for very soon thereafter she became the creator of 'The Love Boat' hit TV series, essentially based upon her novels and her cruise director experience. Coincidences did not end there; the vessel featured in the show was *Pacific Princess*, a P&O ship that was transferred to that company's worldwide cruising company, Princess Cruises, though the company quickly sold it when cruising ballooned in popularity and new and much bigger ships became necessary. Jeraldine was an author of a considerable number of probably-now-forgotten books (apart from 'The Love Boats') that rendered her an American household word in the late 1970s, and she published an astrological column that brought her further fame ... or notoriety, whichever you favour.

The balance of the summer proceeded much as the first cruise. I constantly had to change crew-members every time we returned to Victoria, for reliability problems were never resolved. A prime example of these ongoing issues arose with a young and new bosun who arrived about mid-season and was a real 'hot-shot'. He organised the crew (not all had even been to sea before, let alone possessed an Efficient Deck Hand Certificate) such that they actually became quite adequate; he had unusually good training abilities. But one morning, upon arrival in Skagway, I could not find him, his post being on the foredeck, ready to drop the anchors should that be necessary. Upon enquiring, I was taken down to his cabin, and there I found him lying comatose on his bunk. I was told that he had overdosed, on *what* nobody would tell me. The ship's doctor told me that nothing could be done; he just had to be left as he was until he recovered. He didn't, and left the ship four days later, his replacement being a man called DesRoches, a 'farmer' from Quebec, but in whose demeanour I felt there to be a good seaman. Fortunately, I was right; he remained the ship's bosun until Holland America decided that Alaska cruises were good business, sent *West Star* over the horizon, and brought over to Vancouver a couple of their ships for the cruise season.

Glacial Ice for West Star's drinks

Unfortunately, the deck crew was not the only problem with the ship. As stated, we always endeavoured to get in among some ice, either in Glacier Bay or Tracey Arm, both of which lent themselves to lowering a lifeboat to pick up some glacial ice and serve the thousand-year old product in the bar drinks that evening; passengers loved it, even at extra cost! The drawback was the size of the ship, for the propellers were only a few feet below sea-level, and too frequently we damaged the propeller blades. This induced some noticeable ship vibration, thus necessitating going into dry-dock in Victoria and having the propellers shaved into shape or replaced. By some lucky coincidence, this was easy enough; Victoria had one of the world's biggest dry-docks in the naval base, a relic of having occasionally to service the *Queens* during the War.

This was not all. The ship was a motor ship, and prior to joining it, my total experience had been with steam turbines. The difference was in mobility, for in Alaska one did not use tugs to go alongside, and on occasion it took several movements to properly berth, in some cases meaning that we ran out of 'starts' – the compressed air that was stored and blasted into the cylinders to get the motor to start simply being used up. In those instances, we were obliged to sit out in the harbour off the berth while the ship's compressors refilled the compressed-air storage tanks, sometimes for a half-hour or so; that did not sit too well with our passengers, all naturally anxious to go ashore.

Another problem was a bit more ticklish. Captain Blackwell was not a difficult person with whom to work … but he was moody. His main issue was a relief Captain, or absence thereof, as neither I nor Malcolm had a master's ticket with which we could have taken over the job (not that either of us would have wished to do so; we were both aware that we had insufficient experience even if either had had the ticket). Mr Case found a temporary replacement, whom, I believe, was teaching at a local navigation school. He, Captain Mullin, came on for a couple of cruises and he was very much the calm and quiet type, though obviously not one who had much sea-going experience (not a big issue, of course, because of the omnipresent pilots). The problem was that Blackwell simply did not like him, not, I think because of any professional pride, but because he was a bit insecure in his job, he, Blackwell, having only recently joined *West Star* after leaving a nautical instrument salesman's job in Vancouver, to which he seemed loath to return. And after Mullin did his relief, Blackwell constantly told both of us how Mullin didn't know his job. That opinion had no effect upon us, but what did concern us was that if he could so demean Mullin behind his back, what was he saying to other officers about us and others? Elementary man-management dictated that this is absolutely how not to gain or retain respect.

But September 3rd came around, University started the next day – on our anniversary – and a new chapter began. I took courses that I felt confident would prove easy, because I could then apply for Law School without having to complete an undergraduate degree. I chose courses on South Asian Culture, South East Asian Political Science, Communist Chinese History, Russian Economic Geography and International Mass Violence, and I was accepted into Political Science Honours (one may discern a pattern, based upon my earlier interests, in this group). And thank goodness that I chose six rather than five courses, for the Chinese History course was taught by a most peculiar long-haired Quebecois lecturer who, on most days, favoured wearing a skirt. He rattled off Chinese name after unintelligible Chinese name, all of which we were supposed to remember. He had his Ph.D. from Beijing University, I understood, where rote learning must have been de rigueur. I, however, thought that the class was to teach the history of collective philosophy and Chinese economic imperatives, not to know who or what was Wu Pei Fu!

But all went well, and at the end of the year my marks were good enough, Chinese History excluded, to apply for Law School. And I prepared for the return to *West Star*, which for some unfathomable but pleasant reason, I had to rejoin in Honolulu.

In the meantime, however, by dint of 90 seconds of strenuous exercise, I had managed to get Judith pregnant, and I looked forward to another four months' work and eight months' pay. Again, she came on the vessel for one trip, and by this time I was quite familiar with the routine. One pilot that we seemed to have more than any other was a youngish fellow called Casey (at least, that was what we named him), an ex-tug skipper from Seattle. A watch on the bridge with him could pass in pleasant style, which could not always be said in these sometimes stilted circumstances.

But one could not always rely upon 'routine'. We sometimes fell behind our schedule (late passengers, tours held up, delays in berthing and the like) and on one nice bright night we found ourselves somewhat delayed in departing Ketchikan. There was an alternative route to Juneau that was shorter, but which entailed the transit of Wrangell Narrows, a passage between two of the larger islands that *West Star* had infrequently used in the past. Mullin was concerned about our schedule, largely because many tours were tightly programmed and getting behind could often mean that delay fed upon earlier delays. He therefore asked the senior pilot (Ed), one who spent his winters on his farm in Montana, whether we should use the Narrows. I also asked Casey about this transit, because I had had a previous trip with Ed and thought him a bit amateurish. Casey said that he himself had had insufficient experience with the Narrows and felt that in the circumstances he would not recommend such a transit, an opinion with which Ed 'somewhat' agreed. I returned to Mullin and strongly suggested that we take the longer route, I having seen how convoluted the Narrows were, and Ed's hesitant response bore out my previous reservations respecting his rather loose style with commands. But Mullin declared that the schedule had to be maintained if possible, and that Wrangell it would be. I then ensured that Bob Ward was available as the helmsman.

Mullin, both pilots and I were on the bridge as we entered the passage. As before, it presented an alarming sight, especially as it was a crystal-clear night; so 'twisted' is its winding route (it is twenty-two miles in length) that all one sees is a mass of flashing green, red and white lights, and the perspective is so poor that it is more important to know the point reached rather rely upon a guidance from such confusing lights.

About half-way through the Narrows (when all seemed to be going well) Ed said, "Starboard 10," but signalled with his left hand to put the helm over to port.

Bob said, "Don't you mean Port 10?"

"No," said Ed and gesticulated more vigorously with his left hand ... in seconds, though Bob applied some port helm, we were aground. "Oh," said Ed, "I mixed up left and right" (or something to that effect). Needless to say, I immediately looked at the chart, and observed that we were over 'loose stones and sand', a bottom that relieved some concerns. I told the watchman to go below to call the carpenter to take some soundings, but I did not think that we had sustained any real damage; we were at the time on 'slow ahead'. And so it proved;

we maneuvered back and forth a few times and were safely off, having taken on no water or sustained any damage except perhaps to the pride of a few individuals. I told Bob that, if anything, he had acted completely correctly; never can a pilot be disregarded unless plainly deranged, and his helmsmanship had very nearly avoided the whole sorry saga.

There were no untoward consequences. Upon later inspection, not even a dent was found, though there was perhaps a bit of scraped paint. The real issue, I could foretell, would be Blackwell's use of this incident to impugn the skills of his relief … unfair, but I knew that he was that type of man.

On the whole, though, the summer's fifteen cruises were satisfactory. Plainly, our view from London that there would be little call for mass cruises from and to Alaska was entirely misconceived, in large part, I think, because we had not taken into account the firm ethnocentrism of the great American Lower Middle Class (and others; I recall a US Senator, when asked of his European travels, answered something to the effect, "…Never been there; why would I ever want to go outside the US?"). It was the case, and I believe it remains so, that of the advanced nations of the world, USA has the lowest proportion of passport holders, though, surprisingly, actual statistics are hard to come by. Therefore, while there are lots of fascinating places to travel within the contiguous states, Alaska ranks high because of a 'frontier myth' that it is something outside the norm, and little nonsenses (like the Robert Service paeons of praise to the frigid north, and the legend of the bar that serves whiskey with a petrified human toe therein, to give it taste and cachet) reinforce the conceit of an odd exoticism that envelops the Pacific North West. In fact, the vast state is of interest to hikers, oil men, hunters and misanthropes, but of limited interest to others – although, it has to be said, it even produces its own idiosyncratic politicians.

I was advised upon returning to Victoria at the beginning of September that employment next summer was unlikely, Holland America deciding that the idea of major Alaska Cruising was not only viable, but very promising. I was not much concerned at the time, as the commencement of Law School promised to be demanding, but in fact I found it more than 'challenging'. I did not find the work particularly difficult, as the main requirement was to read vast numbers of cases and texts. What was difficult was to do <u>well</u>, because most of the students were accustomed to getting very high marks and coming 'top of the class', a position generally unfamiliar to me. But there were other compensations; three weeks after starting Law School, Judith was delivered of a son, a big strong boy whom we thought should be, perhaps somewhat conventionally, named David, my brother, in UK, having already been sublimely successful in twice leaving his genetic imprint with two healthy boys. 1972 quickly moved into 1973.

Naturally, the study of law does not give rise to much narrative energy; nor did some of the part-time jobs that Judith found for me; I was the worst fork-lift driver ever taken on by Eatons, as I was on one job charged with moving furniture from the highest of storage shelves to waiting customers, all with a fork-lift, 30 feet up in the air, with a pencil-like joystick to control a machine of sixty horsepower. Several furniture items duly received irreparable damage. On another occasion, I and a friend, the son of a lady working with Judith, were drafted into a group to complete installation of beds and cupboards in a hotel that Eatons was supplying with room fixtures (side-tables etc.). We had difficulty putting up the rooms' bedheads, as a .22 staple-gun was used to shoot the staples into the wall to affix the brackets upon which the bedheads were hung; the problem was that the gun needed constant adjustment. Sometimes the staples seemed fine, but when the bedhead was put in place, it fell right off the wall. The contrary, however, was worse; if over-adjusted, the staple would shoot right through the whole wall! Our supervisor, a young fellow called Bill, was appalled at our incompetence.

There was a good ending to the story, however. Bill, in need of an advance on his pay, went into the personnel office and asked the appropriate person – who happened to be Judith. She signed the requisition but asked how the two fellows that she had sent along were doing. He didn't hesitate; "They are the two most useless individuals I've ever seen," he declared, "Why do you ask?" Judith mumbled some vague reply and off Bill went, blissfully ignorant.

For some reason, we were never fired, nor even warned. But, as I said, these menial tasks paid for the groceries.

Suffice it to say that at the end of first-year law school the summer of 1973 did not present the employment difficulties that I had expected to encounter. There was no *West Star*; Holland America brought two of its smart 25,000-ton vessels over to jump-start the new trade (as did P&O, who delivered *Spirit of London* and *Arcadia* to operate from Vancouver). However, given the experience that I had gained, I thought that there might be other opportunities, so I looked around.

Princess Patricia approaching Skagway

And there, on the end of the cruise ship pier in Vancouver, lay *Princess Patricia*, a vessel of some antiquity, operated by CP Rail, that operated a series of Alaska cruises. I enquired, and found that there might be a position available, for which I had a very pleasant interview with Mr Yates, the company Marine Superintendent. I had lucked out again; his son-in-law, whom I knew reasonably well, was in my law-class. It appeared that CPR operated a number of ships, a Victoria-Port Angeles ferry, a Vancouver-Nanaimo ferry, and a couple of smaller rail-car ferries between the mainland and Vancouver Island. Asked whether I would mind the summer on the Alaska cruise run, my response did not take long to formulate; I was to be 3rd mate this time, but that was because CP had a solid slate of long-term officers.

So, we made our plans. Instead of Judith staying around at home for the summer, we elected for her and David to fly down to Port of Spain (Trinidad and Tobago) where her parents were now stationed and rent out our house. I would work for CPR (they liked the idea that I wanted NO leave) and we would resume family bliss in early September. Before we did so, we had Malcolm over for dinner, and Judith invited over one of her friends from Eatons (with the unlikely name of Mardi), a darkly attractive young lady. Malcolm had obtained employment elsewhere and was in a good enough mood to enjoy a convivial evening. And he did, though I was interested in seeing how his low-keyed charm worked so well on the fairer sex. Not that I now needed any help, but it was a joy to watch a master at work.

I was content to join *Princess Patricia* and to meet Captain Pendry Harris. Needless to say, CPR was a component of the vast Canadian Pacific Empire of railways, passenger shipping, hotel ownership, real estate management and all manner of other commercial endeavours. The ships, of which one could probably call *Patricia* the flagship, had their own traditions that arose from many decades of operating passenger and cargo vessels on this prosperous coast. The ship, of 6,062 gross tons, was a fine example of old British shipbuilding. Built in Glasgow, as was her sister *Princess Marguerite*, in 1949, she was originally destined for the triangular passenger ferry service in the Strait of Georgia and was in 1963 refitted extensively in order to serve the Alaska cruise trade. A very attractive ship, she was riveted, solid in appearance with twin funnels, painted a prim white, and with a speed of seventeen knots, in many respects she operated much as *West Star* could have done had its owners been a company of more solid standing.

As seemed usual on this coast, watches were six on/six off, thereby again being 'day-for-day', much to my advantage, and I again learned much about this coast. There were substantial differences, however, between the two ship-going experiences. The primary one was that we needed no pilots, all of the officers being qualified to handle this tricky coast. And I was glad to see that with a steamship, as expected, there was no need to worry about 'starts'; not that that was a concern, for in all my time at sea, I had never seen such an excellent ship-handler as Captain Harris. He was the permanent Captain of the ship and

Princess Patricia in Skagway

handled it like a motor-boat. He was a rough-hewn sort of man, not given to any airs or graces (passengers were there to earn money for the company; I never saw him evidencing any interest in socialising) and he thought that I was something special, inasmuch as he believed that a deep-sea ticket was really worth more than his coastal masters', and that my being in law school demonstrated something exceptional. My ego was not so overblown, however, as to think that I could ever handle a ship with the facility that he demonstrated. To me, one of the finest of Captains, in all respects, with whom I had been privileged to sail.

Equally important was my view of the other officers, all highly competent and quite willing to impart to a callow youth like me all of the experience gleaned on a coast of such complexity. Additionally, my view of the 'Canadian Seaman' changed dramatically. CPR employed for the long-term; everybody knew their job, no drink or drugs, and all were completely professional. I could see why Yates was a happy counterpart to the sombre Wiggins.

While she was away in Port of Spain a fortunate coincidence occurred and the then Bishop (or Archdeacon, I know not which) of Trinidad, one and the same man who _might_ have married us, was now installed in Port of Spain and thus able to christen David. Neither of us had any particular Christian predilections (I had been to a school where we had to attend three services each Sunday, quite enough to tire one of dogma) so, again, an insurance issue (just in case Pascal's Wager about God held water) for his future welfare, at least in the Hereinafter, if not for this life.

While I enjoyed the experience of *Patricia*, I should say that I could not see how that type of ship could really compete with the big white ships in this arena. The vessel was small enough for passengers to be able to get to know each other, but the facilities included in such ships could not compete with the plethora of pleasures possible in the conventional cruise vessels. It could not be ignored, either, that the Alaska climate was highly variable; of the forty-five cruises that I undertook over the three summers, I could say that only ten or so were accompanied by even good weather. Additionally, the cuisine was unimaginative; for example, on the penultimate day of each cruise, the main hot course at dinner was broiled ox-tongue. I myself had no problem with this myself (Mother prepared the dish superbly) but for American passengers I thought it akin to serving devilled kidneys or tripe and onions, hardly winners in the land of hamburgers. But nobody asked my opinion; and I wasn't going to bite the hand that fed me.

I was greeted on the pier by Judith, again on our Anniversary, after giving due thanks to Captain Harris, from whom I had learned much but never expected to see again, as I thought that the next year would see the total dominance of the big cruising vessels. In driving home, I found myself confronted by a startled eleven-month old, who looked at me with complete amazement; the feeling was mutual, for at that age four months growth is quite a substantial spurt, and he was obviously going to be a big boy.

Back at UBC I knuckled down to another year. Naturally I chose my courses with some care, one of the more important being Maritime Law, of which, of course, I knew a little, at least that of a practical nature. The lecturer was the distinguished Jack Cunningham, a practicing maritime barrister located in Vancouver, who was termed 'Captain Jack' because, not only did he look the part, but he had also apparently served in a corvette during the War. As for the rest, I realised very quickly that I would never make a criminal lawyer. We even had a bit of distinction, when Lord Denning came to the Vancouver Law Courts and visited the Law Library to give us an impromptu lecture. This distinguished man was at the time the Master of the Rolls (as the Chief Justice of the English Court of Appeal is titled) and who was known to have responded to the question of when he might ascend to the House of Lords by "…Well, it's a bit like going to Heaven; you rather want to get there … but not quite yet!" His fame, however, succeeding his Profumo/Keeler report, had ossified.

My final year of any seagoing career was served in far less glamorous (though that is such an inappropriate word for *West Star* and *Patricia*!) circumstances than those to which I had become accustomed. There were no small passenger ships available on the Alaska run, so I spent the summer of 1974 on the dull run of *Carrier Princess* (on whose bridge I heard the news of Nixon's resignation) on the Vancouver to Victoria truck-and-trailer route, interspersed with the even more dull Vancouver to Nanaimo railcar and vehicle ferry route. Of course, I had nothing about which to complain; I was now able to have dinner with my small family at home, being at home to actually enjoy the vaunted Vancouver summer, losing some, but not all, of the day-for-day system, and, as a theoretical bonus, now having sufficient time under my belt to take my Foreign-Going Masters ticket if I ever wished to return to a life that had offered and given me so much.

I never did so wish.

Sunset in Alaska

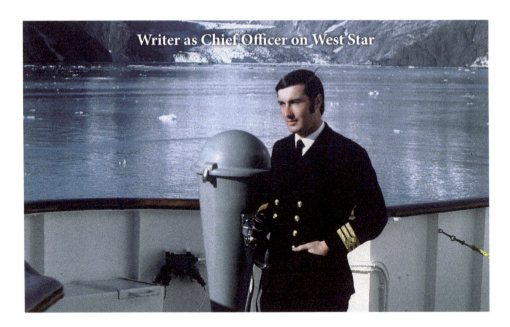

Writer as Chief Officer on West Star

9 Postscript

After gaining my law degree, I thought that gaining Articles would be easy enough (it is necessary to struggle through a year of Articles before one can apply to be called to the B.C. Bar). I was wrong. There were only three law firms in Vancouver that enjoyed practices that emphasised maritime law, and of course, I applied to all three (plus a few miscellaneous firms of generally good repute), but the tumbling-over-themselves to obtain my services seemed not to occur. Fortunately, I eventually received an offer, which I immediately accepted, from Macrae, Montgomery, Spring and Cunningham, the firm, 'led' by Captain Jack, that was in fact my prime target. The year completed I was called to the B.C. Bar as a Barrister and Solicitor (the Canadian way of doing things being in my opinion far more logical than the clumsily bifurcated British system of a divided profession) in 1976, my parents coming from England for the occasion.

I was delighted to see that the rather disorganised office environment that I knew from Leadenhall Street found no parallel in Vancouver. The office was superbly managed, the staff were equipped with the latest equipment (P&O had still used ancient Remingtons!), tight control was kept over time spent on files, and individual expertise, such as mine, was encouraged. I even found some familiar stuff; within a week of joining the firm I found myself in the lower hold of *Massimino d'Amico*, a scruffy cargo vessel that had filed a Note of Protest over some shifting and damaged cargo. I have earlier mentioned that office life in London was a bit circumspect after life on the seven Seas, but in an office of this sort the people and the matters in which we were engaged were, if not always scintillating, invariably of substantial human and intellectual interest. I felt that I had arrived in the right place. Even the most important things worked out well, our younger son Andrew arriving in 1977 to enhance the world with his wit and spirit.

A few months after I began learning my craft, however, I again re-learned the impermanence of life. One day, at home, I received a call from an unknown young lady, whom I found was Malcolm's girlfriend. She recited a horrible tale; during a trip to Houston, where his ship was moored, Malcolm had gone ashore for the evening, and upon his return to the ship had been accosted by two young men who asked him to hand over his money. He apparently had $25 on him, but I knew him to be a parsimonious sort of fellow, and, characteristically, he refused to comply. Having a black belt in judo, he was quite ready to take them on … so they simply knifed him, and he died on the spot! His assailants were caught, and I recall that his mother came over to Vancouver from UK to look after his affairs, which were few enough. A tragic waste of a good person.

And other strange things happened. When Andrew graduated from secondary school, his *inamorata* was a young lady whose father was of Czech descent. As Andrew was the Master of Ceremonies at the year-end dinner and gave the representative address to parents and teachers at its conclusion, we saw little of him during the meal, but as we were on the same table as his girlfriend's parents, we necessarily engaged in chit-chat. Her father, a Czech Count (I was not aware that the Czech Republic even had ranks of ennoblement) seemed not to want to converse with us, the proletariat. So, I entered into a conversation with his wife; at first, it was heavy going. But somehow the subject of *Canberra* came up; "Oh," said she, "I was on that ship in 1967 when the Arab-Israeli War started!"

"In first class?" (as if I didn't know) I responded.

"Yes," she said, "and we had to turn around and go around South Africa!"

It was not difficult to recall that on that voyage (as in the preceding Part 7), there were two young girls, and even over the years, I could see that I was not talking to Virginia. Suddenly the mood changed, and in fact improved beyond all measure when the Count also discovered that David's wife, Sabine, spoke fluent Czech, her parents having arrived in Canada from Czechoslovakia some years before. Except for the worrying effect of the Gothic makeup that the daughter favoured, the evening turned out to be a very convivial event.

(One has to digress at this point, and that is because 'coincidence' plays such a role in any life, even those not 'well-lived'. As the average life encompasses many thousands of chance encounters, that some strange coincidences would not consequently arise would by *itself* be an astonishing coincidence. In particular, chance dictates that I should not have met Judith in the middle of the Indian Ocean on a moonlit night, that there would not have been two J. Shep(herds/pards) of fair disposition and coincident ages on *Cathay* at the same time; that a young man would be in a political science class who could translate 'love' into Sinhalese for the engagement ring; that Judith Smythe would meet both myself and Mother in such disparate circumstances; that Don McGill and I would meet the Beatles in Sydney; and that a fellow student at UBC in a Mass Violence political science class would be from Woolwich and there have lived just a few houses from me; these are just six examples. I could quote many more.)

The final question perhaps is whether the nautical world had matured as had I. There were four main vessel groupings in the Merchant Marine; Passenger (Cruise) ships, Cargo vessels, Tanker (oil, gas and exotic), and the Rest (ferries, pleasure boats, heavy-lift ships, ro-ro vessels, cattle ships and those specifically designed for exotic tasks; coast-guard, ice-breakers, warships, tugs etcetera). Passenger ships of the 21st century could not have been foreseen in the 1960s; now, they seem <u>almost</u> logical; containerisation has resulted in vastly bigger cargo ships, such that now London's Royal Docks, once the biggest in the world, are now an alternative London Airport sitting above and astride what were deep-water terminals, and the ships themselves are gargantuan, yet served by very small crews; tankers are likewise giant in size, as often used as floating temporary oil repositories than as a means of carriage as they await the most profitable ports at which to berth, despite the probable decline in not too distant a future in the world's demand for fossil fuels; and the Rest have all manner of unique designs and new propulsion systems (of which I know little or nothing, other than the fact that not too many now have simple 'propellers' at the stern).

But, I think, for man and ships; plus ca change, plus c'est la meme chose.

~ Glossary ~

Aldis Lamp	A signal lamp, handheld or fixed, with which to send messages by Morse Code.
	(Named after its inventor, Arthur Aldis 1878–1953.)
Bosun (Boatswain)	The senior member of the 'uncertificated' deck (navigating) crew.
Catenary	The curve of a cable or wire when it hangs from fixed points.
Davit	A 'crane' (there are many types) that holds, raises or lowers lifeboats.
Discharge Book	A record a mariner's certification and seagoing experience.
Freeboard	The distance from the load water line to the main deck.
Hawse pipe	Steel pipes in the hull through which the anchor cables run and in seaward (outward) end of which the anchor itself should fit snuggly.
Khat (Qat)	The leaves of a shrub grown and chewed in some parts of Africa. It is a mild Stimulant, which apparently suppresses the appetite and produces some degree of dependence.
Knot	One nautical mile per hour (thus 'knot per hour' is tautological nonsense).
	One nautical mile is the distance subtended at the globe's surface by one minute of latitude; thus, because of the earth's 'flattened' poles, a nautical mile differs in its length from place to place all over the globe.
Mate	The 'navigating' officers rank from Chief Officer down to 4th mate. Normal British terminology is for the senior of them to be termed 'The Mate' and the next senior either the 1st mate (if there is one) or the 2nd

mate, who is traditionally the navigator and cargo officer. Occasionally there is a Navigator, who ranks below the Mate. Engineers rank from Chief Engineer (like the Captain, a 'four-striper'), the 2nd Engineer (equivalent in his own department to the Mate) and on down the line. Electrical, refrigeration, doctors, radio officer and pursers etc. rise to the height of three stripes.

Pitching and Rolling	Pitching is the up-and-down plunging of the ship's head in a seaway, while the stern goes through the opposite see-saw motion. Rolling occurs when the sides of the ship perform a see-saw motion.
Poop	The stern or aft part of a ship.
POSH	'Port Outward, Starboard Homeward'
Quarter	The rounded part of the ship's side aft, on each side of the poop.
Serang	With an Indian crew, he is the head of the head of the uncertificated sailors (see 'bosun'). The Tindal is the rank below that of the Serang.
Shackle	Two main meanings; (a) a harp or 'D' type that joins sections of wire or rope, or (b) 15 fathoms of anchor cable (one fathom is 6 feet).
Sheave	The grooved wheel over which a rope or wire travels.
Stabiliser	On passenger vessels, generally like 'wings' which help keep the ship upright. (There are some other, more exotic, designs, rarely encountered.)
Taffrail	Railing fitted to the aft end of the poop and perhaps elsewhere.
Wheel-Spanner	A spanner designed to provide leverage for men to rotate large valves.

CPSIA information can be obtained
at www.ICGtesting.com
Printed in the USA
LVHW072330030521
686429LV00008B/105